D1766390

WITHDRAWN FROM STOCK

Handbook of Creative Learning Exercises

Building Blocks of Human Potential

This series of books is supported by the American Society for Training and Development as part of its continuing program to encourage publication in the field. Most of the authors are active in ASTD and have contributed to its growth over the years. The Publications Committee of ASTD is a continuing link between the editor and the publisher and the membership.

Handbook of Creative Learning Exercises

Herbert M. Engel

GULF PUBLISHING COMPANY
Book Publishing Division: Houston

Handbook of Creative Learning Exercises

Copyright© 1973 by Gulf Publishing Company, Houston, Texas. Printed in the United States of America. All rights reserved. This book, or parts thereof, may not be reproduced in any form without permission of the publisher.

Library of Congress Catalog Card Number: 73-75394

ISBN: 0-87201-162-3

Contents

Foreword

With the publication of this book, our series adds another dimension. Up to this point, we have covered some of the broader areas of the field of human resource development and some of the ways in which we can release human potential. With this book, we now have in the series a volume addressed to some specific methods and techniques.

Practitioners in our field have sometimes been criticized for being "gimmick" crazy. We tend to reach out for the new, hoping that this will provide the answer to some of our significant problems in improving the learning situation. Over the years, learning techniques have come and gone. Some of them have proven valuable in aiding us to reach our learning objectives.

High among the learning techniques which have survived are the use of case studies and roleplaying. Even today, there are many who hesitate to use these well-established approaches. There are probably many reasons for such hesitancy, and it is our belief that one of them is the absence of clear and distinct literature which describes and clarifies the use of these learning approaches.

Therefore, we are most pleased to present this book by Herbert M. Engel. The author is a long-time leader in the field, and the book comes out of his own experiences in writing case studies as well as using them. He has also designed roleplays and used them. Most important, he has taught others how to develop and use these learning approaches. In this book, he shares with us some of what he has been doing for many years—helping others to improve their understanding of these learning techniques. The cases and roleplays cited in the book have been used in many situations, so the reader will benefit from material which has withstood the test of time and numerous learning situations.

Of course, no book can provide the skill required by the leader of a case study or roleplay situation. Such skill can only be developed over a period of time and with adequate feedback. However, this book does provide the basis to enable the reader to reexamine these learning approaches and to improve his understanding of them.

Washington, D.C.

Leonard Nadler
Series Editor

Preface

Trainers tend to be active persons who wear many hats: human development technicians, change agents, curricula planners, organizational development specialists, instructional managers, teachers and trainers of trainers. Another characteristic of training people is that they emerge from many diverse backgrounds: advertising, engineering, sales, personnel, public relations and education. Having selected training as a career through choice—and not as a result of a chance rotational assignment—you are likely to be marked as "different" by line people. Working as a trainer is not everyone's cup of tea. It's tough—and frequently unrewarding—when compared to other phases of an organization's operation. My own view is that good trainers are worth a lot more money than most of them earn. Struggling for status and monetary recognition should not, however, drain a trainer's energies as he pursues his own personal development. The trainer can hardly expect others to seek personal growth if he himself is completely satisfied with his own level of achievement. But, reinventing the wheel as a form of self-development—an unprofitable pastime for many in education-related fields—serves no useful end.

The trainer should build on what others have done. Several years ago, while searching for some special course of study materials in the trade training area, I learned of the existence of a "gold mine" of filed lesson plans. These were controlled by an elderly bureaucrat who was responsible for adult education in a very large public school system. My request to view and appraise these files—to determine whether they could be used in another jurisdiction—was promptly rejected.

"Do you think that I'm going to turn over a life's work for someone else to use? After I retire, I'll have to decide what to do with this stuff."

Regretably, the gentleman died suddenly about three months after my visit, and his treasure of files was delivered—so it was reported to me—to the trash man.

Trainers who preach about the wholesomeness of trusting relationships are often loath to share their personal handiwork. As far as I can tell, no secrets have been withheld from the reader of this book. About 30 years of personal experiences are made available in a usable form.

The plan of the book is arranged so that individual sections may be consulted for particular information without wading through the entire publication. It has been our intention to help active trainers save time in their work, to assist them in preparing more usable instructional materials and to improve the quality of the instructional output.

I am grateful to my many friends for their assistance and advice during the development and editing of this publication. May I express particular appreciation to Dr. Harry W. Blair, New York State Department of Mental Hygiene, for his suggestions in connection with "Reacting to the Resume." Several years ago, he also collaborated with me on the original version of the "Psychologist as an Administrator." Special gratitude is also acknowledged for the suggestions made by the editor of this series, Dr. Leonard Nadler, George Washington University; also, for the valuable aid and support given by Prof. James Early of Hudson Valley Community College; Mr. Michael Edwards, New York State Office for Local Government; Mr. Ronald James and Mr. John Iocco, New York State Department of Civil Service; and Mr. Gerald Weisman, New York State Department of Transportation. I am also indebted for the assistance rendered by Mr. Peter LeFleche, National Commercial Bank and Trust Company, Albany, for his contribution of the "Branch Manager's In-Basket."

Finally, I must express my indebtedness to my many students in various teaching and consulting activities who probably taught me as much as I have them.

Acknowledgments for the privilege of reproducing selected materials have been noted on the pages where such materials are used.

Suggestions on How to Use This Book

This book was designed as a ready reference for the user. Each chapter contains a summary of major topics covered. Each chapter also stands by itself, with cross references provided where these will assist the reader.

An annotated bibliography and indexes have been included—all intended to lighten the burden on the user. Finally, the cases, roleplays and complex exercises have been identified and labeled as to the applicable principles.

Handbook of Creative Learning Exercises

1. Case Studies

Case study materials are intended for use in the simplest forms of participative learning activities. This book examines the relationship between learning and participatory methods. This first chapter considers the functions of the trainer when he introduces case study materials and the essential requirement that he know his materials thoroughly. The selection of the group members is often crucial; therefore, the size of the group and the optimum number of groups are discussed. The groups' task assignments represent the heartland of the case study training approach. This chapter considers such areas as the selection of a group leader, a group reporter, if unanimity in responses is required and the extent to which minority opinions are considered. The trainer's functions during the group discussion work are analyzed. Finally, this chapter examines the trainer's role in leading the discussions, summarizing and synthesizing group findings: wringing the case dry and making the learning experience as productive and lasting as possible for all concerned.

The Case of the Cost-Profit Squeeze

The restaurant business is tough and highly competitive. No one knows that better these days than Mike Doyle, the manager of the FF/FF (Fine Friendly Family Fare) chain on South Boulevard. As the name denotes, FF/FF caters to the family trade with several "All You Can Eat" nights each week. The three FF/FF Restaurants in Central City are franchises, owned by Milt Peters. Peters has other investments in several business ventures in the greater Central City area.

Yesterday, Peters phoned Doyle, giving him this message:

My accountants tell me that the profit analysis for the first three months for your unit has dropped below where it should be. Figure out some way to cut our costs. Now look, I know that for the salads you can cut the tomatoes into eighths instead of quarters. Also, cut the oil you use in making the biscuits. I'll be in next week and I want you to have some of the ways that we can drop costs.

Doyle knows better than to disagree with his boss. He also knows that he's going to have trouble with Sarah Jones, the head cook. She's a tyrant in the kitchen, and it's a very trying experience to talk to her about how she should cook or bake. Nevertheless, Doyle tells her what his instructions are. She listens in silence and finally says, "O.K., if that's what they want, that's what they'll get . . . ."

Later, Doyle notices that the biscuits being set up by the bus boys are badly burned on the bottom.

Instructions

If you were responsible for training restaurant managers or if you were a restaurant manager at the receiving end of such training, which of the following approaches would you select?

1. A lecture, followed by a discussion, on the day-to-day decision-making problems faced by the manager
2. A case study discussion using, as an example, the "Cost-Profit Squeeze," with plenty of group interaction and a suitable lecture input by the instructor

Is there any doubt that the second option would be best?

Case studies offer a methodology, both imaginative and productive, encouraging the trainee to join in, involving him with what the instructor wants him to learn. Generally nonthreatening, it holds greater attraction than non-participatory teaching approaches and is likely to have a more enduring influence on the trainee's behavior. The intensity with which one becomes enmeshed in the *doing* process influences learning and how well it is applied.

Even if we do not recognize it as such, most of us use case materials nearly every day of our lives. We scan the newspaper, focusing in on the story of the high school junior picked up by the police for having stolen a neighbor's vehicle. Our youngster, who is a high school senior, may volunteer what he knows about this event. Around the dinner table we discuss the reasons for car theft, the circumstances of the family relationships, why kids steal cars, what may happen if one gets caught, and other relevant matters which the family members will raise in what may develop as a heated and lively discussion.

Whether we appeal to our youngsters or not as a result of this case will depend on their receptivity, the communications patterns within the family and other factors. The point is that this *is* a variety of a case situation. A fair selection of the materials found in Ann Landers' columns are also cases, miniaturized to be sure, but case materials nonetheless.

Another way of putting this is to consider how historical writings have been used. History, to a considerable extent, is a chronological collection of cases: what men once did, where and why. Debates occur in every generation as to whether "history repeats itself." Therefore, we should learn to profit from the errors of others who have passed on. While these are perhaps philosophical matters, we know, intuitively and experientially, that a study of the *way* things were once done may help us (we cannot be positive) in future situations which appear comparable. For instance, at one time, before Alamogordo, military men studied the campaigns of Hannibal and the Carthaginians. This material, describing how elephants were deployed against Rome, could be of some instructive value when facing a future enemy in a yet-to-be fought battle. And the case situations presented by Hiroshima and Nagasaki have, so far, taught man that using nuclear weapons is unthinkable.

Thus we recognize and concede that the use of case situations is hardly a new learning technique. Perhaps because of its universality, we become imprecise and even, at times, careless when using it. Our thinking is blurred as we fail to recognize that an exciting "discussion" about a past event is not necessarily a *systematic*, planned experience, tied to learning objectives.

A case becomes a real case study when a group of individuals becomes involved in a planned analysis of the materials found within a case and those other factors which may be inferred as a result of the way in which the case is constructed. The case may be the recitation of a real occurrence, or it can be completely or partially fictitious, put together to present some principle which the user wants to convey in meeting predetermined objectives.

Case studies *always* involve a group discussion and are normally based on written materials which have been provided to the participants within the group. Case studies may be long or short in terms of number of words. This book is generally concerned about materials which are reasonably short; that is, materials which may be read by the average participant in a period of time generally not exceeding three to ten minutes. Case studies provide a ready method for obtaining and exposing a slice of organizational life before a learning group. It can be about a simple grievance, a complex organizational problem, internal communications, morale, training or one of many other phases of how people interact within our societal structure.

The data within the case does not provide clear-cut answers. Because solutions are not readily available, case materials force-feed the resulting group discussions. After having offered their answers, individual trainees are confronted with other facts or inferences which are likely to vitiate simple solutions. They are then required to search collectively for more subtle resolutions to the problem. Each trainee becomes exposed to the ideas of others. All these new ideas together go beyond the responses which were provided individually after a hasty analysis of the case.

What Learning is Sought?

Assume that our trainee group is available and that we have decided what we want them to learn. We recognize and agree that teaching methods should vary because we can better maintain the trainees' interest and attention and make them understand.

When a lecture or lecture-discussion has been conducted in the morning, and if the same group is scheduled to meet with the trainer for an afternoon session, a case study is recommended for three broad reasons:

1. The group participates. People remain alert.
2. The burden of activity is on the trainees. They are required to do much of the work.
3. The interest levels are heightened because people like to know what others in their group are also thinking.

One-way communication, which occurs when the lecture is used, quickly gives way to a multifaceted interchange. People usually welcome an opportunity to express their own views and opinions and, perhaps, to show off and perform for their associates. Even the shy individual can be drawn from his shell to contribute ideas and views which might prove helpful in the total group learning experience. The perceptive trainer will observe how group members react to the case study materials, and this should be part of his overall goal.

Although the principles of learning will not be covered extensively, this chapter will discuss certain relevant thoughts which must be considered when adults are brought together for learning. Many "learning experiences" are nothing more than glorified bull sessions. The instructional plan is, in fact, no plan at all. "Playing it by ear" usually means "I don't know where the hell we're going." This represents a convenient cop-out for the trainer. When people are assembled for training using participatory methods, the trainer needs to be assured that such participation *leads* to learning.

Certain things are known about how adults learn. How does this knowledge influence decisions to use or not to use the case method? A brief analysis is useful to demonstrate the interrelationship of learning theory to the case method.

One of the basic rules of learning is that people learn best when actively joining in what is being taught. The well-constructed case affords an opportunity for the learner to take a spirited role in analyzing and discussing the body of the case. He is encouraged to contribute ideas, opinions and reactions. As the discussion moves forward, these are picked up by other trainees, absorbed in part, bounced back, and then integrated by the total group. The case method avoids the classic teaching situation depicting the school marm, her finger raised above the class, saying: "All right, children: my job is to talk; and yours is to listen. Should you finish first, raise your hand!"

Another rule of learning is that we learn whole things first. At that point, we can disassemble these wholes into elements when we must do so in order to understand how they work. In a sense, a case situation represents the whole. Under direction, the discussants break the case down into the various elements the trainer had in mind when he introduced it. After the group discussion is completed, the trainer is provided with the opportunity to explain how the elements fit together as a whole. This is good summary reinforcement and a fine application of another principle of learning.

Repetition assists learning, but excessive repetition may be boring, particularly to sophisticated learners. The case study method affords the kinds of repetition which tend to reinforce what has already been known but has not been completely integrated. This repetition has been provided by the trainees themselves.

Learning is furthered and strengthened by the trainee being an active member of a congenial social group. The design of the case study method presents an ideal setting for vigorous training activity. As the learner speaks and captures other points of view, he tends to accept the "group view" as his own, a view with which he can readily identify.

Verbalization is possible without knowledge or understanding. As the discussion advances, group members will usually recognize and control the shallow, fast-talking trainee. And even if they do not, the trainer is able to cope with this situation by serving as a backstop for his trainees during the summarizing period. In any event, because past experiences affect how we learn, the fast talker will usually be exposed during the verbal give-and-take between him and other experienced group members.

We learn most effectively that which is relevant to our own selfish needs. Properly developed or selected case materials should be relevant in terms of the trainees' job situations and will, therefore, provide a learning payoff. The "stinginess factor" comes into play when we learn about other situations and how these had been handled, then relating these back to our own experiences.

One learns only when he is ready to learn. The instructional atmosphere and its setting, before a case is introduced, will be most important. Once the proper foundation has been laid for the introduction of the case and the purposes of the discussion have been made clear to the participants, the readiness factor comes into play. Learning is facilitated or hindered according to how well the trainer has prepared his efforts.

Adults learn effectively when placed in situations where they are able to hook up the new to what they already know. Case materials present practical work illustrations with which they are familiar. Instructional strategy calls for using this as the springboard for the acceptance of new knowledge, skills or altered attitudes. The realism of the case provides the intellectual lubricant, assisting the trainee to advance from the known to the unknown.

The more varied the methodology, the greater the likelihood of getting through. The trainer who talks at his trainees most of the time—no matter how exciting his delivery—will ultimately fail. Therefore, appealing to more than a single sensory channel will engender positive learning results. The author has also observed that if he were unable to explain certain significant points to some of his trainees which he wanted to convey, other trainees who understood the items were able to "translate" these to other members of the group. Case studies help deliver the message; not everything within the class must flow through the mind and lips of the trainer.

Deductive and Inductive Approaches

Switching from the lecture or conference methods to case studies should be an effortless, casual move. The initial case may be introduced as an illustration of a principle already discussed and summarized by the group and the leader. This is an example of deductive or analytic learning: a general principle has been established; its application to particular situations is the immediate objective. In terms of logic as applied to learning, one moves from the general to the specific; from the broad principle to the application of such principles.

Interpreting a principle or concept means much more than simply explain-

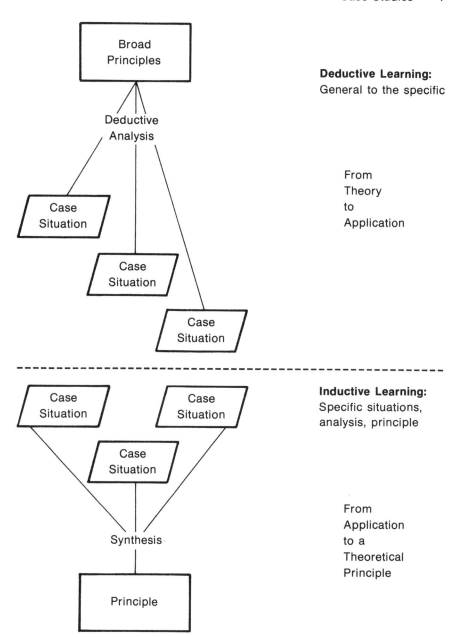

Figure 1.1. Case studies and deductive-inductive learning.

ing to the group how it came to be and showing its relationship to other accepted principles. As group discussion advances from theory to application, the trainees analyze deductively *why* the principle is appropriate in the illustrative cases. Good and effective learning is produced.

However, not everyone learns the same way. Some trainees find it difficult to relate the theoretical concepts covered during the discussion with a case used by the trainer as an example. Therefore, a different approach should be considered. The trainer should forget the principle for a moment and commence with the case. He should use other cases which demonstrate comparable circumstances. He should evaluate what factors, in these three or four case situations, provide a common bond. Then he must guide the trainees so that they themselves will *synthesize* from their study of the cases the broad principle which he wishes them to understand. This approach represents the *inductive* method of instruction. Figure 1.1 illustrates the two learning approaches and the relevance of the case method to each.

Having considered these distinctions and recognizing their value when planning group learning exercises, the reader can advance another step. In the eight examples in Table 1.1, the reader will judge the suitability of each sequence of methods for various learning groups. One can quickly see that for a group of foremen attending their first course in grievance processing Sequence A would be far more effective than Sequence E. Conversely, Sequence E might be a fine arrangement for a group of middle manager participating in a series of sessions organized to improve their decision-making skills.

William Cowper, the English poet, once wrote that "variety's the very spice of life." Variety also belongs in the *how* of teaching—it makes it spicy and zestful. Trainers will be well advised to interweave their methodologies, especially as case materials, roleplaying and other participative exercises are introduced to groups of trainees. The proper variety or mixture of methods will yield more highly motivated participants, greater personal trainee involvement and commitment and higher levels of feedback.

Table 1.1 offers eight ways that methods may be varied for training groups. In terms of possible combinations, the number is nearly limitless. The trainer will, however, select and arrange his methods according to:

1. Course objectives
   a. Precise?
   b. Imprecise?
2. Nature of trainee group
   a. Experienced?
   b. Inexperienced?

Table 1.1. Examples of Case Materials in Combination With Other Instructional Techniques	
Sequence A	**Sequence E**
1. Lecture 2. Lecture-Discussion 3. CASE STUDY 4. Group Evaluations 5. Summary	1. CASE STUDY 2. Roleplay (based on case) 3. Lecture-Discussion (including summary)
Sequence B	**Sequence F**
1. Conference 2. CASE STUDY 3. Group Evaluations 4. Summary	1. Conference 2. CASE STUDY 3. Roleplay (based on case) 4. Conference (including summary)
Sequence C	**Sequence G**
1. CASE STUDY 2. Group Evaluations 3. Lecture (including summary)	1. Conference 2. CASE STUDY 3. In-Basket Exercise 4. Conference (including summary)
Sequence D	**Sequence H**
1. Lecture 2. CASE STUDY 3. Roleplay (based on case) 4. Lecture-Discussion 5. Summary	1. CASE STUDY 2. Conference 3. CASE STUDY 4. Conference (including summary)

    c. Strangers to one another?

    d. Work together?

  3. Timing and scheduling

    a. Training spread out over period of time?

    b. Training condensed in solid time block?

In some of the possible sequences, the trainees advance from the case study directly into the roleplay without first going through the intervening step of a group evaluation of the case. In this approach, the case serves as a warm-up for the subsequent exercise. After the in-basket or roleplay exercises are completed, the trainer may redirect his group back to the case, if necessary. Usually, this is not needed because the trainees will have gained a complete appreciation of the principles through the more active exercise. The interconnection between case materials and roleplays is discussed below.

Before Using the Case Study: A Few Cautions

If learning is strengthened and bonded by moving the learner from simple to more complex techniques, then learning systems must be planned accordingly. A few common sense rules follow.

1. Start with trainer-controlled learning for inexperienced participants.
2. Gradually shift to group learning as the learners become experienced with the methods.
3. Avoid assigning complex learning exercises before learners have acquired the skill necessary to master the simpler ones.
4. Recognize that group "involvement," which is often translated to mean lots of talk, is not necessarily synonymous with learning.

For trainees who have not acquired a firm base in sophisticated methods of presentation, games may become gimmicks. From sessions where there was extensive involvement and much pleasure, trainees emerge with little useful learning to be carried over to the job. If the trainer is sharp enough to recognize this condition, he becomes forced into making a mighty leap backwards, to bridge or link the new exercise with something the trainee never had. This situation is somewhat like encouraging trainees to build a space platform without first understanding how space rockets work.

Another caution to be considered before moving into the case method is this: decide what learning is sought. Is the proposed learning in the areas of knowledge, skills, attitudes or combinations of skills and attitudes? If learners lack the basic knowledge, there is little to talk about. Perhaps this is why trainers often tend to overrely on case studies for "human relations" training, since all are presumably "knowledgeable" in this area. In reality, case studies may be used to cover all three kinds of situations. Obviously, the participants must have a basic knowledge of the subject area under consideration. The degree of knowledge within a group working on a case study will vary. Individual trainees will learn new facts from one another. Where a disagreement occurs during the course of the discussion about whether a particular fact is correct, the role of the trainer is that of a clarifier. A case study may be used in teaching a group how to sell mutual funds; what went wrong during the investigation of a bank robbery; or why a particular employee was

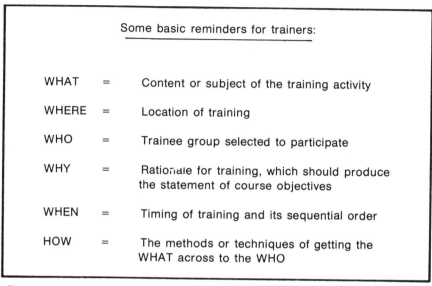

Some basic reminders for trainers:

WHAT   =   Content or subject of the training activity

WHERE   =   Location of training

WHO   =   Trainee group selected to participate

WHY   =   Rationale for training, which should produce
the statement of course objectives

WHEN   =   Timing of training and its sequential order

HOW   =   The methods or techniques of getting the
WHAT across to the WHO

Figure 1.2. Elementary interrelationships found in group teaching activities.

released from service after thirteen years of "faithful" performance. The skills inherent in solving problems are also important as part of many case studies. Frequently this will be a desirable goal in and of itself.

Each case must breed excitement and stimulate learning. If it fails to do this for the particular group, its value is low. What is a good case for one group may have very little value for another. Some basic reminders for trainers are presented in Figure 1.2.

Objectives and the Case Method:
Can We Stay on Target?

Objectives are desirable when they make sense, But one must not be enslaved by them. It is unrealistic to require evidence that, as a result of participation in a particular case study exercise, an individual trainee can now do something which he was unable to perform before.* Case studies by their very

*Herbert M. Engel, "Evaluating Employee Development," in *Employee Training and Development in the Public Service,* ed. K.T. Byers (Chicago: Public Personnel Association, 1970), Chapter 13.

nature may alter the objectives which the trainers set beforehand. New learning "needs" which result from a case study may change the direction of the learning activity.

This leads to the need for a brief treatise on the evident conflict between the content of a training activity and the apparent loss of control by the trainer in achieving the content when he uses participative training methods. Can the trainer be certain of achieving his goal if he shares "power" with his trainees? Clearly, case studies differ radically from individualized learning. Programmed material, carefully drawn to elicit responses from a single trainee is rigid and inflexible when compared to case studies. Norman Crowder's contribution of branching attempted to humanize the seemingly mechanistic programmed instructional process. In case studies, the human element is the center of power; the interchange of thought—wrong or right—energizes the heart of the system. Therefore, the attainment of even broadly stated objectives calls for careful planning by the trainer to stay on target.

The techniques described in this book—case studies, the in-basket, roleplaying and other exercises—cover the *how* of the training program or course. Precise separation between objectives, content and technique will be feasible only when the instructor completely controls the teaching technique at *every* stage. The lecture, as an illustration, includes a body of subject content, transmitted down a one-way street to the trainees. Staying "on target" (i.e., covering the *what* of the course) demands that the trainer control the mode and direction of the *how*.

However, getting the teacher to move away from his objectives has always been a student-instructor duel. The trainer may face this situation in his training session and must learn to cope with it.

Control may also be jeopardized when "active" methods or techniques have been selected or improperly adjusted for the training session. In this case, the trainer may also lose control over the content itself.

Suppose, for a moment, that a trainer has decided to cover the subject of problem solving. This is to be the *what* of the selected training activity. Assume also that the trainer intends to use case studies to cover his subject. The subject is introduced; the group goes to work on the case material relating to problem solving techniques; at least this is what the trainer has intended. The active discussion involving the case, however, quickly leads the group away from his goal (problem solving techniques) toward the intrinsic content of the case itself. Suddenly the group members are uninterested in learning methodology about solving cases. They demand answers to the problems presented *within* the case. The group wants to discuss poor communication in their organization, to lay the blame for the problem described in the case on such poor communication rather than getting into how the case itself might be solved by a typical supervisor within the training class. The active participation of the group has seemingly subverted the original intent of the instructor. What does he do to keep on target and to avoid such situations? A few suggestions follow.

Before the case is used, the trainer will restudy it carefully. If feasible he may want to show it to a colleague for another opinion as to its appropriateness in the proposed teaching activity. Most written material is best "left over-night" for rereading. What appeared to be great at 4:30 p.m. often looks dismal at 9:00 the following morning.

Suitability of any learning materials over which *others* have control requires trainer empathy. The trainer must imagine how the trainee will read the material (even if the material is taken off the shelf or out of a book such as this one). Will the trainee comprehend the subtleties of the case? Will his eyes focus on certain words, which for him have a meaning different from that which you had in mind? Is he apt to be diverted by a phrase or two which remind him of a recent hot issue within the plant? Sometimes trainers unfairly label their trainees as slow or dense when the fault is their own because of the way the training materials were constructed.

The case will focus on real situations and on problems with which the trainees can readily identify. Sufficient facts will be provided to meet the needs of the given situation.

At the time the case is *first* introduced, the trainer makes clear (using the lecture method) what objectives are to be achieved. The discussion which will follow (conference method) should reemphasize that the goal is a better *system* of problem solving, rather than securing an answer to one isolated problem. All of the above are summarized by the trainer *before* commencing the case study.

After the groups have begun to work, the trainer should circulate about unobtrusively. He should listen in and observe the small group discussions to be assured that the participants are working only on the problem. (Not gossiping about who is apt to be promoted or fired).

The trainer must avoid becoming personally involved in the small group discussions unless:

1. The group is completely off the topic. Then he should suggest that members get bact on the track.
2. The group misunderstood the case. He must clarify facts for them and for other groups. Perhaps he did not make all details clear.

3. The group completed its work ahead of other groups still actively occupied. He can assign extra questions for the speedy group to consider.

In spite of these reasonable precautions designed to keep the trainees focused on the topic, situations will arise where the trainees insist on considering the details of the case rather than the principles underlying it and a method for solving similar problems. Repeating that "it's the principles involved, not the circumstances" is apt to leave the trainees dissatisfied. Therefore, the trainer may have to explain (if he knows) what really happened and how the matter had been resolved. Factors introduced to make the case more challenging, but which actually never happened, are also clarified. *Precedent* will be powerful factor in selected areas of training where the case method is used. In labor-management relations involving discipline or grievance handling, the rulings of fact finders or arbitrators carry much weight in future managerial behavior. Nonetheless, it is unlikely that two situations are ever exactly alike. Consequently, the danger of transferring one set of conditions to a similar set may simply result in the recycling of errors. Using the case to teach trainees to think before they talk, to analyze prior to action and to apply a system of problem solving will provide the most productive returns.

Introducing Case Materials

What should the trainer say to his group when he initially proposes the case study method?

Following are some suggested lead-ins when using case materials for the first time.

> This afternoon we're going to work on a problem, which is being presented as if it really happened—and it probably has, somewhere! The material which I'm about to hand out does not relate to anyone in this room. Please rest assured that it's entirely fictional and that any similarity to persons living or dead is simply coincidental!

A bit of humor may be inserted to remove the possibility that a trainee could assume that the case is about him. When case materials are used for the first time, the accompanying discussions are always about "the other guy"—a fictitious character who, of course, is not a member of *this* training group.

Now that we've hit the highlights of the (whatever the subject of the lecture or discussion), let's see how this can be applied to a true-to-life case situation. The printed case which I'm about to hand out is based on a *real* situation, but not one—as far as I can know—which has a personal tie-in to anyone in this group. Be assured that it has been concocted out of my own personal experience, in *another business*, but which should be, nonetheless, very close to your interests.

As was noted in the preceding introduction, the "present company" is excluded by the trainer's explanation. He ensures that the trainees will realize that it could apply to them by linking the case with their probable job circumstances. This helps make it real and germane to their work-a-day world.

If the trainer is uncertain about the previous training experience of his students, he will often ask for a show of hands to this question: "How many of you have had some experience in a training session working with a problem case?"

This information will quickly give the trainer some guidelines as to how detailed and exact his introductions to case materials must be. The trainer also recognizes and adjusts to the problems inherent in the differences between the written and spoken language. Case materials which are read aloud but are not made available in writing to the participants will be perceived differently by the trainees than case materials presented in writing without having been read aloud. Written language lends itself natually to "nit-picking." It is probably asking for the impossible to expect case materials to exclude every word with a double meaning or terms which are vague or ambiguous. If the material is read aloud, the collective memory of the listeners will be different than the reading capacities of all individuals working the identical case. One sound reason for presenting the case both in writing and by reading it aloud is that this provides the trainer's inflections, his emphasis and the verbal underscoring which he might wish the trainees to hear. If this is not important, then the oral rendition may be omitted. In any event, the trainer, as he circulates about the room while the individuals study the case and discuss its contents, should be alert to misreadings, misinterpretations and misapplications of essential points inserted by the trainees even though he had never so intended. After the trainees begin to work on a case, the trainer who knows his business will not leave the classroom and head for the nearest coffee urn.

Cases should be used as parts of other instructional techniques. The conference method is one technique which can be readily converted to the case study approach. The conference leader may also serve as the case study leader. Individual copies of the cases are distributed to all participants, and the case is read aloud by the leader as all participants follow their own copies. This is a good warm-up introduction to a more intensive utilization of case studies. The conference is also a good way for the leader to evaluate the individual group members and determine which ones are likely to be strong or weak, argumentative or supportive, passive or active.

As a reminder, the following check list contains a few items to ensure a profitable, introductory case discussion, when the trainer doubles as the leader of the group.

1. *Seating of group members.* Make certain they can all *see* and *hear* one another. Arrange chairs in a V-shape, circle or square or at rectangular tables, depending on room size and equipment. Plush, overstuffed furniture does not contribute to successful group work. Occasionally, the trainer must work in a room with fine, straight-back chairs, but it also contains lounge-type furniture around the perimeter. Do not permit some trainees to use these chairs. Ask politely, but firmly, that all members sit and work together.*

2. *Group size.* Avoid "starting" groups in excess of 25—too large to handle effectively. An ideal number is around 20.

3. *Writing equipment.* Have a flip chart, overhead projector or chalk board at hand. This is great for summarizing total group reactions, linking facts to principles, etc. Masking tape is desirable when tearing pages from the flip chart and "posting" them on walls, as the group becomes increasingly productive in its output. Do not forget flow pens (color attracts attention) and/or chalk.

4. *Tent cards.* Encourage trainees to learn each other's names. Name cards, folded like small tents, help do this.

Disbanding the Large Group

When the total training group is divided, a means of subgrouping the larger group must be sought. Decision-making as to the composition of the smaller groups is usually best left in the hands of the trainer. For instance, if there are twenty participants in the total group, chances are that some of the trainees are seated together with their friends. It is generally unwise to divide the groups up on the basis of how they seat themselves. Since the purpose of the learning experience is to exchange ideas with others, the "others" should be

---

*Leslie E. This, *The Small Meeting Planner* (Houston: Gulf Publishing Company, 1972).

members of the total training group with whom individual trainees have fewer personal contacts. The best way of dividing the larger groups is to have the members count off from one to four or five and then to seat all the one's in one corner, all the two's in another, and so on. After the subgroups have been assembled in their respective locations and the individual members seated facing each other in a circle, the case materials are distributed and then read aloud together, as has already been noted.

Each small group may have a leader, or it may operate on a leaderless basis, according to what the trainer decides. The small groups may also select a reporter who doubles as a leader, or both a leader and reporter may be used. In most instances, the former is the better approach, particularly when the case is short and uncomplicated. The so-called "democratic" selection of leaders and reporters within training groups is often wasteful in that this cuts into the time available for the actual discussion of the case.

At times, small groups seem to play games with trainers where group spokesmen have not been selected. When the trainer asks Group Three to report, for example, and no spokesman had been selected, there is apt to be some embarrassing foolishness as to who will verbalize the group's report. Ultimately the trainer may have to intervene and designate one trainee to report for the group. The trainer will always allow for minority reports after all of the groups have come through with their reports.

Judging Case Materials

The points developed in the following commentary apply equally to judging another's work and one's own efforts. In Chapter 2 on writing cases, the reader will be reminded of these observations.

Three broad factors should be examined and studied when evaluating case materials: *language, content* and *length*.

Language

Language is a combination of words to give meaning and communication of messages, ideas, attitudes, expressions, feelings and facts.

Because, the written language of the case provides a permanent record, it offers a greater opportunity for contemplation and dissection of the message. Therefore the case language must convey what the trainer intends it to convey to the reader.

To ensure that the trainees understand what it is the trainer wants them to understand as they read a case, the trainer can use the guidelines in the following check list for judging effective language.

1. Case language *suitable* for trainees. Words used are simplest needed to carry thoughts.
2. Exact message and meaning transmitted.
3. Sentences suitably short and clear.
4. Technical expressions can be understood.
5. Ideas and concepts presented in logical order.

Content

The content of the case largely involves its appropriateness for the trainees. What constitutes fine material for one group could well be inappropriate for another. Here are some factors to consider.

1. Complexity of materials is *suitable* for trainee group.
2. Dated, passé material is eliminated.
3. Realistic situations are presented.
4. Emotionality of materials is suitable for the trainee group. This refers primarily to cases where trainee sensibilities are involved. Emotionally loaded language is fine if its inclusion moves the group toward the broadly stated objectives of the session.
5. Mood, tone or humor of materials will elicit the desired outcomes.
6. Total case situation is one with which group can readily identify.
7. Embarrassment or ridicule of individual trainees is avoided. This refers to the possibility that cases devised by trainees may contain well-publicized incidents which make one particular trainee look foolish. If the trainer is not perceptive, one particular member of the group may become the butt of the case.

Length

Common sense rules are applied as to the conciseness and completeness of the written materials. If the case is too complete, little is left for the trainees to mull over. Similarly, if insufficient data is offered, there is apt to be a floundering about within the small group discussions. The following check list provides a few guideposts for the case length.

1. Materials from cases which trainees have worked on previously have

been avoided.
2. The length of case is suitable for the time available for deliberation.
3. All essential material is presented.
4. Extraneous materials, having no relevance to essential facts or to "setting the scene," have been eliminated.
5. Long-winded expressions and circumlocutions are eliminated or rephrased into shorter forms.

Off the Shelf or Tailor-Made?

Many textbooks, especially on supervision and management, provide case materials at the end of each chapter. These are intended to be tied to the teaching activity. A chapter discussing the subject of planning might have a series of four or five cases relating to problems about management responsibility for planning. At the end of each such case, three or four questions, designed to stimulate class members in their thinking, may be posed. Often the instructor—and this applies primarily to teaching in a college setting—will ask his students to prepare written responses to the questions found at the end of the assigned cases. He will use the questions and answers as a means to stimulate class discussion. He may also use the student responses as one basis for determining whether or not they read and understood the material or as means for providing a letter grade.

Occasionally, texts are accompanied by teachers' manuals which offer helpful tips on the use of selected cases, the principles involved and suggested follow-up questions for the teacher.

Published case materials will sometimes seem to be ideal for the trainer because they save considerable time and effort in the construction of comparable materials. Published case materials should not be used, however, if they do not fit the precise needs of the group and the trainer. "Fit" involves numerous factors. For example, a case dealing with a situation in a government bureau might not be suitable for a similar group with seemingly similar problems working in a profit-based organization. Even though the principles and situations are very similar on the surface the mind-set of the individual trainees may be turned off by the illustrative circumstances in which the case is framed. Almost all people have the ability to empathize with analogous situations in varying degrees. However, if trainees are unable to visualize the relationships between the written (canned) case and the situation that the trainer is trying to convey in his own organization, time and effort are wasted and the desired result is not produced. Because cases are so easy to construct, there is rarely any good reason for the trainer to fail to develop specialized case materials for the group with which he is working. This will be discussed in greater detail in Chapter 2.

Questions at the conclusion of cases are provided to stimulate thinking. Therefore, these should (a) be relevant to the case material; (b) provoke thoughtfulness on the part of the reader, and (c) connect with some principle, rule or process which the trainer wishes to cover as part of his objectives.

The questions should be phrased to provide the reader with the opportunity for explaining his responses. Leading questions where a "yes" or "no" answer may be offered as the complete response should be avoided. If this type of question is the only way that the problem can be stated, the word "explain" should be inserted after the question. For instance, a question might read, "Was the foreman justified in his reprimand to Bill? Explain or justify your answer."

Linking the Case to the Lesson Plan

How are case materials correlated with the instructional plan? Some trainers are able to pick up new case materials and quickly envision the principal discussional outputs that are likely to spring up during the group work. Yet even experienced instructors desire an instrument that ensures all key materials within a case are carefully tied to an action plan to be used in the classroom. Such an instrument reminds the trainer that he will not overlook vital issues and, at the same time, is sufficiently flexible in meeting the unexpected.

Training time is a precious commodity. Our aim is to trim the unnecessary, unproductive and repetitious. By linking key language within the case to the lesson's major topics (which, in turn, directly carry out the objectives of the session), we are certain that the group work will be mirrored in the instructor-led discussion or summarization.

The example in the appendix demonstrates how case materials are inserted into the format of a lesson plan. Two primary and different uses of the case study are shown:

1. *Major topics I-VI*: using the case to teach principles of supervision or management.
2. *Major topics VII-XII*: using the case to teach problem analysis and decision-making. (See p. 26 f f for discussion on use of cases in problem analysis and decision-making.)

The amount of time to be allocated for each major topic has not been set. A case such as the one illustrated in the appendix will usually require from two to three hours for each of the two purposes shown. The instructor would ordinarily take the total time available (say, three hours) and equate this to 100 percent. Each major topic included would then be suballocated a percentage figure, the total to equal 100%.

Break Time

Coffee or coke breaks have become institutionalized features of most training activities. Profitable, free-flowing discussion and an attending reinforcement may take place during this "downtime" period. The formal socializing, structured by the trainer, continues in another dimension during coffee. Because trainees occasionally associate such socializing periods with training, they (and their bosses, unfortunately) may fail to recognize that productive learning continues unabated. The frill becomes a necessity for the smart trainer. The key to the successful use of breaks is flexibility. The trainer must avoid becoming schedule-bound. The author has seen modern training facilities which have installed automatic clocks, buzzing every 50 to 60 minutes during the day. Forced ten-minute breaks each hour, in complete disregard for the varied ways that people work and learn in groups, soon effect both instructor and trainees as did the bell developed by Pavlov for his animals.

Breaks should be scheduled at natural break points during the instruction. If four small groups are engaged in the same case problem and Group Three finishes its work three minutes ahead of Groups One, Two and Four, there is no reason why Group Three has to remain seated. This group should be allowed to break (quietly) while the other groups continue working.

Groups tend to operate at different speeds according to the human mix within each. When productive discussions are taking place, the patient trainer will permit his groups to complete their work, even if each is operating at varying rates of speed.

The trainer may have to cut the discussion—but only if the day's schedule is apt to be thrown off badly. If the training facility permits, trainees may bring their coffee into the conference room and continue group work right through their break period.

Summarizations

Participating in a case study and then being stranded in mid-air as to the necessary conclusions is akin to a rifle platoon on training maneuvers moving through dense underbrush without being told if its objectives are being met. Both situations have produced activities, but to what purpose? After they have finished their work, trainees welcome a critique and wrap-up. They want to know where they stand. Adults, particularly, want to know how well they have done. This need must be met by the trainer during the summary. Two ways for handling the summary are suggested.

1. Group assignments may include a mandate that members will be expected to summarize the principles which they consider applicable as a result of working on the assigned case.
2. After completion of group discussion, the trainer *lectures* on relationships between content of case materials and the intended principles. Use of the chalk board, flip chart or overhead projector may reinforce the message. He synthesizes the suggested group findings with the fundamentals that he had in mind when the session was planned. The preparation for this will have been completed and reproduced for ready accessibility in the lesson plan.

Accessibility of Learning Exercises

Well-organized trainers will have study files which can be tapped for ready use. In supervisory training, for instance, the file might be separated into broad subcategories such as discipline, appraisal, employee relations, grievances and similarly relevant headings. However, many case materials, roleplays and in-basket exercises cover more than a single topic. By making extra copies for filing in several suitable file jackets, time can be saved on cross-referencing and later retrieval.

Some topics within cases require a special, precise classification. Trying to fit these into general categories when filing may result in loss. Because the need of some unusual illustration may arise within a course, such materials should be readily available. Figure 1.3 indicates how this may be done.

Live and in Living Color

The written word evokes images within the mind's eye. A person reads, and based on past experience, his brain provides the illustrations necessary to fit the language. If a story mentions a "burly, heavy-set mechanic taking a swing at the foreman," he automatically plugs in certain circuits and the mechanic on his inner screen resembles a character with whom he has had an argument

---

On the Prowl for Safety

Jim Pierce was making his weekly <u>inspection tour</u> through the Z Unit of the plant. As a <u>management trainee</u>, Jim was serving as "safety officer" one portion of a <u>three-month rotational assignment.</u> Jim <u>was looking for violations of plant safety regulations</u>, which he <u>zealously</u> noted and forwarded to the front office.

Dead ahead of him on the walkway, which was supposed to be clear of all impediments, was a heavy electrical cable. It lay across the walk, from where to where Jim couldn't immediately tell as he examined it because the cable ran alongside heavy storage stock. In the dim lighting, one could easily trip and break his neck.

Jim stopped, pulled his clipboard up to his waist and started to write. Just then he felt a sharp tap on his back. He turned to face an obviously angry Joe O'Brien, a maintenance foreman.

"What the hell are you doing, smart boy? Writing up a safety report? Go ahead, write it up! Management wants production but is unwilling to spend a few bucks for more outlets. Safety! That's a joke around here!"

What should Jim Pierce do in response to Joe O'Brien's outburst? Should Pierce report O'Brien's outburst to his boss? Explain. If he does report, should it be in writing? Explain. What conditions and attitudes seem to be prevalent? Explain. What do you believe is the real problem here?

1. Attitudes (toward safety)
2. Safety procedures
3. Professionals and nonprofessionals (relations between)
4. Training (use of rotational assignments)
5. Report preparation

Figure 1.3. Topical areas and/or principles for curricula files.

in the past. In historical nonfiction, which may be "profusely illustrated," readers' images are channeled into the photographic patterns which accompany the text. However if one considers how the novel differs from nonfiction and how in numerous world-famous tales, one identifies the principal character with someone who has portrayed the part on the screen. Bela Lugosi becomes Count Dracula; Basil Rathbone, Sherlock Holmes; and Sean Connery, James Bond.

There is a lesson in connection with these examples when trainers overrely on the cases in forms other than the written word. Some cases are produced as a recorded roleplay, either on a sound tape recorder or on video tape. Other cases come to us as a portion of a 16mm motion picture.

In many training situations, the carefully written case is likely to have practical advantages over the one that is presented visually, on video tape or as a 16mm motion picture. Identification for most trainees comes as readily, and they are less distracted by the theatrical features of the presentation. The same comments may apply, though to a lesser extent, to the case presented on sound tape. While a strict advantage-versus-disadvantage comparison presents some problems, compelling arguments for continuing with the written word can be noted.

In Writing

Written cases are inexpensive and relatively easy and simple to construct. Such materials are easy to transport and to organize for group work in many different training situations. No special mechanical equipment or darkened room is required. The trainer is able to judge the speed with which the participants assimilate the data within the cases. The participants may reread and recheck the data within the case, using whatever time is allocated by the trainer. The participants also have the written case available on which to make notes and to jot down relevant comments that may be used during discussion or taken back to the work situation. Reading a case requires that the reader visualize the action, the people depicted in carrying out the action and the nature of the problem. Obviously, each trainee will interpret differently the language describing the people within the case and their actions. Diagrams and sketches within the case assist in the trainees' focusing process so that everyone is encouraged to see the particular point at issue the same way.

On Film

All participants view the case as a series of live actions. Unlike reading a written case where intake speeds vary, everyone is required to see the same sequences simultaneously. The trainer may stop the film at a suitable break point for discussion of the case situation shown up to that point. He has the option of replaying or advancing the film after a portion of the group discussion is completed. Despite the idea that "one picture is worth a thousand words," the filmed version raises real problems of perceptual differences.

Although everyone is forced to observe everything at the same time (assuming that no one is dozing), not everyone "senses" the same material in the same way. Important factors within the filmed case may be missed. Further, the use of projectors and other gadgetry can be an inhibiting factor when considering whether to introduce case materials. Many people regard films as entertainment; consequently, participants may overrelax during the showing and miss key factors within the case. In one well-known training film dealing with instructional methods, observers are transported into a football stadium. Perhaps this filmed portion was inserted to underscore the necessity for adequate preparation, the big game being the payoff for teaching how to throw a football straight and true. Unfortunately, some viewers are undoubtedly transfixed by the football sequence and are "off and running" toward an objective far different than that intended by the instructor.

However, films are closer to the real thing than written cases in one vital aspect: the genuine case occurs through time and space and its circumstances are seen only once.* Live participants cannot be rewound to reenact the events. What has been perceived is finished. All that is left is memory. Therefore, the one-time film showing of a case comes closer to simulating the real occurrence than does the written version.

As the trainer applies the case study method, regardless of what materials are used, he will remind his trainees that in real life our memories require assistance. That is why the police officer and investigator keep note pads on which to record, as soon after an event as practical, the details of what was observed.

Sound Cassettes and VTR

Usually at or near the end of a written case is a sentence such as: "You are now entering your manager's office to_____." Intended to provide a modicum of realism and to focus attention on the decision-making requirements within the case, this language may be an indication that the case lends itself naturally for conversion into another medium. The total case can be "inserted" into the sound (cassette) tape recorder. Written dialogue material is tape-recorded onto a cassette so that the trainees will listen to what occurred, rather than reading about it. The "then and there" of the case becomes the "here and

---

*This point is well made in emphasizing contrasting perceptions in the Japanese film classic "Rashomon," as well as in the training film "The Eye of the Beholder" (Stuart Reynolds Productions).

now." This must be considered by the trainer in terms of his trainees (their sophistication) and his objectives (how does he want them to receive and interpret the message).

For the trainer, the virtue of cassettes is their ease of use, storage and filing. Another advantage is the accessibility of a practical system of recording the trainees actions as they "solve" the case, as well as the simplicity of playback and analysis by the trainer. The implications for roleplay conversions are also obvious. These are discussed in Chapter 5.

Having considered the feasibility of a transference of a case from the written word onto the sound cassette, the trainer must also be alert to the possibilities of still another step: putting the situation described within the case onto video tape. When this is done, the trainer is faced with many of the features of the filmed medium. However, the completed VTR sequence is unlikely to be as slick as a commercially produced 16mm motion picture. The trainer will want to weigh costs versus benefits of each approach. New technological developments and lower costs have made sound cassette recorders and VTR equipment feasible under circumstances where once both were viewed as impractical or excessively expensive.

Using Case Materials in Problem Analysis and Decision-Making

One learns by doing—but what is it that he learns? Does he learn the *function* or the *process*?

When "chewed out" by his supervisor for punching another's time card, does the worker learn that (a) this was a stupid action not to be repeated (function) or (b) next time he had better be more careful so that he will not get caught (process). The employee may conceivably learn both process and function. Although he realizes it is wrong to punch another's card, when the work group pressures become so great and if everyone else is doing it, he may still risk this action, being more cautious, however, to avoid getting caught.

This illustration is instructive when explaining why case studies are desirable in teaching problem analysis and decision-making. Without a planned approach for training and development (i.e., systematized learning by doing), the learning by doing becomes based on a "watch Joe" technique. "Joe" in this context is anyone—usually a colleague or supervisor—whose "doing" rubs off onto the learner. Such a learning system is hardly to be commended. Obviously, there are better ideas—to borrow a thought from Ford—for streamlining methods that people use to learn problem analysis.

The use of cases provides the means for (a) establishing the objectives in relation to the doing-learning process, (b) controlling the learning conditions which advance the learner in the desired direction and (c) accelerating the learning process. Some authorities concede that experience cannot be beat.* At the same time, they emphasize that this kind of learning may take too long even if it were systematized and arranged to be progressively more difficult and demanding. Therefore, case simulation is used as a desirable and available alternate. Many applications of case studies are concerned with teaching a process rather than how individual functions or situations were resolved. Trainers want to instruct trainees how to apply a *logical system*—one which can be used, regardless of the real life circumstances. If this is the program objective and if this objective has been thoroughly explained to the trainees (this is considered to be of critical importance), then the trainer can proceed with the following outline:

1. *Receive and study case.* Trainees receive material and read it together (for the first time).
2. *Sort and reassemble data within case.* Trainees separate what is *known* from what is uncertain. Trainees sort facts from inferences and agree which inferences may be accepted as reasonable. One technique provides that inferences are sorted into three bins: the probable, the possible and the remote. Trainees then determine the probabilities that particular inferences can be accepted and combined with facts, or which inferences they are willing to bet on.
3. *Reassess the material.* Trainees discuss what is the problem. Is there more than a single problem? Group consensus is obtained. Logic of group agreement must be supported under Steps 2 and 3.
4. *Decision-making.* Trainees consider and agree on solutions. Which alternatives are available and which alternatives are feasible and practical? How important is time as a factor in getting the problem solved? Must this be done immediately, or may the problem be deferred? Finally, trainees accept a single solution after a group agreement, justifying why this is the best of all alternatives.

As is true with other kinds of off-the-job education, the case method does not guarantee an automatic transfer of learning to the job situation. Topside organizational knowledge, support and reinforcement are mandatory. But, if this is accepted fact, how does case studies training produce more effective problem analysis and decision-making.?

*Charles H. Kepner and Benjamin B. Tregoe, *The Rational Manager*, p. 229.

Analyzing problems and making decisions are what supervisors and managers are paid to do. Problems which are analyzed quickly and handled acceptably save money and reduce future criticism. When adopting the case method, a training goal is to teach a trainee to refrain from speaking before thinking. Special qualities within the case study method which are peculiarly effective when teaching problem analysis and decision-making follow.

1. Trainees learn to separate facts from inferences. Problem analysis requires that inferences be identified. Decisions based on unrecognized inferences may produce unexpected and undesirable results. Ultimately, when actions based upon problem analysis are carried out all should understand the degrees of risk involved.
2. After group analysis, multidimensional problems become redefined, and the consequences of proposed actions become clearer.
3. Alternative approaches are outlined and described by the group. The individual trainee is exposed to broader concepts than he normally would receive on the job.
4. Shooting from the hip, when analyzing problems, is unacceptable. The "gunman" is forced to defend his way of doing things to the group members and is invariably shown to be in error.
5. Because cases often tend to focus in on the kinds of problems with which supervisors and managers deal (communications, morale, motivation, interpersonal relations, discipline, etc.), the participants learn how to handle particular situations which will arise within their own areas of authority and responsibility. Although no two cases are alike, the trainees may transfer information gained through the study of a case to a real-life occurrence. For instance, in grievance handling there are certain things which a supervisor or manager does not do. The learning which comes out of a case involving grievance handling should be transferred back to the job for some future situation.

There is a distinction between problem analysis and decision-making. (Note that the term *problem analysis* is used rather than *problem solving*.) Problems must be identified through analysis before they can be solved. Few, if any, problems are automatically solved simply through emergence after analysis. Analysis of the situation or case leads to identification, which, in turn, leads to decision making, a point illustrated in Figure 1.4.

Seen from this perspective, the analysis phase must precede the solving phase. The solution or decision will be either a single or multiple action. What is done or not done subsequent to problem analysis will depend essen-

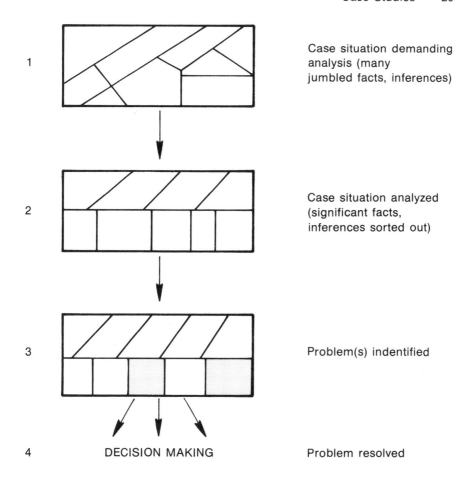

1		Case situation demanding analysis (many jumbled facts, inferences)
2		Case situation analyzed (significant facts, inferences sorted out)
3		Problem(s) indentified
4	DECISION MAKING	Problem resolved

Figure 1.4. Analysis of a situation or case leads to identification which in turn leads to decision making.

tially on which open alternative for resolving the problem is most attractive. What is likely to be done will be decided on the basis of past knowledge or personal experiences. Innovative decisions (i.e., ones which have never been tried) are applied because, given a particular analysis and problem identification, what has been done in the past in precisely similar circumstances has failed to work.

Therefore, decision-making is more likely to be experiential and intuitive.

Consequently, case materials are most beneficial for learning when used during the analysis process. The importance of avoiding rushing the group through to how the case "came out" cannot be overemphasized. Doing this is analogous to the reader of an Earle Stanley Gardner mystery turning to the final chapter to find out how Perry Mason solved the case. Getting there should be more than half the fun!

Harvard Cases

The American Association of Collegiate Schools of Business and Harvard University's Graduate School of Business have collaborated to create the Intercollegiate Case Clearing House (Soldiers Field P.O., Boston, Massachusetts 02163). This represents a coordinated effort to pull together major case study contributions, primarily by the academe. The case "method," for which Harvard may legitimately claim credit, harks back before the turn of the century. Generally speaking the methodologies just described are simply variations of the Harvard Case Method. Of course, many of the cases are highly technical and are strictly oriented for use in schools of business administration. Cases vary from a few to nearly 100 pages.

Information about available versions of the published cases may be obtained by writing to the clearing house. Cases are classified into six broad categories:

1. Controls, Accounting and Statistical
2. Finance and Financial Institutions
3. General Management: Policy and Social, Economic and Political Aspects
4. Human Aspects of Administration
5. Marketing
6. Production. Other cases available cover functional problems in data processing, foreign trade and similar technical topics.

The Incident Process

A variation of the case method was developed several years ago by Dr. Paul Pigors, Massachusetts Institute of Technology. Referred to as the incident process, it has been widely used in supervisory and management development. The cases produced by Dr. Pigors have also been employed for courses in decision-making and problem analysis. The time required for the incident process is generally longer than for traditional case studies. The term, *incident process*, has been used as synonymous with other variations of the case study method, often distinctly different than which Dr. Pigors originally had in mind. The description of the incident process which follows is based on the official explanation of this training method, as provided by the Bureau of National Affairs.*

A brief problem situation (the incident) is presented to the group by a discussion leader who has at hand the background facts surrounding the situation. He gives out pertinent facts only as participants ask for them. This forces participants to reconstruct the entire situation from start to finish.

This pattern duplicates real-life business situations where all pertinent facts are not always clearly laid out for the man who must make the decisions. He must dig for the facts through questioning and analysis before he can arrive at a sound decision.

Companies using the method have found that it emphasizes the development of leadership skills, develops or reinforces the habit of getting a full set of facts before making a decision, and helps participants understand how their decisions affect the goals, practices, policies and established procedures of the company.

Each session follows a planned, five-step approach toward the best solution of the problem presented. This five-step pattern-of-attack on a problem soon becomes a built-in work habit. After participating in a series of these sessions, the supervisor or manager finds himself following this pattern-of-attack routinely:

1. Analyze the incident.
2. Get the facts.
3. Define the major question for immediate action and the subquestions on which the decision hinges.
4. Weigh alternatives and decide.
5. Follow-up decision and evaluate the facts for future action.

Simultaneous Case Studies

Seasoned trainers using case materials are sometimes frustrated by the pattern of group reports which are provided after four or five small groups have worked on the same material. What occurs is that Group One reports its

---

*The Pigors Incident Process," developed by Paul Pigors and Faith Pigors (Washington: BNA Incorporated). Reprinted with permission.

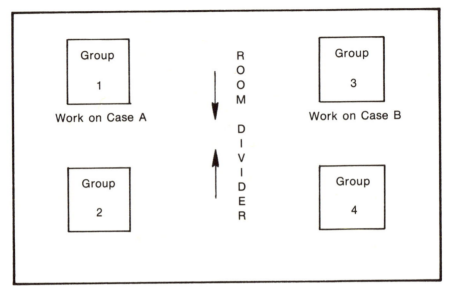

Figure 1.5. Seating arrangement for simultaneous case studies.

findings, Group Two adds more in its report; Group Three provides some additional details; and Group Four, somewhat unhappily, confirms that its report essentially contains the same substances as has already been reported.

When more than a single case is to be used during a session, the trainer will often reverse the order of reporting for the next case. This means that the group that reported last now reports first. The solution, intended to give every group an even break, still fails to resolve the dilemma of the last group's report.

This is disappointing to both the trainer and to the group reporting last. Its members ususally feel that they have been thwarted out of participation in the problem—and they undoubtedly have. Their product has been preempted by another group.

What can be done to overcome this predicament? The author has found simultaneous case studies very effective.

Two different cases covering the *same* topic or principle are assigned to the trainees. Half of the trainees receive Case One; the other half, Case Two. If the room has a divider or if two adjoining rooms are available, the trainer divides the entire class into an even number of small groups. Half of the small groups work on Case One in one area; the other half on Case Two in another area. (Figure 1.5 shows the seating arrangement.)

Both cases must be about the same length so that the time required for reading, discussion and analysis by each small group is about equal.

Before starting the reporting process, the trainer explains that two different cases have been worked on. Reporting then begins. Groups One and Two, which worked on the first case, report; then Groups Three and Four, which had the second case, report. Since the principles involved in both cases are the same, the trainer is able to reinforce these principles from one case to the other. The interest level is high within the small groups, since they are not listening, in terms of the events in the cases, to a rehash of what has already been covered. Intergroup questions are encouraged so that details of the cases can be clarified.

2. How to Develop and Write Case Study Materials

Numerous training and development subjects lend themselves to original treatment by the case writer. Suggestions are provided as to where and how to start with raw case materials and how to transform these into appropriate learning exercises. Several methods which may be used to effect such transformation are demonstrated. A diagrammatic system is provided to assist the reader in case writing and to ensure that the essential elements are present in the finished case. This chapter also contains a discussion of suitability of language, case styles, humor and several other related factors. Examples of case studies are offered to demonstrate the application of technical suggestions. Also provided are attractive variations in case writing methods.

What Topical Areas Are Suitable for Case Studies?

Some suggested areas where case materials will be effective may be found in Table 2.1. Nearly every case is effective somewhere in a suitable teaching situation; not all teaching situations, however, lend themselves to the case method. Fitting particular cases for use in course materials means that:

1. The needs of the trainee group have been identified.
2. Instructional objectives have been written.
3. Methods have been selected and approved which permit the use of case studies.

34

Table 2.1. Areas Where Case Materials Can Be Effective

Absenteeism	Job Pressure
Alcoholism	Leadership
Appraisal	Line-Staff Relations
Authority and	Listening
Responsibility	Morale
Budgeting	Motivation
Chain of Command	Order Giving
Change and	Organizing Work
Resistance to Change	Performance Standards
Communications	Planning
Controlling	Problem Solving
Coordination	Productivity
Cost Reduction and Control	Public Relations
Customer Relations	Purchasing Practices
Decision Making	Receiving Instructions
Delegation	Recruitment Methods
Directing	Rumors
Discipline	Selection and
Drug Abuse	Placement
Employee and	Span of Control
Labor Relations	Supervisor-Subordinate
Employee Development	Relations
Fiscal Controls	Tardiness
Grapevine	Teaching Methods
Grievances	Tensions
Interviewing	Training
Inventory Control	Union Relations
	Work Improvement

For example, if constraints have been placed on how long a course may last, the methodology will be affected, as well as the effectiveness of the course in meeting the instructional objectives. The case method takes more time than the lecture method. Because of this required expenditure of time, it is important to consider the practicability of particular cases when this method is to be used. The case has to fit the needs of the trainees—not the other way around. (For further discussion on judging case materials, the reader should turn to p.17 f f).

In developing and writing case materials, the trainer should strive for a good product, keeping in mind that the product—the case—will be instrumental in achieving the objectives of the training session.

The author's contention is that every trainer, every instructor, every training manager should be able to write with reasonable facility. Effective writing is an acquired skill. Just as one learns how to draft a suitable reply to a customer's complaint, so can one acquire the requisite skills needed to construct usable cases. The basic tools of the writer are a good dictionary and a thesaurus. If he is uncertain about precise English usage, he may consult one of many useful handbooks on grammar and sentence structure.

A prime objective of this book is to encourage trainers to create their own case materials. The cases and other learning exercises included may be applied as supplements to your own course materials. These materials are also intended as examples of form and style.

Creating one's own product provides many satisfactions.

1. It is yours and is the result of your perceptions and mental labor; not someone else's. Because it is yours, you understand and appreciate its contents better than anyone else. During the follow-up discussion and summarization, all the nuances which you intended during its construction are yours to manipulate.
2. Through your creative efforts, an uncommon training need has been met.
3. The very act of generating new, fresh, pertinent cases provides a sense of professional accomplishment.* Although an intangible factor, its impact is strongly felt after one's own material has had the desired impact on the training group.

Writing cases is not unlike work performed by an author. Cases constructed especially to fulfill a particular objective (which normally includes teaching a principle) are produced *to order.* That is, writing the case situation after the objective has been fixed means that in all likelihood the trainer must either recall or invent ideas based on past experiences, real or imagined. A commissioned job, it is analogous to an author under contract with *Redbook* to produce a short story dealing with a teenage narcotics addict because *Redbook*'s editor might want to feature this material as part of a spread on youthful drug abuse.

The other system involves "the inspired idea." The substance of the bright idea is set down by the writer in hope of a sale at some future date. In case

---

*Every trainer must, inevitably, struggle with the issue of plagiarism. Original materials—your own writings which have not been reproduced elsewhere—should be so identified. It is our view that even though an idea was first introduced by a trainee, after the trainer revises and restructures it into a usable training exercise, it is his to claim. Professional courtesy requires that ideas based on completed exercises, prepared by others, should receive suitable acknowledgement. The use of electrostatic devices to "borrow" materials from published writings of others is, obviously, another matter. Such "borrowing" becomes compounded when these works are used without permission, clearly intending to imply that they are the original product of the user.

writing this means that cases are noted and constructed as situations occur, based on vivid recollections, documents, personal notes and those of others, without trying to adapt the case to any immediate, specific use. Obviously, one notes and writes up only those occurrences which seem worthy of use in future courses. Experience comes into play when deciding what should be annotated. However, it is a desirable practice to get into the habit of recording such material. Even if some write-ups are not used, little has been lost.

Case Construction

A rule book approach to writing creatively is contradictive. To attempt to fix an immutable system of putting words together is silly. Writers and readers both know that there are an infinite number of ways of telling a story. Certainly, in reciting a few suggested patterns for case construction, it must be emphasized that if one can organize written materials, in style utterly different from that described, he should. He will know if he has been successful by the user's reactions to his handiwork. Although conceding that no single procedure will suffice when writing cases, we are pragmatic enough to recognize that several systems are worthy of attention. Our efforts here are concentrated on the most productive and widely used techniques of case writing.

Two major techniques are open to the writer of case studies. Unlike the home builder, the case writer may initiate his creative product either from the top down or from the bottom up. He may start with a situation and develop his materials towards a principle or reverse this process by moving from a principle to a situation.

Situation to Principle

1. Choose a situation out of the work environment, one with which you are familiar. It should be job-related and possess intrinsic value as a potential learning exercise.
2. Evaluate or judge the situation. Do this by:
   a. Analysis of available facts and inferences.
   b. Deciding what the problem probably is and to what principle it relates. For instance, a situation involving excessive waste of raw material perhaps would relate to the principles expressed in work improvement systems.
   c. Finding out, if feasible, how the situation was resolved. Since many problems are never completely solved or, if they are, perhaps

erroneously, this factor is not vital to the construction of the case. Nonetheless, it is helpful to know what really happened.

3. Establish a fictionalized version of the original situation. Names, titles, places and time are changed. Normally, the fictionalized version will encompass additional data. The new version must hang together as a believable entity.

Principle to Situation

This technique, while seemingly more logical, is more difficult than where the writer moves from the specific situation to the principle. With practice, perseverance and perhaps with the help of a colleague, one can construct a fine useful case, especially designed to fit some principle which is to be covered in an upcoming course.

The writer selects a general principle to be illustrated as an instructional objective. Example of such a principle: *Supervisors have a training responsibility when breaking in new employees.*

This principle is then clarified and elaborated on as it will be used within the written case. Continuing to use the same principle as an example: The desirability for supervisors to adhere to the four-step method when teaching new subordinates. The writer explains what occurs in a job situation if the defined principle is not applied by a supervisor. Continuing with this example, such factors as the following would be listed:

1. Teaching will be incomplete, if the four-step method is not followed.
2. Subordinates may be unhappy with their progress.
3. Supervisor will be dissatisfied with employees' on-the-job performance and blame them for his own deficiencies.
4. Morale within work group may be effected.
5. Excessive turnover may be experienced.

The writer then establishes, using his imagination, a problem situation which includes as many of the listed factors as may be fictionalized in a *realistic* fashion. The writer draws on his own experiences and recollections as the case is written. He will want to obtain reactions to his creative ideas from an associate.

Having assembled the material in either of the two systems described above, the writer now applies the finishing touches. The case is rewritten into a three-or-four-part format. This rewrite job is done for the benefit of the reader—the trainee within a course. In form, the final product generally looks like this:

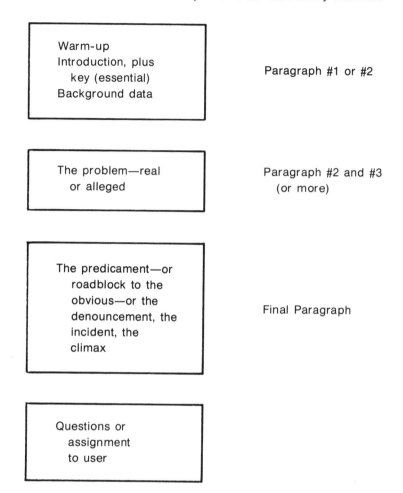

Figure 2.1. Diagram of rewritten case. Some cases can be condensed into a single paragraph.

1. The introductory section which includes the essential factual background date.
2. The "problem" which is either real or alleged.
3. The predicament or roadblock to an obvious resolution of the problem. The incident which creates the situation is included within this part.
4. The questions or "charge" to the users.

In a diagrammatic form, the rewritten case now looks like Figure 2.2.

The following case, "Managing a Change Scene," provides an illustration of the above format in two paragraphs and questions.

Managing a Change Scene

David Thomas supervises a district office of the U. S. Division of Rehabilitation (a fictional organization) which has recently added additional staff members. There are five counselors in all, three of whom are new employees. The office is expanding, as added responsibilities are acquired covering new facilities and services, with an attending increase in counselor case loads.

Because of the large geographic area to be serviced, Thomas estimates that about 50% of his time must be spent in the field. A new federal program of support for mental retardees is due to commence within this fiscal period. Assume that the two experienced counselors are approaching retirement. Both are likely to leave during the next two months.

How can the new counselors best be trained for their jobs, especially since Thomas will not be able to see them as often as he would like?

Explain how you can ensure that your Division's procedures are uniformly applied.

What kinds of staff support should you be looking for from your divisional headquarters?

Rewriting the Case

Getting started on a rewrite job is admittedly difficult. Some helpful starts for paragraph one may be found in these lead sentences:

You are the supervisor of ten laboratory technicians, working on cancer research in _____.

Harry Dexter, one of the employees in Unit Z, has been _____.

Mary is an extremely efficient stenographer who has been _____.

Recently, you selected a new typist for your unit, Mabel Morris _____.

You have an employee who has a real problem: she doesn't use her head. She has been making some stupid mistakes.

Your boss has called you in concerning the amount of alleged pilferage in the shop.

You've been working for nearly ten years as the Chief Maintenance Supervisor for the W.W. Company. Two months ago, the company was sold to Super Industrials, which is a large conglomerate listed on the NYSE.

I've been transferred to the Northfield Works and promoted to plant manager. Seven years ago I worked at Northfield as a foreman. My first impression since returning to Northfield has been _____ .

The wrap-up of a case is as exacting a job as its introduction. The following are examples of *climax, predicament* and *roadblock*. These are usually stated as the lead sentences in the final paragraph.

Two weeks ago, the three stenographers started coming in to work late together. You reprimanded them. Now they are beginning to take days off together.

Phil seems to be faced with three unhappy possibilities:

1. If _____ .
2. If _____ .
3. If _____ .

This morning Jones came into your office and _____ .

There are some truths in his accusations, but the situation is not nearly as bad as he depicts it.

Your boss now feels that you should have returned the damaged merchandise and is hinting that your Christmas bonus may be drastically reduced.

Yesterday, you learned that Sam and Phil were given the responsibility to clear up this matter. Your boss has evidently decided to bypass your unit.

Writing Good Case Material

Good writing and good case material do not appear on paper without studious attention to detail. The writer wants to convey a series of messages. What should he do; what should he avoid? Here are areas worthy of attention so that ease in case writing can be accomplished.

Language

Write in a straight-forward fashion. Express your ideas in the language of the user. Follow the principles of good written communications as outlined in many fine handbooks dealing with letter and report writing. Slang is acceptable, if it fits the vernacular of the training group which will use the material. If technical expressions are included, beware of nit-pickers within the trainee group. Be certain that you understand what you are writing about, that the technical terms mean what you want them to mean and that the trainees will apply the same interpretation.

Comments on Characters

Well-known, non-controversial names (Smith, Brown, Miller, Cooper, etc.) generally should be applied to the characters within the case. When adopting and applying names, avoid the wiseacre approach, unless for some special reason you deliberately set out to do so. If the case, for instance, deals with a supervisor's attitude toward a minority member of his crew, it is probably unnecessary to name the supervisor "Archie Bunker."

Use fictional names, or "you" or "I." See p. 56 for an example of a case written in the first person. This case is, in terms of the content, identical with case shown on p.27, which is written in the third person. Consider how the two versions, both identical insofar as details are concerned, have different effects on the reader.

The case writer must decide how he wants to use his material. He has an option of revising third person materials into a first person version. Such a revision will, of course, provide a ready bridge to a roleplay. See p. 44 f f for a discussion of how this is done.

Cases using the pronoun "you" encourage the reader to identify with the situation. This is another facilitative mechanism for converting the case into a roleplay.

Case Style

Some case writers advocate that there be within the case a "do-righter" and/or a "do-wronger." The do-righter is the typical "Mr. Straight" who makes few, if any, mistakes. Presumably, he is the hero whom we want to get out of the particular pickle in which he finds himself. The do-wronger or anti-hero is apt to be sarcastic or terribly introverted, or he may be someone who needs training, and certainly *no one* like him exists within the training group!

If such characters emerge—and in many case situations they will—label them with plain names. Their personalities will come through without unnecessarily stigmatizing them with peculiar appellations.

The "do-right"-"do-wrong" presentation is an acceptable, simplistic style for framing a situation. For new, inexperienced learners where cogent reasons exist to have them see things starkly highlighted as correct or incorrect, this approach is excellent. But for worldly-wise trainees, such a style is unlikely to appeal to anyone. The case must be rewritten putting the situations into gradations of black and white, with shadings of meanings so that careful thought be given during the ensuing discussion.

Humor

Humor *in* a case is somewhat similar to the problem of humor outside of the case in the conference room. For the conference leader or instructor who lectures, humor will be most effective if it fits at the point of introduction. Gagsters who are good at telling a story can get away with poor teaching while meeting their group. Afterwards, trainees will realize that they have been entertained and not taught. Consequently, if humor adds to the instructional output, use it. The same general rule applies when writing case materials.

When constructing cases, stay away from "clever touches" unless these add to the product.

Naming the Case

Cases may be identified by code number or by title. The latter system seems to be generally more acceptable, since it humanizes the event. The name should reflect the problem. The word "case" frequently appears in the title, and this may be helpful in communicating to the trainees that they have got a problem with which to work. In one sense, this is akin to problems faced by fictional detectives. All the materials are there: use your senses, your experiences, your group's give-and-take to fulfill the mandate given at the end of the case.

The comments about humor also apply to the naming of case studies.

The Antagonist-Protagonist Case Situation

Often, case situations pertaining to problem solving present the "facts" to the trainees in such a way that only predirected courses of action are open for solution. As the group commences its study, it is handed a "story" which it unconsciously senses is one-sided. It is as if a jury heard only the prosecutor's version and then was asked to render its decision.

In roleplaying both "sides" get presented, although unevenly because the nature of the spoken word precludes an evenhanded, balanced presentation. However, in written case materials, what is written and how it is presented can be controlled. One method that helps ensure such a balanced portrait follows.

First, a problem which concerns people and their behavior must be present. It is a problem for which answers are sought. Second, within the problem two "sides" exist even though one side may appear as obviously "in the wrong."

If conditions such as these are present, then the original case can be rewritten. The case assumes two facets: that of the antagonist and that of the protagonist.* The examples which follow ("I'm Your Baby Now" and "He's Your Baby Now") clearly demonstrate the way in which the language is structured. There are few real factual differences between the two versions except that the *perceptual* attitudes are clearly different and perhaps hostile to one another.

When using this approach, the total training group is bisected so that an equal number of small groups work on the case but from either the antagonist's or protagonist's viewpoint. Each group is assigned to solve the problem. Each must, therefore, gather and interpret facts and inferences, define the problem, consider and construct alternative solutions and then select a single one, which it effectuates.

In real life the ability to carry through with certain decisions resides in whoever possesses the requisite organizational power. A conflict between a superior and subordinate may be resolved by suitably altered subordinate behavior. Or the superior may decide to do whatever he believes has to be done. That fact must be borne in mind when applying the antagonist-protagonist method. The small group which has the case presented from the subordinate's viewpoint can hardly recommend, as a solution, that the boss be reassigned. Thus, even if seemingly biased, an empathetic solution must be provided by the trainees.

In the follow-up discussion between the two halves of the total group, the trainer will have an opportunity to encourage and foster an appreciation of empathy. The "best" solution may lie in neither group but perhaps somewhere else. Pat answers, emerging during some traditional case study sessions, frequently have little tie-in to live situations. Hence, whatever can be

*See p. 81 f f for discussion of these terms in connection with roleplaying.

done within the training sessions to infuse a sense of realism will be worthwhile and provide a payoff.

Further comments on the antagonist-protagonist case approach will be found under "How to Develop and Use Simple Roleplaying" in Chapter 4.

He's Your Baby Now!

Yours is a nonprofit organization which has as its mission the rehabilitation and counseling of "people with problems." It has several branches throughout the community. Recently, a "seasoned" older counselor requested a transfer to your office from an office in another part of the city. His reason for the transfer was that his abilities were not being properly utilized. He asked for "no special privileges." He simply wanted "to be treated like everybody else." The transfer was accepted.

The counselor immediately demanded special privileges and dispensations. He looks down on the younger counselors, does not accept responsibilities for his own actions and blames his coworkers for their lack of cooperation. He either denies having received verbal instructions from his immediate supervisor or changes the instructions and then states, "This is what you told me." He dislikes field work and thinks up dozens of reasons why he should stay in the office. In general, he is a rather mediocre counselor.

How can this person be made aware of his inadequacies and helped to raise his level of job performance?

Where did we "go wrong" in taking this man on as a transferee?

I'm Your Baby Now

My name isn't important. What you need to know is that I am a seasoned counselor, with many years of experience. I work for a nonprofit organization which has as its mission the rehabilitation and counseling of "people with problems." This organization has several branches throughout our community.

Not too long ago I requested a transfer to a different office from another part of the city. My reason for seeking a transfer was that my abilities were not being properly utilized. I asked for no special privileges; I simply wanted to be treated like everyone else. My transfer was accepted.

Recently, I have been having problems in the new office. It is staffed with younger counselors, most of whom are less experienced and have less knowledge of the business than I do. They are not especially cooperative and probably resentful of my having moved in from the other office.

One of the reasons that I transferred to the new office was that I would have additional responsibilities and would be able to work, to a greater extent, on my own. However, my supervisor is constantly on my back. He changes my instructions frequently so that I am often confused. Further, I do not have an opportunity to exercise the responsibilities which I know I can carry out. Also, he has given me several field assignments which I am not especially fond of. Frankly, I would prefer to stay in the office; therefore, I have been forced to concoct excuses to avoid going out into the field.

What can be done so that my new supervisor will allow me to assume those responsibilities which I feel I can handle?

If I made an error in transferring into this office, what can I do to straighten matters out?

Case Materials from Trainees

Run-of-the-mill experiences suitable for rewrite into cases are easy to find; the unique and out-of-the-ordinary are more difficult to obtain. Therefore, trainers can reach out to the trainee population for ideas. If sufficiently motivated, trainees will readily share their significant experiences in written form. Initially, this means that each understands:

1. The ground rules concerning the use of written experiences to be produced.
2. The format to be followed when submitting such written materials.

Most trainees are more than willing to contribute written cases which they realize are likely to be used during instruction. Care must be taken, however, to avoid a commitment guaranteeing that particular cases submitted will be used. Flexibility as to usage must rest with the trainer. Trainee contributions should be received in a reasonably usable form. Therefore, the instructor will brief the trainees as to types of materials being sought. Copies of acceptable written cases should be handed out as examples of what is sought. As a general rule, it is wise to suggest to the trainees that they alter names, titles and places as well as other pertinent factors which easily identify contributors and create the possibility of embarrassment at a later date.

Cases may be used within the training sessions in which the trainees submitting the materials participate. Such cases become part of the instructional curricula. (See p. 22 for suggestions on filing.)

For sophisticated trainees with previous exposure to the case method, it will be practical to assemble the trainees well ahead of the formal start of training. Perhaps a month before the course begins, the trainees meet briefly as a group. They are provided with information about the objectives of the course and are instructed to prepare written cases which will be discussed and analyzed during the course. A deadline for submission is agreed to and fixed. The time between the deadline set for submitting cases and the formal start of the course is used by the trainer to:

1. Edit and revise case language.
2. Analyze cases for principles which will be tied to lesson plans and any additonal input provided by instructor.
3. Sort materials to avoid overlapping. (One key idea may be submitted by several trainees. This usually means that this subject demands in-depth attention.)
4. Introduce cases, from other sources, *not* produced by the group, but which the trainer believes should be included. Such cases are used to provide a bridge or link between topics.
5. Consider the order of presentation, based on what has been turned in.

Questions, Questions, Questions

At the conclusion of written case materials, the writer usually provides a few questions to stimulate the reader's thinking. Questions are introduced to spark discussion and to require the trainees to read and synthesize data. Many key words employed by trainers in questioning have been borrowed from the academe. Following are a few examples of starters that may be helpful to the writer when phrasing a question: *apply, appraise, construct, determine, develop, discuss, evaluate, explain, illustrate, list, outline, provide and suggest.*

And do not forget: *why, how, what, where,* etc.

Good questions accomplish two things: they challenge the group, while at the same time channeling its energies quickly toward the intended instructional axis. While ordinarily it is much easier to ask questions than to answer them, good useful questions should not be tossed in at the end of a case simply to bring about group activity. The activity must be headed toward a worthwhile outcome. Questions should be reread to ascertain that the necessary linkage between instructional objectives and this part of the instructional input is clearly supplied. If it is not, the questions should be revised or replaced with others that do the job.

Finally, if the objectives are not that vital (perhaps several goals are of equal importance) and if enough time is left, the trainees can construct their own questions. A trainer may be surprised by their perceptiveness and he must be certain that he have more than a cursory knowledge of the case. If questions are raised which the trainer had failed to consider, he will, nonetheless, be called upon to summarize and tie together the case, the questions and the principles. Case studies will challenge the trainer, and unlike other, more static teaching methods, boredom is unlikely to overtake either the trainer or his group.

Multipurpose Cases

Case material suitable for more than a single topic is very difficult to obtain. An observer with tunnel vision may well overlook alternative implications of a given case situation. Imagination, inventiveness and ingenuity are most helpful when constructing a case. Often the writer will bounce ideas off an associate, and the temporary mental collaboration triggers gestalts, enabling both to see factors which individually they had missed.

The straight-forward, single topic case may be so structured that it ultimately encompasses several equally useful subjects for study and analysis by the class. In the example which follows, "Work Simplification in a Freezer," the reader should note how such matters as (a) Harry Hobart's apparent failure to communicate fully to his foremen, and (b) the fact that the job analysts are rather secretive. Both of these factors contribute added dimensions to the case. Even if the communications within the plant were ideal, one or two problems would be encountered. The inclusion of the communications factors enables the trainer to exercise additional options with his trainees. At any point he may alter the circumstances for his group, if this is deemed desirable in meeting the learning objectives. Situational layers may be added or removed during the use of the case. For instance, in the same illustration, after leading an appraisal discussion of the plant's communications, the trainer may ask the group: "How would the basic situation be altered if Harry Hobart had conducted a free-wheeling staff meeting with all of his supervisors, and if he introduced the job analysts, he had asked them to explain what they planned to accomplish?"

This "either-or" type of question is expecially beneficial as a teaching technique; it is provocative and forces the trainees to think analytically. The multipurpose case permits trainers to function at these different levels.

Work Simplification in a Freezer

Hardly unique is the situation at your firm, Labrador Refrigeration, where the union recently agreed to a revision in its two-year contract. Throughout the region in which the plant is located a number of companies, large and small, have seen their previously hostile employees expressing a more conciliatory view when faced with a possibility of plant shutdowns and loss of jobs. This represents a very real change over the situation in recent years.

Your boss, the plant manager of Labrador Refrigeration, Harry Hobart, has now embarked on a work simplification kick. Even though the employees have agreed to a 5% reduction in salary, Hobart has brought in four staff specialists from corporate headquarters to conduct an "intensive job analysis" of production line B activities. Production line B manufactures an inexpensive series of refrigerators sold under private labels by several well-known, nationally prominent retail chains.

There is nothing in the union contract which precludes an analysis of work performance, and Hobart has not discussed this activity with the union representative within the plant. Hobart is convinced that there's a lot of fat in several sections—and he is evidently determined to cut costs, even if some guys don't like it.

Within the B-line crews there is very considerable anger about the way in which the four job analysts are proceeding. The crew members say that they have already made too many concessions and they are not about to give up any more. There have been threats of slowdowns, and in several specialized incidents, there is every reason to believe that sabotage by the assembly line members has resulted in serious damage to sealed refrigerator units.

Most of the first-level supervisors (foremen) believe that Hobart's hard-line approach, coming directly after the voluntary wage cut, is wrong. They also think that his present concentration on work simplification is wrong-headed. The only real information the first-level supervisors have had to date is a written memorandum from Harry Hobart explaining the general objectives of work simplification. He has asked for an "open-mined attitude by all levels of management," while at the same time charging that there had been too much complacency in the way in which the assembly work had been handled in the past. The job analysts have been staying pretty much to themselves and have not offered any real information as to what may result from their studies.

What problems do you see in this kind of a situation?

Assume that you are the personnel and labor relations manager. What advice, if any, would you give Harry Hobart? Justify your answers.

If the union plant president asked for a meeting (presumably to discuss the "work simp" project), what response would you provide and how would you plan for the meeting?

Subject areas available for discussion:
1. Line-staff relations
2. Basic labor-management relations
3. Introducing a work improvement program
4. Managerial communications
5. Employee discipline

(Suggestions to trainer: each of these areas may be considered as a major topic—*if in line with objectives* set for trainees. Case will then be integrated into instructional format, its timing depending on sophistication of trainees, when session is being held and other related factors.)

Permutations and Combinations

Securing a basic case situation and revising it in alternative forms provides a valuable expedient for the trainer. In a sense, this practice is not unlike the little girl who dresses and undresses her china doll in several different costumes. The essential condition is present. But, what can be done with it to provide maximum usability? The case can be presented in different forms and in varied settings. This technique offers the trainer a very great savings in time and effort. Good ideas are available for reuse, and the amount of writing is considerably reduced.

In "The Building Custodian," a basic case with four additional alternative forms is presented. Undoubtedly, many other variations could be added, but for the purposes in this section, these should readily demonstrate the point. The basic case, reproduced as *Possibility A*, tells of a personnel problem involving a custodial employee who may have been a bit forward with some of the female help.

In *Possibility B,* the situation is changed by introducing the custodian as an employee of a third party, the firm's rental agent. *Possibility C* provides the setting for a discussion of racial attitudes, as does *Possibility D*. However, the tension within the case is heightened through the insertion of strong racial and political attitudes by one of the key parties within the case. Finally, *Possibility E* returns pretty much to the facts as stated in the first possibility; however, the setting has been altered into a script-like dialogue between two managers.

All five situations involve the separation of facts from inferences; heresay from factual evidence. On the other hand, each will be uniquely suited to a slightly different set of instructional objectives. Each can be "converted" into a roleplay situation which is discussed at greater length in Chapter 5. *Possibility E* can be readily transformed. Here, the form of the case demands that the dialogue be continued between two parties. This requirement is not specifically constructed within the other possibilities.

The questions for group discussion at the end of each possibility are not intended as all-inclusive. Others, also in revised form, are available to the writer, or, as noted elsewhere, the trainee groups might be charged with devising their own study questions, based on the content of the material.

The Building Custodian: Possibility A

James Brice is one of your custodial employees. Brice's duty is to enter the building about an hour and a half before closing time, to mop, dust, and clean, working until 11:00 p.m. When the head janitor is ill, or on vacation, Brice covers for him.

Several female employees in your firm have recently complained to your boss that Brice has been coming in earlier than usual and fallen into the habit of discussing with them his personal domestic problems. An unmarried female employee reported "in a state of panic" an elevator incident where, instead of bringing her up to the fourth floor, he started the elevator to the basement. When she complained, Brice immediately reversed the elevator and brought her to the proper floor.

Some of the women expressed fear for their safety. However, when talked to privately, most said they saw no harm in Brice. A few said he was no more forward than several men among your firm's office employees. Three said they were afraid of him, but could offer nothing substantial, other than the single elevator incident noted above.

You are called in by your boss and, as his executive assistant, told, "Cliff, I want you to look into this business involving Jim Brice. If necessary, don't hesitate to get rid of Brice. We must protect our women."

You have observed James Brice to be a good worker who has performed well for 12 years without incident.

You believe there is a more constructive solution to the problem. What action should you take?

The Building Custodian: Possibility B

James Brice is a custodial employee hired and employed by your landlord's rental agency. Brice's duty is to enter the building about an hour and a half before closing time, to mop, dust and clean, working until 11:00 p.m. When the building "super" is ill, or on vacation, Brice covers for him.

Several female employees in your firm have recently complained to your boss that Brice has been coming in earlier than usual and fallen into the habit of discussing with them his personal domestic problems. An unmarried female employee reported "in a state of panic" an elevator incident where, instead of bringing her up to the fourth floor, he started the elevator to the basement. When she complained, Brice immediately reversed the elevator and brought her to the proper floor.

Some of the women expressed fear for their safety. However, when talked to privately, most said they saw no harm in Brice. A few said he was no more forward than several of your firm's male employees. Three said they were afraid of him, but could offer nothing substantial. other than the single elevator incident noted above.

You are called in by your boss and, as his executive assistant, told, "Cliff, I think we should ask the agent to get rid of Brice. We must protect our women." Immediately thereafter, you did some checking and found that Brice is a very active member of Local 32F, Building Services Union (AFL-CIO). He was one of the first union employees in your building. It is highly unlikely that the agent would want to stir up trouble with the union.

You have observed James Brice to be a good worker who has performed well for 12 years without incident.

You believe there is a more constructive solution to the problem. What action should you take?

What relationships are likely to be involved here, if pressure is applied by the tenant against the rental agent of the landlord? (Assume that your firm's lease has four years yet to run.)

If yours is a unionized firm. What impact may this fact have on the situation?

The Building Custodian: Possibility C

James Brice is a black custodial employee hired and employed by your landlord's rental agency. Brice's duty is to enter the building about an hour and a half before closing time, to mop, dust and clean, working until 11:00 p.m. When the building super is ill, or on vacation, Brice covers for him.

Several of your female employees, both white and black, have recently complained to your boss that Brice has been coming in earlier than usual and fallen into the habit of discussing with them his personal domestic problems. An unmarried female (white) employee reported "in a state of panic" an elevator incident where, instead of bringing her up to the fourth floor, he started the elevator to the basement. When she complained, Brice immediately reversed the elevator and brought her to the proper floor.

Some of the women expressed fear for their safety. However, when talked to privately, most said they saw no harm in Brice. A few said he was no more forward than several of your firm's male employees. Three said they were afraid of him, but could offer nothing substantial, other than the single elevator incident noted above.

You are called in by your boss and, as his executive assistant, told, "Cliff, these women are concerned about Jim Brice. Personally, I think it's a lot of nonsense. Look into this for me and see what you can do to straighten it out. Take whatever action you deem necessary."

You have observed James Brice to be a good worker who has performed well for 12 years without incident.

What action would you take? Explain feasible alternatives.

The Building Custodian: Possibility D

James Brice is one of your custodial employees. He is black. Brice's duty is to enter the building about an hour and a half before closing time, to mop, dust and clean, working until 11:00 p.m. When the head janitor is ill, or on vacation, Brice covers for him.

Several female employees in your firm have recently complained to your boss that Brice has been coming in earlier than usual and fallen into the habit of discussing with them his personal domestic problems. An unmarried female employee reported "in a state of panic" an elevator incident where, instead of bringing her up to the fourth floor, he started the elevator to the basement. When she complained, Brice immediately reversed the elevator and brought her to the proper floor.

Some of the women expressed fear for their safety. However, when talked to privately, most said they saw no harm in Brice. A few said he was no more forward than several of your firm's office employees. Three said they were afraid of him, but could offer nothing substantial, other than the single elevator incident noted above.

You are called in by your boss and, as his executive assistant, told, "Cliff, I want you to look into this business involving Jim Brice. If necessary, don't hesitate to get rid of Brice. We must protect our women." Immediately thereafter, you did some checking and found that Brice is perhaps a member of the Black Panther Party. He has been seen reading Black Panther literature during his breaks. Brice is also actively involved in union affairs and serves on the firm's grievance committee.

You have observed James Brice to be a good worker who has performed well for 12 years without incident.

You believe there is a more constructive solution to the problem. However, you are concerned because your boss has strong feelings about groups such as the Panthers. While you have avoided discussing politics with him, you are aware that he stands well to the right of center. He is a regular subscriber to William Buckley's "National Review."

What action should you take?

The Building Custodian: Possibility E

Cliff C. serves as executive assistant to Leo H., the chief administrative officer of your firm. The business employs about 250; most are women. Leo requested that Cliff see him about a personal matter. Cliff enters Leo's office.

C: You asked to see me . . . . .

L: Yes, Cliff. You know Jim Brice, one of our janitors. Well, I think that we should consider letting him go.

C: You mean because of his so-called harrassment of a couple of the gals?

L: Well, I hear that one of the girls was in a state of panic in the elevator. Brice was supposed to have brought her up to the fourth floor, and as I understand it, he started to take her down to the basement. When she started complaining, Brice reversed the elevator and brought her up. Also, I've been told that Brice has been coming in earlier than usual and has fallen into the habit—which I'm not especially keen about—of discussing his personal, domestic problems with the women. Jane Stewart, one of our older women has expressed fear for the safety of her crew. That's why I think we ought to do something about dropping Brice.

C: Leo, take it easy . . . . You know that Brice has been working with us for twelve years without an incident, and as far as I'm concerned he's a good worker, who has performed quite well. You're also aware, Leo, that Brice is an active member of the Building Services Union. We'd probably be in a pile of trouble if we dropped him without cause.

L: Well, that's your problem and I'm *not* taking it easy! *Please*, Cliff, straighten this business out. And you should know that as far as I'm concerned, the sooner we get rid of this guy, the better. I don't want any harm coming to any of the girls.

3. Sample Case Materials

Nineteen different kinds of cases in the area of supervisory and managerial training and employee development are presented in this chapter. The cases illustrate various situations in communications training, managerial planning, decision-making and similar topics.

They show case writing styles and are available for application in courses where suitable.

On the Prowl for Safety

Jim Pierce was making his weekly inspection tour through the Z Unit of the plant. As a management trainee, Jim was serving as safety officer, one portion of a three-month rotational assignment. Jim was looking for violations of plant safety regulations, which he zealously noted and forwarded to the front office.

Dead ahead of him on the walkways, which was supposed to be clear of all impediments, was a heavy electrical cable. It lay across the walk, from where to where Jim couldn't immediately tell as he examined it, because the cable ran alongside heavy storage stock. In the dim lighting, one could easily trip and break his neck.

Jim stopped, pulled his clipboard up to his waist and started to write. Just then he felt a sharp tap on his back. He turned to face an obviously angry Joe O'Brien, a maintenance foreman.

"What the hell are you doing, smart boy? Writing up a safety report? Go ahead; write it up! These bastards want production, but they're unwilling to spend a few bucks for more outlets. Safety! That's a joke around here."

What should Jim Pierce do in response to Joe O'Brien's outburst? What conditions and attitudes seem to be prevalent in this situation? Explain.

If he does report, should he put it in writing?

What do you believe to be the *real* problem here?

Potential Exercise

This case has been included not only as an illustration of case format but also as a potential exercise for the reader. We are concerned about the relationship between a case and a lesson plan. Therefore, employing the methods shown on p. 248ff the reader may wish to convert the data into a usable teaching plan. The following additional facts will be helpful when organizing the lesson plan.

More Case Facts

The plant has a very good safety record. It has gone for almost three years without a major accident. The insurance rates are low.

Traffic in the area where Jim Pierce was making his inspection is relatively light. The only persons who are supposed to be in this area are those drawing stock. The plant currently has a large inventory which is one of the reasons why material is piled so high. Consequently, the light level from the ceiling is reduced.

Joe O'Brien is a chronic complainer. Another problem with Joe is that he has been reprimanded several times for violating safety regulations. He has available a small tent-type florescent sign marked "Danger," which should have been placed over the cable. This is not the first time that O'Brien has been "caught" violating safety procedures. He has been hurt once in a fall from a ladder which slipped out from under him when it was not propped correctly.

On the Prowl for Safety (First Person Version)

My name is Jim Pierce. Recently, I was making my weekly inspection tour through the Z Unit of the plant. As a management trainee, I am serving as safety officer, one portion of a three-months rotational assignment. I was looking for violations of plant safety regulations, which I zealously note and forward to the front office.

Dead ahead of me on the walkway, which was supposed to be clear of all impediments, was a heavy electrical cable. It lay across the walk, from where to where, so that I couldn't immediately tell as I examined it, because the cable ran alongside heavy storage stock. In the dim lighting, one could easily trip and break his neck.

I stopped, pulled my clipboard up to my waist and started to write. Just then I felt a sharp tap on my back. I turned to face an obviously angry Joe O'Brien, a maintenance foreman.

"What the hell are you doing, smart boy? Writing up a safety report? Go ahead; write it up! These bloody bastards want production, but they're unwilling to spend a few bucks for more outlets. Safety! That's a joke around here!"

What should I do, in response to Joe O'Brien's outburst? Should I report Joe O'Brien's outburst to his boss? Explain. If I do report, should it be in writing? Explain.

What conditions and attitudes seem to be prevalent? Explain.

What do you believe is the real problem here?

After Johnny Came Marching Home

Your company's policy has been to permit returning veterans to be reappointed to the same positions which they held before leaving for military service. Harold B. was one of your professional subordinates prior to his being drafted. He was serving in a trainee capacity and just before his departure for military service, you had determined that his work was unsatisfactory.

A written appraisal had so stated, and a copy was transmitted to Personnel: "*Essential Negative Features:* Is lazy (needs to be prodded). Takes little real interest in work or in self-development. Completed work rarely comes in when due. On one occasion, brought girl friend into office during work hours. When supervisor appeared, tried to hide girl friend under desk."

One year has now elapsed and you have learned that Harold B. has returned to your organization. You are dismayed to discover that he will be reassigned to your unit. You have protested this assignment to your superior, he tells you to make the best of it.

What approach should you take with Harold when he first reports to your unit, which will be tomorrow?

What organizational problems seem to be implied by the facts recited within this case? Explain and list options open for correction.

The Problem of the Missing Automobile

Your firm maintains a large fleet of automobiles with a fixed number of cars assigned to each major division. You are responsible (as an "additional duty") for assigning and keeping track of the autos used by your own division. Your supervisor had directed you to assign, for the period of one week, a year-old Buick Electra to a former division chief, H. Wilmot Carpenter, who works part-time in an advisory capacity for your division. Mr. Carpenter, now retired, has the reputation of being a rather eccentric individual and, at times, rather tyrannical. He has strong "topside" personal connections within the firm and is a large stockholder.

When checking your records two weeks later, you discover that the Buick which has been loaned to Mr. Carpenter has not as yet been returned. At the direction of your supervisor, you contact Mr. Carpenter by phone and inquire as to when it will be returned. Mr Carpenter replies: "The car has been turned in."

A careful search is made, and the car is *not* in its assigned parking area. No one has received the key or even seen the car.

With your supervisor present, you phone the former division chief and are abruptly told the same thing: "The car has been turned in" and that "I do *not* wish to be bothered about this matter again!" He hangs up on you before you can question him further.

What steps would you take to locate this vehicle?

What is the basic problem and how should it be resolved?

What are your responsibilities in this case?

The Takeover*

A small local agency was legislated out of existence and its functions taken over by a larger agency performing the same general type of work. Key staff in the larger agency had known of the takeover long before the effective date of the change. The professional staff of the smaller agency (but none of the clerical or stenographic staff) was transferred to the larger agency.

Prior to the merger both agencies had the same public goals but had operated under different laws. Management of the larger agency had not consulted with management of the defunct agency to plan for the combined operation. In the view of the transferred professionals, management has failed to utilize their experience to resolve the many problems that have recently developed.

Management within the smaller agency is isolated from the "real" management. As they see it, communications have not been adequately established. Morale of the transferred workers is poor. Neither first line supervisors nor middle management know what is expected of them. A verbal directive may come down in the morning from top management, only to be followed in the afternoon by its written counterpart, which is entirely different from the verbal directive. Still later, the written directive is rescinded before the supervisors can execute the previous directive. When the supervisors ask what action or procedure they are to take, they are told to wait until they receive further instructions. Meanwhile the employees seek instructions from supervisors who have been immobilized.

*Note that the conditions within this case parallel those within the private sector, involving the purchase of a small business by a coglomerate.

Assignment for Trainees

1. Rewrite this case, as it might have been written from the viewpoint of personnel in the large agency.
2. Enumerate the problems inherent in this type of situation.
3. What are some acceptable solutions? Discuss their implementation.

The Open-Door Policy

Open-dooring is likely to mean risk taking! Rebuffed by your boss on a proposal which you are convinced is sound and will save the company money, you can take your idea over his head without his permission to your manager's manager. He *must* open his door to you, listen to your proposals, evaluate their worth and render a decision. If you're right and your boss was wrong, the payoff may be considerable. If it goes the other way—well, there's the rub!

All of us can think of situations in our own plant where such a policy would have produced exciting results as well as lucrative savings to the firm. Discuss the advantages and disadvantages of such a policy. What trust levels are called for to make such a policy effective? How would you go about initiating such a policy in (our) (your) company?

Leadership or Group Apathy?

Here is a problem relating to a community-based organization which has been in operation for many years. Its general "mission" is *socioreligious*. Meetings are held in a well-equipped meeting center at regular intervals. Although the organization has about 150 paying members, only about 25 regulars show up for the meetings.

Karl L. is the newly designated president.

He and others who have been among the regulars and concerned about the feeling of apathy which has grown among the members, most of whom are over 50 years old.

In an effort to restore activity and interest, Karl and his board of directors developed and circulated an opinion survey poll to the membership. This was done to determine what the membership felt was important and where the priorities should be fixed. The responses were either neutral or, in those areas where initiative and personal involvement were demanded, wholly lacking. All members still expressed an interest in its continuance.

Eventually, new members were thrust into major committee appointments. An attempt was made at imaginative publicity. This was handled by individuals who were professionally competent in public relations.

Only limited success was noted. The membership did *not* increase. Attendance at the meetings declined in spite of a program which was "objectively" viewed as "best of its type in the area."

Evaluate This Situation

What are some of the reasons that people join organizations but on the condition that they need not become personally involved?

What steps can be taken to rejuvenate this organization?

Case of the ASTD Conference

It has been the tradition in the Training Bureau to rotate, among its senior staff members, assignments to attend the annual ASTD (American Society for Training and Development) Conference. There are four senior members: Art, Bill, Charlie and Doug. Art has been with the firm six years; Bill, seven years; Charlie, six years; and Doug, eight years. This is a large training unit, employing 15 professionals.

Charlie is the boss, but this had made no difference insofar as attendance at the ASTD Conference is concerned. Charlie reports to Ed, the director of employee relations and training. Ed's unofficial policy had been not to interfere in this matter.

Last year, the Conference was held in New York City and because of the proximity to the firm's location (Philadelphia), Charlie—whose turn it was to attend—made some cryptic comments about being cheated.

This year's conference is being held in Honolulu, and Doug has been looking forward to attending. He has just learned that Charlie had discussed and secured an approval from Ed permitting *Charlie* to attend the Honolulu Conference. This was done despite the fact that Charlie had attended the session in New York City.

1. If you were Doug, what would you do? Explain. What seems to be the basic problem here? Explain.
2. Clarify the difference between a "tradition" and a "policy."
3. What "take home learning" should the conference participant be expected to provide to his associates who were unable to attend?

A Case of Quid Pro Quo

Background information: Marcus H. is the chief of the plant's Union Grievance Committee. Larry B. is the personnel administrator. Marcus has asked Larry for a conference, to which Larry has agreed. Larry is assuming that the conference will concern six grievances covering out-of-title work for which Marcus has responsibility to follow up for his members. These actions have been pending since March 7. Today is March 15.

M: Hi, Larry. How're you doing?

L: All right, What's cooking.

M: Well, I wanted to see you about a summer job for one of my boys.

L: What do you mean, "one of your boys?"

M: You know, one of my kids; John, the sophomore at Old Ivy.

L: Oh. What do you want me to do? You know things are very tight and. . . .

M: Well, Larry, as you know, I've been pretty cooperative with you recently, and I felt that it would be most advantageous for all parties if we could develop a little "quid pro quo."

L: What do you have in mind?

M: Well, you're well aware that the six grievance actions on the out-of-title work are pending, and I thought. . . .

L: Are you suggesting that if I take care of your son, you will let this matter—uh—drop?

M: Well . . . let's just say that I won't push too hard to get this resolved our way . . . .

Instructions for Group

Assume that early last year the union struck your plant for three weeks over an unresolved employee grievance. Ultimately, through government intervention the case went up for arbitration—and your firm lost. What would you say to Marcus?

A Problem in Communications

Mr. Biggame, the chief executive officer of the organization, pursues what he considers to be "good communications principles." The key aspect in Mr. Biggame's approach is his monthly staff conferences during which he passes along to his twelve top level administrators his views on organizational policies, problems to be overcome, plans for future activities and other special matters which may require attention. At each meeting one of the twelve (known euphemistically as the "disciples") is expected to make a presentation on his own particular program. At the end of each sectional presentation Mr. Biggame leads the discussion, and all present are expected to pitch in, providing questions, suggestions or comments. The purpose of these presentations or "confrontations" (as Mr. Biggame refers to them) is to broaden the participants' point of view and to strengthen the fabric of the organization.

During last month's session a highly embarrassing situation arose, causing some considerable, subsequent humiliation to several "disciples." Here is what happened.

Mr. Biggame revealed certain facts about important plans for the future growth of the organization. He considered these plans to be highly confidential and known *only* to himself. Yet during the discussions following one of the disciple's presentation, it became apparent to Mr. Biggame that about six or seven of the disciples not only knew about the confidential plans but were already working on implementing them.

Mr. Biggame expressed his displeasure in unequivocal terms. He accused these men of jumping the gun, of undercutting his own authority and of spreading confidential or classified information. When two of the disciples sought to explain that they were only doing what any good staff person would do—anticipating and preparing for the future—Mr. Biggame became angry and called them "empire builders" who were disrupting the entire organization. He said that decisions "should flow from topside and topside only." He adjourned the meeting abruptly. Everyone, and especially Mr. Biggame, was hurt and dismayed by what had occurred.

For Participants

In what way did Mr. Biggame err?

What should he have done?

What should he do now?

What should the disciples do? Explain.

What is the basic problem here?

How did some of the disciples learn about the confidential proposals?

What are your views on the manner in which Mr. Biggame conducts his monthly meetings?

To what extent should a manager seek to control communications within his own organization?

Some Suggestions and Directions
For Conference Leader

Tie formal and informal communication networks together, where points within networks overlap.

Consider purposes of formal communications network.

Consider purposes of *informal* communications network.

Relationship of communications patterns and styles of leadership in an organization.

How groups (such as "disciples") influence organization communications.

How the manipulation of information influences organizational behavior.

Posture of effective management toward the various networks of communication.

Handling a New Line

Note: This case is intended to transfer abstract principles of how to plan into a real situation, which the branch store manager of a major retail conglomerate would have to face in taking on new products for distribution.

Procedure

Each trainee is given a copy of case, to study and to develop a solution prior to group training activity.

Trainees are organized into two- or three-man teams, based on the free choice of participants. Each team works to synthesize the best ideas of its members, preparatory to giving a team presentation. Each team's presentation is open to support or criticism by other teams. Trainer summarizes, using flip chart or chalk board, to cover areas of agreement. Disagreements are resolved using conference method or roleplays.

Case for Study

You are a branch manager of the Super Economy Lumber Corporation. Your branch contains a rental area of about two acres. Inside space, which is occupied with building equipment, plumbing and electrical supplies, hardware, etc., is located in a building of about 100 x 200. This building also houses the office, sales floor and all displays. Outside space is used for items which are not affected by the elements. Three large open sheds are also used to store lumber.

Assume that your branch has been selected to experiment with the sale of *boats* (up to 18 feet long) and *outboard motors*. You are to integrate the sale of this equipment into your *regular* stock. Shipments of boats and motors must be made in one month. It is your responsibility to advise Divisional Headquarters as to the number you can handle and expect to sell. There are three basic boat models (12-, 14-and 18-foot) and two types of motors. Today is February 1 and you must get shipment in by March 10.

No additional warehouse space has been allocated, nor do you have any additional help to handle this new item. What *planning* must be done? State *steps* and justify actions taken.

The Case of the Punch Press Painters

The Precision Punch Press Products Company manufactures punch presses for the domestic and international market. This is a medium size firm operating on a dual-shift. One of the final steps in manufacturing, prior to packing and shipment, is the painting of assembled punch presses.

The color scheme is important to a punch press operator because it improves his visibility during operating time and reduces the possibility of accidents. Workers employed during the day as painters are generally young men, and it has been their practice to use masking tape when performing the job in order to line up the different color markings neatly and clearly.

The evening painters are older men who are quite meticulous in their work and who prefer the free-hand method of putting on lines between colors.

The completed work of each shift is apparent to the other when the men show up for their respective shifts.

The day painters gripe about the "sloppy," uneven work of the evening painters and suggest that the evening painters use masking tape to get their lines straight. These suggestions have been made orally to the foreman on several occasions.

The evening painters, on the other hand, complain bitterly about the tape which the day painter use. They point out that the tape is frequently not removed prior to shipment. If the paint hasn't dried properly when the tape is pulled off, its removal results in some of the paint being pulled off the steel. At times, each shift must touch up the work of the other just prior to packing.

The friction between these two groups has reached a point where something has to be done. Excessive amounts of time are being devoted to criticism and the competition, which at one time seemed "healthy,"is now getting out of hand.

You are the plant superintendent and both shift foremen report to you. Both are scheduled to see you about this problem in an hour. What should you do?

Discuss the advantages and disadvantages of intergroup competition. What do you see as the basic cause of this problem and how can it best be resolved?

Coffee and Milk: A Case
in Problem Analysis and Decision Making

Over the past four years the company* has supplied coffee and milk when excessive overtime has been worked.† This has been intended as a "voluntary" activity by the firm, and nothing has ever been said about it formally or written about it in any policy procedure. The plant manager who approved the action on free coffee and milk has since been promoted to corporate headquarters.

Recently, this extra coffee and milk break has become a nuisance. The present plant manager is especially unhappy. Employees have not only left the containers and sandwich bags lying around but have created quite a mess which has had to be cleaned up by the cleaning crew after hours.

The employees have also insisted that the free coffee and milk is part of their "bargained working conditions" and that the company is obliged to furnish such free coffee and milk as part of the "normal working conditions." In addition, they are insisting, through their representatives in the plant, that they want to get paid for the 8:30 to 9:00 p.m. break at overtime rates.

*Some 500 production employees; union establishment; part of a billion dollar conglomerate.
†For about five months each year; about 300 employees effected.

What is the problem? (Define precisely)
What steps would you follow in solving this problem?
Cite alternatives and probable consequences of each. Justify solution.

The Flexible Print Shop Crew

The print shop crew in the organization (non-union establishment) is under the direction of Phil Brown, a first line supervisor. On occasion, his nine-man crew receives work to do which may require more than their normal eight hours. However, the men do not always have to complete these jobs within that period of time and in such instances each man will pick up the following day where he had stopped, working until he competes the assignment. Sometimes the men work as a team on "long runs." Most of the work is done on offset presses. Electrostatic copies are also used. Collators and related equipment are employed extensively.

Nominally, Brown reports to the assistant director for administration. As a practical matter, organizational unit supervisors place their job orders directly with Brown, who in turn assigns these to his men in the order received. "Emergencies" are handled on the basis of past experience.

Higher ranking personnel (upper and middle management levels) tend to take advantage of the "flexibility" of the print shop crew and the lower rank of its supervisor, Phil Brown. They request his men (unofficially) to perform jobs which could be accomplished within their own units but which may be construed as print shop functions. Some of the work also seems to be for personal (i.e., non-organizational) purposes, such as reproducing bowling schedules, country club activities and similar matters.

What should Brown do?
What is the problem from the viewpoint of Brown?
If Brown takes this problem up to his boss, what approach should Brown take?
Define, in writing, what you feel to be the *real* problem expressed by this case.

The New Middle Manager
(Does He or doesn't He?*)

Joe Berkowitz has been one of the better first-level supervisors for the past three and a half years. He has a good crew and his production has generally been superior. During the past six months Joe sat in on several staff meetings for his boss. Joe is considered the unofficial Number Two man in his section.

Last week it was decided that Joe would be a prime candidate for promotion to a middle management slot. Such a position may open up in the next few months.

*Only the buzz group knows for sure!

The organization possesses a "closed" promotion system, requiring that one pass an exam before moving up to the next promotional level. The division chief has called Joe into his office. The chief's objective is to ask Joe a few questions, such as might appear on an oral exam—which Joe would be required to pass high enough "to be reachable" for promotion.

The questions put to Joe are these:

"How does the job of a middle manager differ from that which you have been performing?."

"What do you see as the greatest problem(s) which a middle level manager is likely to encounter? Explain what you mean."

Assume that you are Joe. How would you respond?

Note for Trainer

Some hidden items within this case (the perceptive group should pick this up): Is Joe the fair-haired boy; the heir apparent? What are the office ethics of providing such special treatment for Joe, presumably excluding others of equal rank within the section? What consequences might follow from Joe's boss's decision to help *only* Joe?

One Study Leads to Another

You are Gerald Bates, a relatively new line supervisor in the finishing department which employs an average of seventy production workers. These employees are mainly females who are assigned to ten conveyor lines as operators. The "efficiency experts" (your manager's expression) have reported that your department has run into a gradually increasing problem of lost time. After a brief study, you were told that the mechanical department blamed your operators for "ruining" the machines. The operators, on the other hand, stated that they were being forced to work with "inferior" materials. In any event, the machines have not been working properly, and the older workers can't maintain the pace of production.

You find some of this information to be true. Through the combined effort of shift foremen, foreladies and engineering staffs, some reduction of lost time has been accomplished. You, feel, however, that better results are yet to be obtained.

During the investigation, you find that coffee breaks are being abused. Also, hourly changes in position by operators on the lines are taking five minutes or more in some cases. Comfort trips by female personnel seem to be occurring more often than necessary. Company policy dictates that all lost time be paid for at the employer's base rate and that two ten-minute coffee breaks and five minutes wash-up time shall be paid at the same rate. Breaks are taken at midpoint in the morning and afternoon.

You are inclined to seek further cuts in lost time by various forms of disciplinary action and through a strict enforcement of company rules and regulations. However, you are told by your manager that "we must keep the confidence of the people" and "not to rock the boat."

What seems to be wrong here?

What steps can Bates take to help correct the situation?

Are department or company policies at fault or outdated?

What should be done to correct the situation?

What difference in actions might be called for if (a) this were a non-union establishment, or (b) it is a unionized establishment?

Universality

The universality of the case method helps to explain its popularity and its ready acceptance by trainees as a starting point in learning how to learn. An example of this feature is to be found in the following case. It has been selected because its style of writing has a very special British flavor. Nevertheless, one can see that it is easily adapted to many other cultures, including the American. Acknowledgment is given to Michael Ivens and Frank Broadway (editors), and to Business Books, Ltd., London, for permission to reproduce it (see annotated bibliography).

The New Trainer

Henderson has left the Army and, after a management course, has taken on the job of training manager in a group of companies that has never had formal training. He is anxious to learn what kind of training is going on in industry and, through a friend, arranges to have lunch with Donnelly, the training manager of a large company.

The two men get on well together, and, over coffee, Donnelly offers some frank advice.

"Look old boy, it just depends what you want to do. If it's being popular with management, getting a higher salary and promotion and having the quiet life, just don't get involved in the operational side of business. Put on some nice innocuous course with bags of management principles, plenty of discussion (they like the sounds of their own voices), good food and drink and the occasional director to come down and chat to them in the evening. If you can, get a nice country house for your training centre; it gratifies their wish to become country gentlemen.

"On the other hand, if you are a masochist, you can go round and see what's wrong with production, marketing, accounting, administration and research and make some recommendations for putting it right. You won't be terribly popular. There's also the problem that you don't know much about production, marketing, accounting, administration and research, whereas after you've read the odd book you'll know as much about management principles as anyone.

"The choice," concluded Donnelly, "is up to you. It depends on what you want. Well, good luck."

Questions

1. What truth is there is Donnelly's remarks?
2. What should Henderson do?
3. What should be the approach of a new training manager to a firm that has never had formal training before?
4. Draw up the objectives of a company training plan with recommendations to ensure maximum management acceptance and participation.

MIS: Up and Down the Echelon

Cost reduction is one of those ephemeral terms which means little until the reduction is equated to the firing of staff. This is what has happened in Al Frost's district office recently, and Al is hopping mad!

Al has been with the organization for nearly thirty years. Having come up through the ranks, he has reached the point in his career where he is both respected and feared as a result of the candidness with which he voices his opinions. Al's district office contains well over a hundred employees and handles the processing of licenses and related matters for the general public.

One of the things that has been bothering Al lately is the continued emphasis, within the upper levels of his organization, on the need for effective *management information.* But, according to Al, the multitudinous reporting systems demanded each month, and which seem to be revised every year, cut seriously into the productive effort for which the district office is responsible. After a recent revision on how reports are to be prepared, Al analyzed the costs visibly required to produce the information which management was demanding "for the upper echelon." Al's analysis, figured conservatively, showed the amount to be in excess of $300,000 per year for the entire organization.

When Al ran into his old boss, who has since been promoted and is now the second highest official within the organization and with whom he can speak on a first name basis, Al obtained a tacit confession that most of the effort being devoted to the MIS was a waste of time.

Al's old boss conceded that the decision to produce the management information was generated by a concern that someone in Washington might demand such information, and "we better be prepared to have it, in the event they ask for it."

Recently, the cost reduction program, which is an organization-wide application of dollar savings fixed on a percentage basis of the total budget, has resulted in layoffs. Al has argued that the management information program should be abolished and the savings taken here, rather than in personnel reductions. Besides, Al points out that such uniform manpower cuts result in reduced services at points where the organization interfaces with the public and where sensitive public relations are involved.

Assignment for Trainees

1. What do you see as the three most important issues here? Obtain group agreement, as these are stated in writing.
2. Develop responses to these issues.

Rotating the Junior Executive

Each year your organization recruits approximately twenty-five young hopefuls directly from colleges to fill openings as upward mobility occurs within the company. The firm's recruiting staff attempts to bring in those new employees who will properly reflect the organizational image and who will possess the necessary potential for career development. After reporting to work, usually in August and September, these junior executives are placed in various open slots within the organization for their work and job training assignments. Initially, they receive about a week of orientation to the entire organization and then are placed under individual middle manager, who have themselves come up through the ranks.

Jerry York, a middle manager handling product development for several key areas, has been given the responsibility for one of the new junior executives, Larry King.

What steps should Jerry follow in introducing Larry to his new responsibilities?

Assume that Larry will be assigned to Mr. York for approximately three months and then will be rotated to other units of the organization for a period of approximately two years before a decision is made concerning final placement.

Based on the foregoing, assume the following situations within your group and consider alternative approaches, as if you were Mr. York:

1. Larry King is sharp but overly eager and impatient.
2. Larry King needs prodding, is slow meeting deadlines and seems, at times, to be a bit "thick."
3. Larry King has made several sarcastic and disparaging remarks about the company—especially its heavy involvement in defense contracting.
4. Larry King has been "fooling around" with York's secretary.
5. Each group should develop three additional reasonable problems which could occur in this type of situation. Leader collects and redistributes to other groups for additional consideration.

This might be termed a sequential case in that it may be cut at any point—even after the very first question, if that is as far as the trainer wishes to proceed. Were he covering the basic principles of job instructor training, this might be a suitable cutoff for group review. On the other hand, additional input into this kind of situation—where conflict may occur between the older and newer generations—is readily provided. When the groups have the means for introducing conditions which the trainer has not personally provided, he must be alert to factors which could cause embarrassment to individual trainees. For this reason, the additional problems will be screened before redistribution for further group consideration.

In this case situation the following training areas are open for analysis:

Job instructor training
Matching people and jobs
The "Now Generation" and its special needs*
Conflict between personality types in superior-subordinate situations.
Planning effective learning experiences for new managerial personnel
Reporting on progress
Relations between line managers and personnel office
Appraisal methods
Coaching

*David Nadler, *The Now Employee* (Houston: Gulf Publishing Company, 1971).

4. Roleplaying: Basic Concepts

In this chapter the basic concepts of role playing are surveyed, and the reader becomes acquainted with what roleplaying really is. Areas where roleplaying may be used effectively and the historical development of roleplaying are also given attention. Detailed explanations are provided covering *open* and *covert* roleplaying and types of roleplay situations applicable to each of these approaches. Also continued are general discussions of the distinctions between converting a written case into a roleplay situation as opposed to converting an oral case. Covert roleplaying and the effective use of written role materials are analyzed, as well as process roleplaying. Finally, implications of roleplaying are examined as an adversary exercise.

Roleplaying: An Active Learning Experience

The role of the trainee effected by the training methods is illustrated in Figure 4.1.

The lecture is, to the weight conscious person, comparable to reading a pamphlet about dieting, whereas the roleplay or in-basket can be compared to jogging or working out in a health club.

Words often transmit unintended meanings. Take roleplay,* for instance. To *play* a role may imply (a) a dramatic endeavor, (b) an impersonation, (c) pretending how someone might behave or (d) to have fun. Actually the word *play* is open to many other interpretations. When a trainer announces to his group that "we're going to do some roleplaying this afternoon," his trainees

---

*For simplicity of spelling, a single word is used.

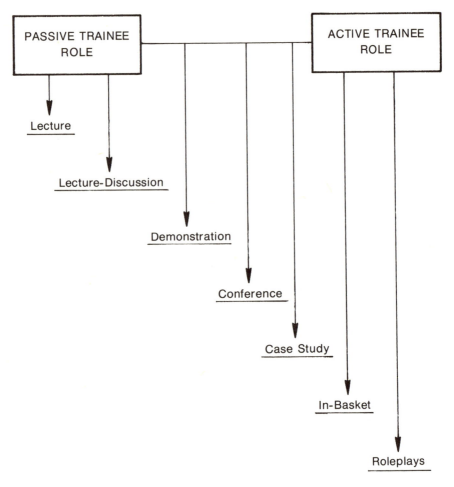

Figure 4.1. Roles of trainees effected by different training methods.

will register various internal reactions—depending on previous understandings of the term or how they translate "roleplay." Frankly, another term, such as "role enacting," would be preferred, but since roleplay has already been designated its internal weakness *as a term must* be understood. Its use as a technique is another story.

One of the threads running through this book is that people have to learn how to learn. If roleplaying is learning, then learning how to *accept* and *use* roleplaying is not an automatic condition of life. It may be a natural process—but it is not automatic. The success of roleplaying depends to a great extent on how it is introduced to the trainees and at what point in a course of instruction. These decisions must belong to the trainer who knows the strengths and weaknesses of his group.

Roleplaying: What Is It Really?

Roleplaying is directed human interaction which creates and capitalizes on imaginary situations. It is people simulating real life behavior. Its purpose is to *teach* (using that word in its broadest sense).

Spontaneity is a hallmark of effective roleplaying. The participants improvise their script as they speak, and the make-believe situation is acted upon by the participants as if it were "for real."

The historical background of roleplaying is to be found in both sociology and psychology. In sociology the process of socialization—how individuals, beginning in infancy, interact within their environments—is studied. It is recognized that the human personality is largely influenced by the most fundamental of groups, the family. Personality is, according to the sociologist, based on the functioning of the social situation in which the child is born and raised. A child's personality is molded according to how others view him.* The child tries out *roles* and judges the reactions of "significant others." Young children appear to *take* roles in the same sense as they try on clothes during dress-up games.

Responding to the way other humans react, children—and adults, too—*play* roles which are more subtle adaptations of behavior and which ultimately seem to become *merged* with the basic personality. In this sense, sociology sees *role-taking* as being more analogous to what the actor does, whereas roleplaying is the continuous adjusting of the way one acts, at all points in his life. Often he is unaware of this kind of roleplaying.

Within the methodology invented for the treatment of the emotionally disturbed is found the psychological basis for roleplaying. J.L. Moreno, M.D., director of the Moreno Institute†, is generally recognized as the principal contributor to roleplaying as it is now used. Because roleplaying, when it is used for therapeutic purposes, often needs an explanation, Moreno developed the term *sociodrama*. This is a kind of roleplay employed to explain the ac-

---

*These concepts are founded on the classic work of Charles Cooley, *Human Nature and the Social Order* (New York: Charles Scribner's Sons, 1902).

†The Moreno Institute, Inc., 259 Wolcott Avenue, Beacon, New York 12508.

tion to the viewing audience and to *involve* the audience. In Moreno's roleplay approach used for treatment purposes, which he termed *psychodrama**, the emphasis is on the spontaneous action of the roleplayers. In the sociodrama, the emphasis is on the audience: explaining the action and involving the audience.

The reader will appreciate that the technical vocabulary of roleplaying is by no means universally accepted by all authorities. This is not only confusing to the neophyte practitioner but contributes, in a peculiar fashion, to the mystique surrounding this method. Terms used within this book are intended to strip away as much of this mystique as is possible. The labels applied to the types of roleplaying and the roleplayers were chosen because they are descriptive. This should serve the nontechnical purposes required by the vast majority of trainers.

The index at the end of the book provides cross-references to the technical terminology of roleplaying.

For trainers the principal recommended uses of roleplaying follow.

1. In supervisory and management training, roleplaying is particularly valuable in providing meaningful opportunitites for practicing the principles of leadership in human relations situations, which are usually required in these kinds of training activities.
2. In many phases of organization development, where openness and trust are mandatory prerequisites to change, roleplaying is a natural adjunct to other techniques. Roleplaying is a most important tool for the trainer or facilitator in removing barriers to change.
3. Roleplaying is employed to train personnel people, line supervisors and shop stewards in such potentially difficult situations as layoffs, handling discharge or exit interviews, merit rating appraisals and related kinds of intricate personnel situations.
4. The roleplaying technique is well suited to teaching how to handle grievances in superior-subordinate relationships.
5. Roleplaying is an excellent method for the study and analysis of problems involved in supervisory-worker or shop steward-worker communications.
6. A relative newcomer to the list of possible users of roleplaying is the field of collective bargaining. Management and union officials have

---

*Ira A. Greenberg, *Psychodrama and Audience Attitudes Change.* (Beverly Hills, Calif.: Behavioral Studies Press, 1968) found it extremely useful to roleplay before presenting their demands within formal bargaining sessions.

7. Roleplaying is used to teach trainees how to follow specific methods which must be applied in the job—for example, selling a customer a product or, for interviewing, following a reasonably precise format.

If studying case materials represents learning by doing, then roleplaying is a further intensification of the doing—by the learners. Roleplaying, or situational enactment, implies an honest acting out of some interpersonal circumstance. The word "playing" has, as has been noted, an unfortunate connotation. The participants' enactment must be sincere and as true-to-life as is attainable. Theirs is neither a game nor charade. The participants have not rehearsed or memorized their lines. They are interacting as if they were alone, without others listening and observing the action. The only play-acting desired is that each party make a genuine effort to behave as if the action were "for real." Therefore, the following are looked upon with *extreme* disfavor:

1. Any attempts by the enactors to play for the galleries.
2. Hamming it up and showing how brilliant one may be with repartee and witticism.
3. Deliberately confusing and confounding the facts by inserting erroneous or misleading information into the role enactment.

The atmosphere or the tone for a roleplay is set by the trainer. To a great extent, he becomes the surrogate manager of each member within the training group (regardless of the relative rank of the trainees in relation to the trainer). In other words, during roleplaying, he is more than a trainer. He sets a firm, no-nonsense direction when moving his group into roleplaying. He clearly delineates the ground rules and boundaries for good taste. He also directs the roleplaying action—with the power to cut it off at any point if he believes this to be necessary.

Roleplaying is a training tool—a method of getting people to learn something or other from one another. It is not—or at least it should not be—a period of downtime during a course when the instructor "exposes the group" to fun and games for the sake of fun and games. Pseudosophisticated trainers, impressed with what they understand T-Group or laboratory training has done, feel constrained to expose their people to lab training techniques. Much of this uncoordinated exposure is a blatant waste of time and money. While there may be claims by trainers that their people learned a great deal, no one can prove or disprove such claims. Enjoyment and discussion by themselves do not indicate that people are learning—although learning is facilitated. Learning, in the context viewed in this book, is proven when some reasonably demonstrable change begins to take hold among the participants back at the job that is traceable to the instruction.

Roleplaying may be viewed by some instructors as a formidable mechanism to handle, but even inexperienced trainers who adhere to the general guidelines which are provided in this book will have little to be concerned about. If uncertain, they should proceed on a step-by-step approach.

Roleplaying will, at the right moment in a course, cement theory and knowledge solidly into application. Even attitude changes may be brought about. But mishandled, roleplaying can create a devastatingly unsettling influence. Trainee confidence in an instructor, built up over weeks of personal contact, may be eroded in moments. There are reasons why this may happen.

1. Most important is that trainers forget that learners must learn *how* to learn.* Participative methods may be frightening experiences to people who have been mainly exposed to the nonparticipative. A warm-up period—a testing process—is needed.

2. The "folklore" of highly participative learning methodologies contains many myths. Most myths have their genesis in some remote incident which really happened. Rumors about how and why roleplaying is used are easily reinforced when terms such as *sensitize* or *psychodrama* are introduced—often in complete innocence. Some trainees—and admittedly a minority—are turned off by such terminology. Rumors about "brainwashing" seem to be suddenly confirmed. *These* are the people to reach; these are the ones that need training. To avoid losing them, explanations must be handled with extreme caution. When applying roleplaying, the low key, step-by-step approach is a must.

3. Trainers must not rush to expose the trainees to *every* kind of roleplay exercise which he has available or knows how to handle—no matter how eager they may appear. Flitting about with the trainee group, sampling

---

*See discussion of research on this point, concerning levels of involvement by roleplayers and various types of observers to roleplaying, by Leland P. Bradford, Jack R. Gibb and Kenneth D. Benne, editors, *T-Group Theory and Laboratory Method: Innovation in Reeducation* (New York: John Wiley and Sons, Inc., 1967), p. 431. *See also* I.L. Janis and B.T. King, "The Influence of Role-Playing on Opinion Change," article reprinted from *Journal of Abnormal and Social Psychology in Attitudes*, edited by M. Jahoda and N. Warren (Baltimore: Penguin Books, Inc., Penguin Modern Psychology Series, 1966), pp. 211-18.

exercises, may be entertaining, but learning has been misdirected. Nothing is lost and much is to be gained by concentrated attention on the principles taught by the roleplay rather than on the techniques of illustrating such principles.

4. Trainers who have had successful experiences with roleplaying—based on reasonably reliable feedback from trainees—are apt to get hooked by this method. Nearly *everything* gets to be roleplayed! The common sense rule is *everything in moderation*, and this includes use of and concentration on roleplaying as a teaching method.

Open and Covert Roleplaying

Either of two basic roleplay conditions exists prior to the initiation of the process. Under *open* conditions, all information leading to the role enactment is known to the potential participants. There are no secrets, hidden agenda or special instructions directed at any of the parties. Under *covert* conditions, data is held in reserve by one party or another and may be released to the other party. Under covert conditions, the material held by either party has to be read and assimilated before the roleplay commences. Each party must fully comprehend the specific instructions provided within his role. Under covert conditions, a period of time is normally provided prior to roleplaying when each party studies his assigned role. The amount of time will depend on the length of the role and the sharpness of the roleplayers.

The trainer, who doubles as the role director, will ensure that each roleplayer understands his role.* The trainer should not ask, "O.K. Do you understand your role?" Such questions are worthless. Instead, the *roleplayer* should be asked to explain what he understands his role to contain. If sections of the role are confusing to the trainee, they should be clarified. Explanations by the trainer of covert material should be handled privately, out of the hearing range of the other roleplayer who holds the other covert role assignment.

Under open conditions, less time is needed to move into the role enactment. All of the material is out on the table at the outset of the exercise. Therefore, if covert conditions are present, time for briefing roleplayers must be scheduled.

The trainer who can hardly be in two places at the same time will remember that while he may be briefing the roleplayers in connection with

---

*When two roleplayers are involved, this is known as a *simple* roleplay. Any number greater than two provides a *complex* roleplay situation.

their covert roles, the other trainees are unoccupied. Probably the best time for such briefings is toward the end of a break period, just before the group reconvenes. Further comments on this point may be found on pp. 95 and 125.

Under covert conditions, there is an ever present concern that the trainee enacting one of the roles may introduce extraneous or erroneous materials into the role. Of course, the other roleplayer would be unaware of what was believable within the total context of the role situation. This is unlikely to occur when roleplaying operates under open conditions. Therefore, when instructing roleplayers, the trainer-director has a very special responsibility to emphasize the necessity for sticking to the roles.

Improvisation is acceptable and encouraged, but only when it dovetails with the role's requirements. The roleplayer who carries the major burden* cannot invent or concoct solutions based on the introduction of improbable concepts which are unlikely to be found in the simulated situation. In all roleplaying the rule is that the verbal give-and-take must be true to life. Further, farfetched resolutions vitiate the intent of the learning exercise and are likely to make the entire process appear foolish and wasteful.

The trainer, by his classroom demeanor, sets the tone. He is serious; neither dour nor cleverly witty. Certainly, he must evaluate his group and look for individual members who may distort the intent of the role out of childish mischievousness.

Types of Roleplays

Roleplaying exercises are classified into four major types.

1. Written case material converted into roleplay. *Open roleplay* conditions exist.
2. Oral case material (i.e., a case that develops spontaneously within a training session) converted into roleplay. *Open roleplay* conditions exist.
3. Written roles prepared ahead of time and made available to roleplayers. *Covert roleplay* conditions exist.
4. Process roleplay. Either *open or covert conditions* may exist.

This grouping has been devised on the basis of the methods used in preparation for and during the roleplays. The order of listing for the first

---

*See p. 82 ff for further discussion on this point.

three categories signifies that the trainee proceeds from the simple to the advanced in his learning methods. In addition, the first three forms frequently concern what are referred to as human relations problems. The term is used as it is traditionally thought of—no two people interacting to a problem in exactly the same way.

The fourth type roleplay has a different purpose in that its objective is to teach a *process*.

Written Case into Roleplay

What people say should be done to remedy some problem and what they do to bring forth a remedy are frequently at variance with one another. In an adversary case study, as is often seen in superior-subordinate relations where the superior must act, the trainer encourages the trainees, working in small groups, to study the case carefully and then report what needs to be done.

Group A's spokesman will say: "Our group has decided that the foreman should . . . ," proceeding then to relate how clever Group A was in disposing of this problem.

Group B might take a slightly different tack and be perhaps a bit patronizing toward the decision reached by Group A and so on. Each group decision is immaculate in the sense that it need never be tried out in the real world. Each problem has been analyzed and settled. And the trainer's clinical evaluation has tied together all the loose ends.

These comments are not intended to disparage what has been done. The designated training groups have learned to work cooperatively on a problem. A case situation has been analyzed and problems identified. Suggested solutions have been developed and considered. Finally, the learning has been looped and reinforced by bridging the results of the discussion with given principles.

This is fine, but how can learning be escalated from here? Most people tend to be attracted to action situations rather than to passive ones. No matter how imaginative trainees are, they inevitably learn more and appreciate the shadings of required actions (to resolve a case problem) when their participation is built into the class exercise.

In Type One roleplay, the potential roleplayers know all facts and all background information in the case. The case has been read, discussed, analyzed and summarized. On p. 90 is a diagram to show how this process takes hold.

Oral Case Material into Roleplay

Cases which are provided spontaneously by individual trainees during a group learning activity are often best handled through a roleplay. After a discussion of some principle, a trainee will say: "In my place, I've got a problem, and I'd like to hear from the rest of you what you would do. . . ." The trainee then describes his special situation. Given orally, it is not constructed with the precision of a written case. But the facts are there and a problem is evident. Some of the other trainees will give freely of their advice since often they have neither commitment nor obligation to solve the problems.

The trainer, however, may suggest that the problem (or incident) be roleplayed. The experience of a single trainee is transformed into a genuine group exercise. Converted into a group problem, it becomes a group learning experience.

Prior to beginning such an open roleplay, the trainer should first clear up any obscure or contradictory factors within the case. This is done by asking for additional data from the trainee who initiated the case. When data cannot be provided on essential points, logical assumptions are made which all group members accept.

Covert Roleplaying: The Use of Written Role Materials

The typical roleplay condition—the one which most people seem to know something about—is where covert, written instructions are provided to the learners. Conflict and confrontation seem to be the essential ingredients within such exercises. Each roleplayer is involved. Each approaches the other with caution, fearful of being trapped. Trainers are urged to lead their trainees—as learners learning how to learn—through an open roleplay exercise *before* exposing them to covert material. Levels of talking and listening, especially in the role held by the protagonist, are factors to be measured. As a rule, more listening and less talking are sought. Usually, however, it comes forth the other way around. Participants, who are learning what to do and what to avoid, generally agree that the open roleplay produces less of a threatening experience than does the covert roleplay. For the trainee who talks too much and listens too little, the open roleplay, as a starter, is less likely to be ego-shattering than if he had commenced with covert materials.

Another very human element is involved when covert role situations are used. The intrinsically secretive nature of the roles held by each participant is similar to a session of poker. Each party knows something which the other does not. Obviously, trust levels are influenced—no matter how sound they are alleged to be. Open-type materials build trust as well as instructing the trainees how to cope confidently with this method of learning.

Covert roleplaying is equally valuable when trainees are ready to use it. The similarity between reality and covert roleplays is clear, and this is what makes this form most appealing to trainers. The covert exercise simulates the genuine article. Herein lies a self-evident threat, both for the trainees and the trainer. Occasionally, the trainer appears to take a sadistic pleasure in structuring the covert roleplaying to imitate a damned-if-you-do—damned-if-you-don't type situation. The result is a humiliating—although faintly humorous—experience for one of the parties. When this occurs, not only have basic program objectives been ignored but common sense as well. Further, elitist manipulators who, after a covert roleplay, patronize the trainees with a discourse on "how smart I am" are to be graded "F" as instructors.

Covert roleplay can teach many things: to listen judiciously, to probe for facts and to sort out the unimportant. It also shows how and when to convert and apply theory into practice. Having acquired a feel for roleplaying through experience with the open type, the trainee advancing into covert roleplaying deserves empathetic support. The trainer using this roleplay form will himself adopt and apply the real life roles of coach, facilitator and mentor. On p. 134 ff the construction of covert roleplays is illustrated and described.

Process Roleplays

In process roleplaying trainees are taught how and why to adhere to some particular procedure or a mandatory requirement of the organization, usually when dealing with the public. If a police officer, a collection agent or telephone interviewer is to perform his or her job in the precise way that the employer wants it done, process roleplaying exercises provide a method for accomplishing this. Prior to the application of the process roleplay, trainees are taught how to react to given situations. When the trainee makes a telephone sales call, the potential client answers. The trainee is taught exactly how to reply to each major type of customer response. An illustration of this form is shown on p. 105.

Roleplaying As an Adversary Exercise

Roleplaying embraces many of the inherent characteristics of an adversary

Table 4.1. Examples of Roleplay Protagonist-Antagonist Titles	
Protagonist	Antagonist
Board Member	Stockholder
Chief Negotiator and Spokesman	Negotiating Team Member
Counselor	Client
Fiscal Officer	Line Manager
Husband	Wife
Wife	Husband
Instructor	Student
Interviewer	Interviewee
Manager	Supervisor
Military Officer	Common Soldier
Parent	Child
Pastor	Parishoner
Physician	Patient
Salesman	Client
Salesperson	Customer
Shop Steward	Employee
Staff Specialist	Line Manager
Supervisor	Employee

situation. At the outset, the parties are apt to see each problem differently. In covert roleplaying, especially, these perceptual differences are what energize the learning exercise. To ensure such perceived differences during this exercise, the structuring of the covert roles has been deliberate.

In the courtroom where the dispute between adversaries is carefully controlled and regulated by a judge who defines the law, the conflict is highly stylized. In the roleplay, the adversaries (the roleplayers) are placed in juxtaposition, not for the purpose of creating and encouraging additional conflict but to teach how to move from unresolved conflict and confrontation to the resolution of such conflict. The roleplayers must generally achieve this by themselves. The trainer is, of course, not analagous to the judge. His function is to facilitate learning, not to judge either the protagonist or the antagonist as being right or wrong.

The protagonist-antagonist* nature of roleplaying requires that attention be directed to those identifying attributes which usually belong to one or the

*The protagonist is referred to as the "hero" of the action in the definitions provided in *Roleplaying in Business and Industry* by Raymond J. Cosini, Malcolm E. Shaw and Robert R. Blake. (New York: The Free Press of Glencoe, Inc., 1961)

other of the roles. The reader will find, in the following listings, recognizable factors or traits which distinguish the protagonist from the antagonist *within assigned roles* (see Table 4.1). The desirable/undesirable behaviors are listed for each party as the roleplay develops and proceeds toward that point where the action should be cut by the trainer.

Protagonist

The one who carries the burden or responsibility for decision-making.
He has the power or authority to act or to reconcile a conflict.
He generally outranks the antagonist.
The trainee to whom the *issue* is presented.
The roleplayer who is on the hot seat.
The one who supports or advocates a position when seeking to solve a problem.

Protagonist: Desirable Behavior

Listens
Open-Minded
Noncritical
Nondirective
Nondogmatic
Supportive*
Focuses on problem
Sincere
Looks at antagonist

Protagonist: Undesirable Behavior

Talks excessively
Pitches his approach to "sell" his point of view
Fails to listen
Close-minded
Shows displeasure
Argues
Sarcastic

---

*Applying transactional analysis (TA) terminology: the protagonist acts as an *adult* rather than as a *parent*.

Insincere
Talks to the wall

Antagonist

Generally subordinate to the protagonist
The aggrieved party
One who is displeased with some action, past or present; or likely to be
    taken in the future
An opponent
Someone who is unconvinced
Challenges the authority of the protagonist
One adversely effected by some action
May be frightened

Antagonist Behavior

Normally, the antagonist will, at the outset, reveal behaviors reflecting the
requirements of the assigned role.

These behaviors typically emerge as:

Talks excessively
Needles
Sullen (needs support to "open up")
Facial expressions of unhappiness or displeasure
Critical or sarcastic ("It's not my headache!")
Argues

These antagonist behaviors should be reflected *naturally* by the roleplayer
taking this role. Trainers should not tell the antagonist precisely how his an-
tagonism should be expressed within the roleplay. For example, during the
pre-roleplay briefing, the trainer might say to the antagonist that "you're
angry with . . ." whatever the situation happens to involve. The trainer should
not, however, advise the antagonist to express such anger by pounding the
table or cursing the protagonist. If the antagonist does this of his own voli-
tion, that is fine. That is the antagonist's behavior, not the trainer's operating
through the antagonist.

As a rule, the roleplay's immediate goal is some overt change in the antagonist's behavior. This is often brought about by how the protagonist acts
toward an antagonist. Each case will provide different outcomes, and

predetermined, idealized results are often extremely difficult to achieve. Nevertheless, if, after a reasonable period, the antagonist still maintains the same views that he held when the roleplay commenced, then the protagonist has not been successful.

Here is an example of what is meant.

An objective of a roleplay exercise is to teach a supervisor to listen to a subordinate with a legitimate gripe. In the resulting roleplay, the supervisor hardly permits the subordinate to get a word in edgewise. The protagonist expends all of his effort telling the antagonist what a fortunate fellow he is to have such an "understanding" boss. The true feelings of the antagonist are never permitted to emerge; they are smothered with smooth talk.

The trainer's function is to surface these facts during the post-roleplay discussion and analysis. At that time, his principal chore is to bridge the results of the roleplay to the longer term objectives of the exercise. He points out that the protagonist-antagonist nature of the roleplay must not permit it to be distorted into a "win-lose" game. In the truly successful roleplay—as in real life under similar circumstances—a double win is achieved. In other words, "win-lose" results are really double losses.

Caution

While much of roleplaying is founded on concept of the protagonist-antagonist confrontation, that does not imply that *every* roleplay must contain an adversary component. In several of the titles shown in Table 4.1, the roleplayer may be *either* the protagonist or the antagonist. A situation may have a husband confronting his wife, the wife aligned against her husband, or both, in a nonadversary, team-type relationship. Through roleplaying, simulating solutions to the problem situations of life is sought, not merely demonstrating the forces of conflict.

5. How to Convert Case Study Materials into Roleplaying Situations

Many varieties of case study materials may be readily converted into highly productive roleplaying situations. When comparing these two methods, levels and intensity of learning are quite different. After struggling with a case study which has been introduced by the trainer, the typical training group concludes by saying, "We would, therefore, recommend that. . . ." Roleplayers responding to the same situation *do not* recommend; they *act*.

The case study is useful in initiating and stimulating group participation and intragroup communications. However, as in real life, the *passive* thought processes of the group, as it evaluates the case study, frequently go awry in the active *doing* processes of fulfillment. It is fascinating and exciting to compare the activities of the group which "recommends" the achievement of certain objectives with the actions of roleplayers selected from the group who actually simulate the "carrying out" processes.

In this chapter the reader will be shown how to plan the case study to roleplay conversion and how to advance on a step-by-step basis from the case study into an *open* roleplay. Three levels of open roleplaying are explained, and the introduction of the trainees to the *convert* roleplay and the various levels of convert roleplaying are discussed. Finally, several examples of roleplays are included to demonstrate its flexibility as a training tool.

Planning the Case Study-to-Roleplay Conversion

Trainees who must learn how to use roleplaying will require more time adjusting to this method than experienced participants. A trainer must avoid

86

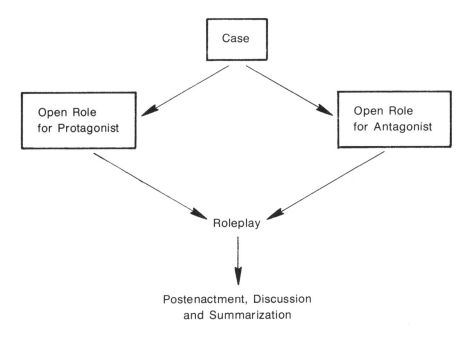

Figure 5.1. Option One.

rushing through the process simply to reach a point where some principle is to be discussed because he may find that he has lost his trainees. They should know why roleplaying has been required and why a straightforward case discussion would not have been preferable. Rushing through roleplaying often makes the process appear gimmicky. The trainees are apt to feel that they are performing for the benefit of the trainer instead of realizing that it is they who are learning both principles and methods.

Three broad options are available to the trainer when planning to convert case materials into roleplays. Deciding which option to use will largely depend on trainees' familiarity of roleplaying, the objectives which the trainer sets before the session begins and the time available. The choices are shown diagrammatically in Figures 5.1, 5.2 and 5.3.

Option One

This is the simplest form of case to roleplay. The trainer commences with case materials and converts these into an *open* roleplay between protagonist and antagonist (See Figure 5.1).

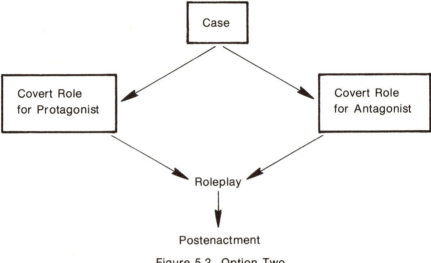

Figure 5.2. Option Two.

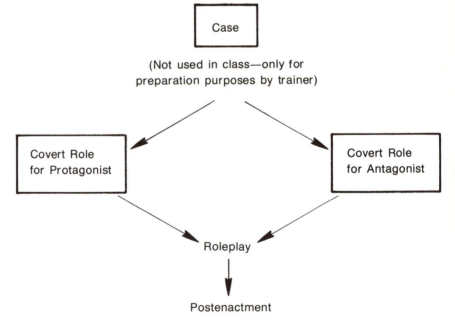

Figure 5.3. Option Three.

Option Two

Here the trainer commences with case material and converts this into a *convert* roleplay between protagonist and antagonist, (see Figure 5.2). When a convert roleplay is used, the trainer must prepare the roles before the exercise is used. (See pp. 97 f f for example of a typical case and converted roles.)

Option Three

The trainer commences with roleplay by skipping the case study portion within the lesson, (see Figure 5.3). However, the trainer has employed the case beforehand to construct the covert roleplays which are based on the written case.

Advancing from Case Studies to Open Roleplaying

Having considered the theory, philosophy and basic techniques of roleplaying, we now proceed to demonstrate how the trainer shifts his participants from one fundamental method to another. Three learning levels have been designated for typical conditions of open roleplaying. Each level is illustrated with a chart to guide the reader through the process. Level One represents the easiest entry. The steps should be followed carefully. Problems and their recommended solutions are discussed in Chapter 6.

Open Roleplay: Level One

Step A: Trainer hands out case material to the trainees for study.
Step B: Group discussions of case by trainees.
Step C: Group reports on case by trainees.
Step D: Trainees are divided into two-man teams. Each team consists of a protagonist and an antagonist. All teams roleplay the case situation concurrently.*

---

*The term *concurrent roleplay* is used to designate this type of group exercise. It is considered to be descriptively accurate as to what takes place. Some authorities use the term *Multiple Roleplay* (MRP) to describe the same type of group work. However, this term is also applied to a roleplay involving more than two roleplayers engaged in a single problem. For a discussion of MRP, see N.R.F. Maler, A.R. Solem and A.A. Maier, *Supervisory and Executive Development: A Manual for Role Playing,* New York: John Wiley and Sons, Inc., (Science Edition), 1964, p. 8.

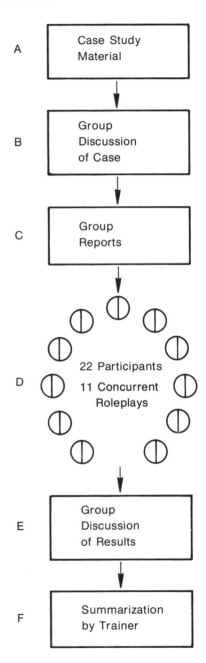

Figure 5.4. Open role-play, Level One.

Step E: Trainer leads group discussions on results of roleplays.

Step F: Summarization by trainer covering results, including principles involved in problem.

As an example, Figure 5.4 illustrates a class of twenty-two participants divided into eleven teams.

Open Roleplay: Level Two

Step A: Trainer hands out case materials to the trainees for study.

Step B: Group discussions of case by trainees.

Step C: Group reports on case by trainees.

Step D: Trainees are divided into two-man teams. Each team consists of a protagonist and an antagonist. All teams roleplay case concurrently.

Step E: Trainer stops roleplay after reasonable period of time has elapsed. Antagonists and protagonists exchange seats and start all over again *from the beginning.*

Step F: Trainer leads group discussions on results of roleplays, including the impact of role reversal.

Step G: Summarization by trainer of results, including principles involved in the case study.
Level Two roleplay is illustrated in Figure 5.5.

Open Roleplay: Level Three

Step A: Trainer hands out case materials to trainees and reads case aloud. He then summarizes key factors within the case.

Step B: Trainees are divided into two-man teams, each team consisting of a protagonist and an antagonist. All teams roleplay case situation simultaneously.

Step C: All antagonists and all protagonists are divided so that antagonists sit on one side of the room and protagonists on the other.

Step D: A single volunteer is obtained from the antagonist group and another from the protagonist group. These two individuals are seated facing both the antagonists and the protagonists. In a sense these two individuals represent their total teams. The

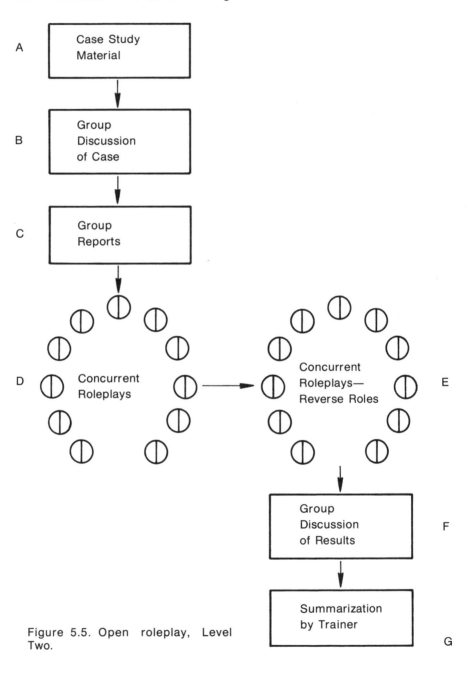

Figure 5.5. Open roleplay, Level Two.

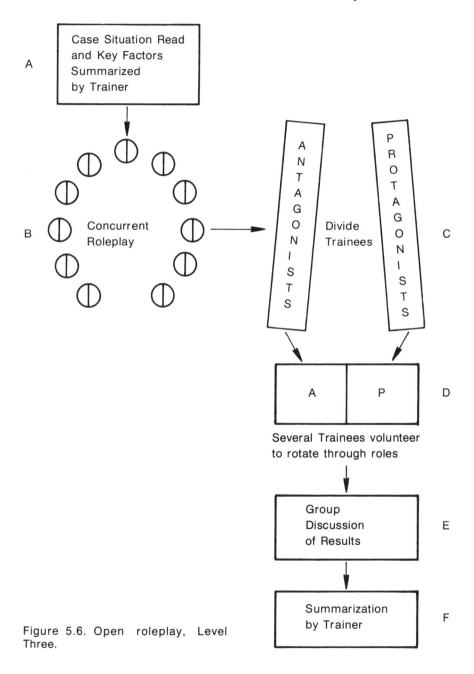

Figure 5.6. Open roleplay, Level Three.

roleplay commences. Additional volunteers may rotate through the roles as individuals exhaust their input.

Step E: Trainer leads group discussion of results.

Step F: Trainer summarizes results, including principles involved

All of these steps are shown in Figure 5.6.

Introducing the Trainees to Covert Roleplaying

Trainees should receive covert roleplaying materials after first having worked with open roleplayings. Those who have progressed through all three levels of open roleplaying will be much more successful at handling covert materials than those who have been provided with such materials as a first-time roleplaying experience. Fewer explanations will be needed; trainees are less apt to misinterpret the intent of the covert exercise.

The most elemental form of covert roleplay has depicted on p. 134. What are the major differences, insofar as trainee participation is concerned, between an open and covert roleplay? What special responsibilities does covert roleplaying impose on a trainer?

In covert roleplay the roles must be preconstructed; they are not spontaneously produced by trainees. Therefore, the briefings of protagonists and antagonists must be controlled and regulated by the trainer *before* roleplaying commences. The trainer distributes the two covert roles after the trainees have been matched with their respective partners and after they have received their assigned roles. Just prior to handing out the written roles, the trainer's instructions will sound like the following discussion.

"Each of you has received your written role information. Will all the Al Browns please raise their hands?" (Trainer checks to see if all proper hands are up.) "Fine. Now, all the Laura Smiths please let me see your hands." (Trainer checks here also, as he did earlier.) "Excellent. Now, please study your assignments carefully. Do *not* discuss these with your neighbor. If you have any questions, just wave, and I'll come over. Please don't ask any questions out loud at this point."

Trainees uncertain of their covert roles are thus able to raise questions about which they are unclear. The trainer explains and clarifies, out of range of hearing of other trainees. If his response is a general one, which should be given the other trainees, then the trainer will restate the question for the group together with his explanation.

Copies of the written roles are generally expendable. In some complex covert exercises, the trainees may wish to make notes on these. Covert materials are intended as a point of departure for the roleplayers. The trainer should emphasize to trainees that they not get hung up on the written language. During the discussion of a completed roleplay, nit-pickers within the trainee group may become engrossed in a hairsplitting examination of exactly what was meant by some particular phrase. The trees obscure their view of the forest. Undoubtedly, this is a problem in any written material of substance: the time available to diagnose words has caused the reader to become intensively interpretive of language in a manner that the writer had never intended. Only by concentrating on the substance of a covert roleplay may the trainer avoid becoming sidetracked in semantic discussions.

A final suggestion and caution: in an open roleplay, all parties (protagonists, antagonists and observers if any) possess identical data when the action begins. For example if the problem in the upcoming roleplay concerns an expired lease on a branch department store, necessitating a relocation, one of the roleplayers cannot introduce contrary facts, such as, "I managed to obtain a lease renewal at the old rental rate last week."

Covert roleplayers are not permitted to solve problems by introducing farfetched or silly solutions. This is a basic rule in all roleplaying. In covert roleplaying especially, where the roleplayers are in the dark as to what the other person can or cannot do, the trainer must remind each trainee of this basic rule.

The total step-by-step process for introducing trainees to covert roleplaying at the most elemental level covers eight steps.

Covert Roleplay: Level One

Step A: Trainer hands out case material to the trainees for study.
Step B: Groups discuss case.
Step C: Groups report on case.
Step D: Trainees are divided into two-man teams. Each team consists of a protagonist and an antagonist.
Step E: Trainer distributes role material and briefs the roleplayers.
Step F: Trainees roleplay covert materials.
Step G: Trainer leads group discussion of roleplay results.
Step H: Trainer summarizes covering results, including principles involved in problem.

Figure 5.7 illustrates these steps.

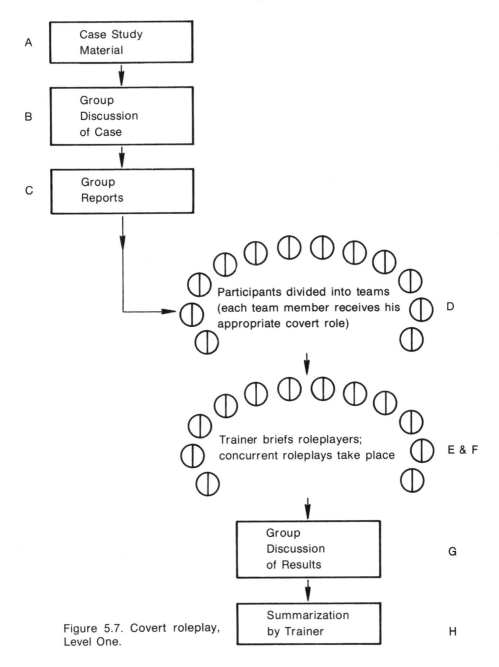

Figure 5.7. Covert roleplay, Level One.

Covert Roleplays: Level Two and Beyond

Step A: Trainer hands out roles to preassigned trainees ready for a concurrent roleplay.
Step B: Trainer briefs trainees.
Step C: Trainees roleplay covert materials.
Step D: Trainer leads group discussion of roleplay results.
Step E: Trainer summarizes results, including principles involved in a problem.

Here the trainer has eliminated several intervening steps. His trainee group has been directly immersed in the roleplay exercise without first having worked on the case analysis. Beyond this point, the next logical step for covert roleplaying is toward single roleplaying where two trainees roleplay before the entire group. They may initiate their roleplay after the entire group has been divided into protagonists and antagonists, as is shown on p. 93 under the example of open roleplaying, Level Three. Trainees who have arrived at this level of experience are probably ready for a number of alternative roleplay approaches as the trainer deems useful to achieve his objectives.

Roleplaying Examples

Several sample covert roleplays have been included in the following section. The "Case of the Blind Ad," shown on p. 106, while a bit unusual in its format, is presented to illustrate a variation of both a case study and the resulting conversion to a covert roleplay. Other materials are intended to demonstrate the wide versatility of simple roleplaying as a training technique.

A Change of Assignment (Case Study Format)

After months of study, the Ajax Company has decided to install a new EDP System in Division A. This decision was taken to improve productivity and to cut costs. During the conversion process, some employees will have to be reassigned. One of these is a senior clerk, Laura Smith.

Laura Smith has been employed by the Ajax Company for a long time. A senior clerk for 25 years, she hopes to hold this position until she retires. She enjoys her work, and in previous periods she made many useful contributions to the company. Eight years ago she received a letter of commendation for her efforts from the company president.

During the past two weeks, the supervisor of Division A, Clarence Coffee, has been instructing his subordinates in the operations of the new system. He has just advised personnel that Laura Smith should be transferred. He states that she has refused to adapt to the new work procedures, is inattentive at training sessions and has even called in sick when she was scheduled for practice in using the new electronic system.

Laura, for her part, has found it exceedingly difficult to adjust to these new changes. Her stomach seems to get upset when she thinks about all the work pressure which the new system requires. She has seen a doctor recently concerning her health, and he has advised her that she should take it easy.

In accord with Clarence Coffee's request and after studying the matter, the personnel supervisor of the company, Al Brown, has decided to meet with Miss Smith. His purpose is to suggest that she transfer to a senior clerk position in Division B. The new position will be somewhat different from the work that Laura is presently performing and is located in another building. He is aware that after 25 years in one job, she may be less than enthusiastic about such a switch.

What is the function of the personnel supervisor in a case such as this?

How should Brown proceed in this case?

'A Change of Assignment' as a Covert Roleplay

Role of Miss Laura Smith
Senior Clerk (Antagonist)

You are a Senior Clerk in Division A of the Ajax Company. You have been in your present position for 25 years. You like your present work very much, and you hope to stay in this position until you retire. The company has been very good to you throughout the years. You have seen many supervisors and many fads come and go. Your present supervisor, (Clarence Coffee) has been with the company for three years. He joined the company right after college and is now trying to convert many of Division A's functions to electronic computers. The changes in your work and the way it has been performed have come rapidly, and it is difficult for you to grasp them so quickly. Lately your supervisor has been correcting your work frequently. Because of the arbitrary deadlines that he has set, you have been unable to do your work as accurately or completely as you would like. His pressure approach to work causes your stomach to do flip-flops. Last week you got so upset you went to the doctor. He advised that you should "take it easy," but who can do that these days?

Why are these "boy wonders" always in such a hurry? Sure it's difficult adapting to all these new "hot-shot" procedures, but you have given the company 25 years of good, loyal service.* The least the company owes you is a little patience.

*Eight years ago you received a letter of commendation from the company president.

Mr. Al Brown, the personnel supervisor, has just asked you to report to his office. You don't know what he has in mind, and you intend to listen before complaining about your treatment on the job.

Role for Al Brown, Personnel Supervisor (Protagonist)

You are to inform Laura Smith that, effective the first of next month, she will be transferred to Division B. A new EDP system has been installed in Division A where Laura has been a senior clerk for 25 years. In planning the system's installation, it was made clear that Division A would be able to handle expected increased workload with one less senior clerk.

A supervisor of Division A* has had the past two weeks to instruct his subordinates in the operation of the new system and to observe their reactions and performance. He has recommended, without reservation, that Laura be transferred. He states that she has refused to adapt to new work procedures, is inattentive at training sessions and has even called in sick when she was scheduled for practice in the new system.

You were partially instrumental in winning approval of the electronic data processing system and are convinced it will work. The supervisor of Division A has stated that the retention of Laura Smith in his unit will seriously hamper its effective operation.

Past reports on Miss Smith's work have always been satisfactory.† When the supervisor of Division A informed you that Miss Smith would be the employee to be transferred, you sought and found an opening for a comparable job in Division B. The new position is somewhat different from her present work and is located in another building. While you realize employee morale is important, there is the pressure of increased profits. The EDP system is one way to do this.

Roleplaying for Supervisory Development

Despite presumed differences in the government and the private sector, experts in organizational theory generally concur that what happens at Johnson & Johnson, Pepsico, General Electric or Union Carbide is often no different than what takes place in the governments of the cities of New York and Los Angeles or in the state of Michigan. "People problems" develop and flourish in every large organization.

The covert roleplay exercise which follows, drawn from a public sector experience, is a practical illustration of how roleplaying may be applied in a

---

*Clarence Coffee, a college employee with Ajax for three years.
†According to the personnel folder, Miss Smith was awarded a letter of commendation from the former company president some eight years ago.

supervisory development program. The trainer should consider the advantages of roleplaying as a tool for ensuring trainee participation over the traditional lecture-discussion or conference methods of teaching.

The traditional case study rendering has been omitted; instead, the material is presented as a covert roleplay with common introductory information.

Background Data for Both Roles and for Observers

Lois Lane has recently been promoted to the position of principal purchase clerk in the Department of Public Information. Previously, Lois had been employed in the Department of Private Records as a senior purchase clerk. She received her appointment as a result of scoring well on an interdepartmental promotion examination. The purchase unit in the Department of Public Information processes all vouchers for equipment, supplies and for special services. It is a unit within the fiscal section. Figure 5.8 illustrates the organizational makeup of the department.

During the past week it has been apparent that Lois has been experiencing difficulties with Mabel Mayberry. Mabel has made no secret of the fact that she felt that she should have been appointed to the principal job. Although she did not pass the last exam, she felt she should have been given another "crack at it." In the interim Mabel felt that she should have been appointed provisionally until the next exam was scheduled.

Her unit head, Jim Jones, did not wish to do this. He wanted the principal job filled permanently and, hence, decided to promote Lois from the interdepartmental list.*

Today Lois has called Mabel aside (although real privacy is difficult to find in this crowded office) in order to discuss work assignments in Mabel's subunit. The time is 10:15 a.m.

The Case of the Purchase Unit: Role for Lois Lane

You are Lois Lane. It's about two weeks since you have been on your new job. The promotion was most welcome since you certainly need the money. Most of the people with whom you are working are pleasant, and you enjoy this kind of work. However, there seems to be a fly in the ointment; namely, Mabel Mayberry's attitude toward you.

Mabel has been around for about five years, and she resents you. On several occasions, she has questioned your authority when you have given her assignments.

*This information to be given to observers only.

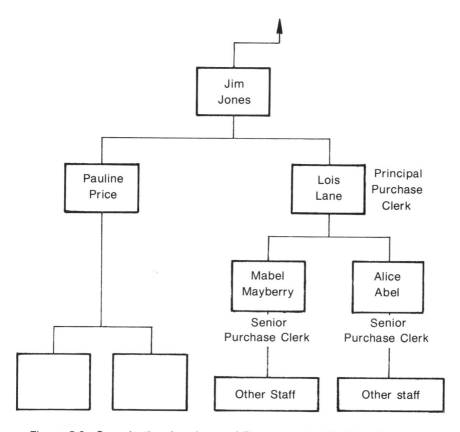

Figure 5.8. Organizational makeup of Department of Public Information.

You have overlooked these incidents and hoped that the situation would improve. However, it has not. Yesterday, Mabel went to Jim Jones to complain, but he sent her back to you. (Jim told you this during coffee break. It is no secret that Jim cannot abide Mabel—which may be why she was not promoted.)

Mabel also seems to spend a good deal of time discussing her "problems" with Pauline Price. Frankly, you have tolerated Mabel's behavior up to this point because you wanted to become acclimated to your unit and to get the feel of things. Today, however, you have decided that you must assert your authority. You gave her an assignment yesterday which was to have been completed by 10:00 a.m.; it is still in her in-basket, untouched. It is obvious she is doing routine work which can certainly wait.

You have called Mabel aside (following the good rules of supervision) so that you can speak to her privately. You are planning on talking to her about this rush assignment, about her attitude to her job and about her relations with others in the section. The time is 10:15 a.m.

The Case of the Purchase Unit: Role for Mabel Mayberry

You are Mabel Mayberry. You have been working in the purchase unit for over five years. Your work has always been most satisfactory. At least—up until now—you have been reasonably content. The new principal purchase clerk, Lois Lane, is a real pain in the neck. How she passed that exam is beyond your comprehension! It's obvious that she must have plenty of "pull"—at least that is the impression that you get from Jim Jones. He claimed that he was "forced" to appoint Lois, even though he would have liked to have promoted someone from the inside.

You have long felt that as the senior member of the purchase unit, you should have been promoted. The department didn't have to use the interdepartmental list.

Anyway, now your problem is Lois. Since she came on the scene, it seems that she is always on your back. Yesterday, she cooked up a "special" assignment which she claimed had to be out by 10:00 a.m. today. What a lot of baloney! You've handled dozens of assignments like these before; there has *never* been any sweat about getting them completed by a deadline. You have your own work to complete, and if you don't get this done, who will do it? You talked to Jim about his opinion concerning this assignment, but he's a weak sister. He gave you a song and dance about not interfering in Lois's decisions! Anyway, thank heaven that you can talk to your friend Pauline. She is so understanding and appreciates your problems.

Lois has just asked you to talk to her. If she pesters you about that so-called special assignment, you will call her bluff. If need be, you will tell her that both of you should meet with Jim.

The time is 10:15 a.m.

When the Antagonist Becomes a Helpmate

The following two roleplay exercises have been made available through the courtesy of Ms. Wendy Fleder, New York Telephone Company. They were developed by the Training Research and Development Staff, General Personnel Department, for the Basic Jobs Training Program in the New York Telephone Company, New York City.

The Basic Jobs program is geared for the training of entry-level personnel. In the roleplays which follow, the typical protagonist-antagonist conflict has been tempered by the nature of the trainee population. The true objective of these roleplays is to teach the *antagonist* (the new employee) that he has a vital responsibility to the company, and that he must develop a commitment to support his supervisor or foreman. Consequently, although the protagonist seemingly has the burden, the antagonist also must make every *reasonable* effort to work within the organizational system.

For instance, Bob Johnson, who apparently has taken an occasional nip with Tom Butler's (his foreman) acquiesence, is likely to endure what will appear as an unjust punishment.

Will he "throw in" his foreman—even though the latter's style of leadership has been hypocritical? Or does he tell his foreman "if you punish me I'll tell *your* boss what you've been doing!"

Covert roles for use by relatively unsophisticated employees must be short, easy to understand and contain situations which are completely job-oriented. The language used should avoid all unneeded multisyllabic words. Information within the role which requires additional reading time, should be eliminated. When roleplayers read comic books the vocabulary of the *Times* or *Newsweek* should not be introduced. Chapter 7 contains more comprehensive discussion of how to write covert roleplays.

An Occasional Nip

Role of Bob Johnson, B&S* Man (Antagonist)

You are a B. & S. man with almost two years on the job. You have worked nights all this time and have often seen your foreman, Tom Butler, take an occasional drink on the job. He has commented that as long as there's no one around at night and he only takes a little drink, it's okay.

Tonight you came to work straight from a party and brought the remainder of a bottle of whiskey with you. You've just finished your work and have gone to your locker for some change for a soda. While you were there, you remembered the bottle and your foreman's words, "As long as there's no one around at night and I only take a little drink, it's okay." You open the bottle, gulp some down and just then you see your foreman with his supervisor in the doorway. You pretend not to notice as they stand there and talk. You put the bottle back and close the locker. Tom Butler is walking toward you and he looks angry.

---

*B&S refers to Building and Supplies Department, New York Telephone Company.

Role of Tom Butler, B&S Foreman (Protagonist)

You are the B. & S. foreman in charge of the night shift. You have a good group of men working for you—all hard working guys. Tonight your supervisor decided to pay you a surprise visit. He wanted a tour of your building and was interested in meeting the staff.

You'd just finished showing him around when you turned the corner in the men's lounge and spotted one of your men, Bob Johnson, drinking. You hoped your supervisor wouldn't notice, but he did. He just reminded you that drinking on the job means two days suspension and he said he'd wait outside while you spoke to the man involved.

You've told your men that an occasional nip is O.K., but don't get caught!

Making an Impression

Role of Bob Blackman, Group Leader (Protagonist)

Since you came to the Company two years ago, you've gotten along well with your co-workers. They're a friendly, hard-working group.

A few months ago, a new guy named John Delson was assigned to your crew and has been causing trouble ever since. He wants to get ahead—even if it means making everybody else look bad in the foreman's eyes. When he finishes his work early, he does a job assigned to someone else and makes sure the foreman hears about it.

You and the other guys are getting fed up with him. Until he came along, everybody got along fine, and the work got done, too. Now, whenever he's around, everybody gets very tense. The guys have talked about telling him where to get off, but it just seems easier to ignore him.

You're on coffee break now and, wouldn't you know, Delson's coming over to sit with you.

Role of John Delson, New Employee (Antagonist)

You've been on the job for six months and have been trying hard to make a good impression on your foreman. Each day you finish your assigned work early and find extra work to do. Your foreman has commended you for this, and you're hoping he'll recommend you for promotion, even though you don't have as much seniority as the other men.

Recently, you've noticed that your co-workers have been avoiding you at lunch and breaks. You're not sure why but figure they're annoyed because you've been getting so many compliments from the boss. This doesn't seem fair to you, so you've decided to talk to the leader of the group, Bob Blackman, to discuss the problem.

You're on break in the cafeteria and see Bob Blackman sitting alone at a table. Now seems like a good time to hash it out.

The Process Roleplay

The personnel interviewer performing this work on a full-time basis becomes adept at obtaining information from the job seeker. Usually a job application form serves to assist the interviewer in ferreting out withheld facts which should be revealed.

The small businessman frequently carries out many duties which are considered specialized "staff functions" in large organizations. Interviewing new employees may be one such activity. Following is a simple roleplay situation which may be adapted as an exercise for several different types of hiring conditions for unskilled or semiskilled labor. The independent service station operation, the vending machine business owner, the linoleum and carpet installer, the nursery and greenhouse owner or the retail store owner fit this description. All recruit lower level workers for job training to more advanced skills. In workshops for such small, independent businessmen, elementary instruction in interviewing is a need which can be met through roleplaying. This is largely a *process*-type roleplay in that the interviewer must be certain that all major blocks of time in the interviewee's background are accounted for. Gaps may indicate periods which he does not want to reveal for one reason or other.

The process to adhere to is a reliance on questions such as: "And what did you do before that?" At the same time, a log of work periods is kept on scratch paper, going back to the time when the interviewee left school and before, if thought to be necessary.

The procedure for handling this exercise is to develop a simple data sheet for the roleplayer who becomes the interviewee. (see p. 106 for an example). The interviewer, who previously has placed an advertisement in the local paper under the "Help Wanted" section, knows nothing about the applicant. This exercise is suitable for a concurrent roleplay.

An Exercise in Interviewing

Facts on Edward Heath (Interviewee)

1. You are 23 years old, married, with no children, and have two years high school education. You were a fair student, but were not "sold" on need for study. You liked shop work, however.
2. You were draft exempt because of poor eyesight when you don't wear glasses. You do get by O.K. with glasses but not good enough to pass the physical.

Most of the time you try to get by without glasses. (This is optional item to be included if roleplayer wears glasses.)

3. Currently you are working as a helper for a house wrecker. Work is not steady and often; it is dirty and dangerous. You've been on this job for about two years. You have an operator's license to drive.

Previous Job History

1. Janitor's assitant at Catholic Home for Wayward Boys (1 year).
2. Various odd jobs (about 1½ years).
3. Two years at Catskill Training School (sent there for car theft). You left there five years ago and have gone straight ever since. You got in trouble because you got in with the wrong gang. You're well straightened out now, but you will not tell about your record unless it's forced from you. You won't deny it, but neither will you volunteer any information. You can give good references and recommendations, if these are needed.
4. Your wife is due to have a baby, and you need a steady job with a future badly! You think this job may be the break you've been looking for.

The Case of the Blind Ad

Instructions for Trainer

This case is available as a traditional case study. It is also shown here to illustrate a case that may be adapted through roleplaying for team building purposes.

The crucial ingredient within the case is the *trust level* between J.W. and his boss, R.H. J.W. is well content with his position, and he views R.H. as a pretty decent fellow.

The initial parts of the case imply that J.W. is a restless individual who may still be looking for greener pastures. His ulcer could be an indication of emotional problems—although this inference is, admittedly, somewhat tenuous. In any event, J.W. is upset for several reasons: (a) the ad itself, (b) whether to *risk* confronting his boss, R.H., with the ad, thereby admitting that (c) he does not trust R.H. and (d) that he has been watching the want ads for, perhaps, a better position. He possesses knowledge, perhaps critical to his future career but is undecided how to use it. This exercise will force his hand. Here is how to proceed.

1. Trainees are divided alternately so that they either will be identified with J.W. or R.H.
2. All trainees receive the *first two paragraphs* of the case.
3. Those trainees identified with J.W. receive paragraphs 3 and 4 as well.

4. Trainees identified with R.H. will receive either paragraph 5a or 5b on *an alternate basis*, but *not both*.
5. After each trainee has received and read the assigned material, the trainer reads the following instructions to the entire class:

All J.W.'s please stand up. You are going to talk to your boss, R.H., about a certain matter which is described in your portion of the case. Remember, R.H. is a "pretty decent manager." At this point, the trainer, certain that each trainee knows who he is, should encourage each J.W. to shake hands with each R.H. and to commence the discussion.

In this single, simple case, the potentialities for several kinds of interpersonal relations between J.W. and R.H. are exposed. One may observe the experience of openness and candor as well as some superior-subordinate game-playing.

In paragraph 5a, R.H. is encouraged to be supportive. The trainer, as he reviews the team results, will be carefully watching whether such encouragement was indeed forthcoming. J.W.'s insecurity may not be lessened, for instance, if R.H. admits and flaunts his knowledge of J.W.'s Sunday ad watching!

Paragraph 5b encourages R.H. to give J.W. a difficult time of it. At the worst, J.W. thinks he is being released; at the best, when he finally gets the facts, he discovers that he is to have a co-equal who will share his authority. And, of course, he knew nothing about this important decision beforehand. How does R.H. break the news and how supportive is he as J.W. digests the impact of the blind ad?

In one respect, this case varies from a traditional roleplay exercise. Normally, the superior carries the burden and is the protagonist. The subordinate is the antagonist. In this case, these traditional roles are deliberately reversed. The *real* burden, of course, continues to lie with the superior, R.H. It is he who must live with the consequences of his actions!

Role Information for J.W. (R.H. Receives Paragraphs 1, 2)

1. On Sunday afternoons J.W. enjoys relaxing with the *Times* as he tunes in to his favorite FM stereo station, playing classical music. One of his preoccupations is the financial section where job offers are listed. Perusing the section offers J.W. a fair cross-section of business and job opportunities in his speciality—security analysis and its application to retirement systems.
2. J.W. is the investment specialist for pension funds in his bank. Even though he is not seeking other employment and is well satisfied with his present job,

he has acquired the insatiable habit of scanning the *Times* for opportunities elsewhere. J.W. has been with his present employer for nearly three years. He considers his boss, R.H., to be a pretty decent manager. R.H. is a vice-president in charge of the bank's trust division.

3. J.W. almost jumps out of his seat as he reads the blind ad, seemingly describing his own job. Although the name of the bank is not listed, the details are *so* specific and seem to be so precise that it *must* be his own job which is being advertised. The ad did *not* state, as many ads often did, that "our own employees are aware of this opportunity."

4. J.W.'s weekend has been ruined, and his ulcer is acting up. What should he do?

Role Information for R.H.

5a. R.H. is aware of J.W.'s weekend idiosyncrasy of checking want ads of newspapers. He realizes that J.W., although personally somewhat insecure, is an excellent security specialist. R.H. is pleased to have J.W. as a subordinate and hopes that J.W. will continue to be associated with the trust division for many years to come.

5b. R.H. is aware that J.W. has been looking for other employment. Won't J.W. be surprised when he reads your ad? You are recruiting for an addition to the bank's staff so that the security analysis area, in which J.W. is assigned, can be expanded. If J.W. spots the ad, he's so insecure that he will probably think you intend to fire him! It might be fun to see how he reacts, assuming he sees the blind ad.

Modification on Simple Roleplay Procedures

A supplemental technique for *guaranteeing* full participation by each member in a small group, which has completed its discussion of a case study, is to employ the following plan. An antagonist, who is *not* a member of the discussion group, is selected and is seated opposite the group members. The antagonist must be sharp; but not necessarily a gifted actor or a wiseacre. The trainer may, if he wishes, choose to take this assignment himself. Before the exercise begins, the group members will have discussed the roleplay problem thoroughly, reaching a *consensus* on what should be done to resolve it, if they (collectively) were the protagonist.

The roleplay is opened with *one* of the group members acting as protagonist (P), welcoming the antagonist (A), into the office, or wherever the roleplay setting is supposed to take place. The selected antagonist responds, and the roleplay proceeds, with each member of the small group *in turn* carrying one bit of the protagonist roleplay forward, step by step. The dialogue might go like this:

P1: Mike, come on in. You know I wanted to talk with you.
A: Yes, and I've wanted to see you, too. You're aware that I'm keenly disappointed on not getting the Harrisburg territory. I was surprised that Joe rated that over me. To be frank, I'm more than surprised; I'm pretty sore!
P2: You seem to be upset. Let me reassure you . . .
A: (Cutting into conversation) You're damn tootin' I'm upset. I was counting on that promotion.
P3: Mike, let's start over again. I asked to see *you* and to talk to you. Why don't you listen for a moment to what I've got to say?
A: (pause) O.K., so I'm listening.
P4: You've been with us, as a fine salesman, for almost three years. You've developed a territory which was pretty sterile until you took it over. Our competition is really hurting, largely because of the way you've managed the clients, their special needs and all the follow-up which they never had before you came along.
A: So, I've done such a great job that you rewarded me by handing out the best plum in the region to someone else!
P1: Mike, have you ever thought of doing something besides just selling?
A: How do you mean?
P2: (Dialogue continued)

Besides ensuring full participation by every group member, this exercise encourages and, in fact, demands very careful listening. The trainees also experience the application of the group consensus in a "conversation piece," wherein their consensus is put to the test. Should one of the protagonists wander off the agreed path, a succeeding protagonist must try to bring things back, even though the "damage" may require some repairing. Tape-recording this technique is helpful during the postenactment discussion as to who said what, voice inflections, etc.

So What's the Story?

This exercise is suitable for the training group which is able to function at open roleplay, Level Three. The trainer introduces a completely unstructured situation to the trainees who have been previously divided as concurrent roleplayers on a protagonist-antagonist basis. In other words, the total group has been arranged into two-man teams. The trainer begins by reciting a suitable incident, such as may be found in the following two examples.

Incident One

It's a mean, miserable day in mid-February. People have been coming into work a bit late. As he enters the office from the company parking lot, Joe, the boss, tells Frank, one of his favorite subordinates, that Frank has neglected to turn off the headlights on his (Frank's) car. Frank is *positive* that he had turned his lights off. Joe *insists* that Frank go out into the lot and check the lights. Frank is afraid that he's got a bad cold coming on, and besides, there's freezing rain outside. Frank feels that once again Joe is being overly solicitous about his personal affairs.

Incident Two

Joe is our boss. He fancies himself to be an authority on automobiles. In Joe's opinion, the USA Motor Car Company produces the finest vehicle for the general, lower priced market. Frank, one of Joe's favorite subordinates, has mentioned that he's decided to buy a BRW, a motor car manufactured in Western Europe. Joe, convinced that Frank is about to make a very serious error in judgment, insists that Frank test drive a USA Model G before signing the papers for the new BRW. Frank feels that once again Joe is being overly solicitous about his personal affairs.

The situation is roleplayed by all teams simultaneously. One player is Joe; the other, Frank.

After a reasonable period of roleplaying, the trainer asks each team to write out, in the form of a case study, the "story" as they now view it. The written case must reflect those major items which arose during the roleplay.

The trainer must not reveal the intent or objectives of the exercise before the roleplay begins. The instruction to write the case is given *after* the roleplay has ended.

Each team reads its completed case aloud to the entire group. The trainer uses the board or the flip chart to record *similarities* and *differences* in cases as reported by each team.

This exercise illustrates that people tend to *act* and *react* to a single set of circumstances in many different ways. Some of these differences are due to preprogrammed experiences. Other differences are based on selective perceptions. An objective, when using this exercise, would be to teach how to develop *objectivity*!

Some uses for this exercise follow.

1. Handling and reporting grievances
2. Training inspectors and investigators

3. Training correction personnel and others involved with criminal justice systems
4. In report writing
5. In supervisory/management development

A variation in this exercise includes the assignment of observers to each team roleplaying and developing the written case. The observer's main assignment should be to determine how accurately the written case reflects what occurred as a result of the roleplay.

6. Procedures and Problems in Roleplaying

This chapter consists of a series of commentaries in which practical advice is given on the resolution of *procedures* and *problems* when roleplaying is selected as the method of instruction. The contents of the chapter are arranged according to the flow of the action: introduction of roleplaying, the operation of roleplay within the training session, halting the roleplay and the post enactment process. Each topic has been considered as a discrete sphere of information demanding simple, straightforward treatment. Consequently, each of the following listed topics is handled as a separate treatise or essay.

1. Time Allocation for Roleplaying
2. Organizing Training Group into Roleplay Teams
3. Roleplayer Breaks the Action
4. Male into Female?
5. Not True to Life?
6. Observers: What Do They Do?
7. Odd Man Out
8. In Concurrent Roleplay, Team Fails to Get Down to Business
9. Assignment of Roles: Trainer or Casting Director?
10. The Low Speaker in a Single Roleplay
11. Roleplay Is Drifting: No Evident Progress
12. Advanced Methods
13. Cutting into Action
14. Applause for Roleplayer?

15. Revealing the Secrets of the Roleplayer
16. Tape-recording the Session
17. How to Direct a Role Reversal
18. Roleplaying into Case Study: A Problem in Reporting the Facts

Time Allocations for Roleplaying

Time allotments are crucial in planning any training activity. How does one measure the time required for a roleplay exercise?

This factor was discussed in the use of case studies. When roleplaying, the trainer must allot time for each of the following actions:

1. The introduction and the "bridge" to the previous session
2. Setting the scene for the roleplay
3. Briefing the roleplayers and related arrangements for the roleplay selection
4. The roleplay itself
5. The post enactment process
6. Session summary

As a rule, all of these actions, except No. 4 (the roleplay), are controlled by the trainer. The functioning of Item 4 is largely in the hands of the roleplayers. As they talk, the roleplayers may wander and enter topical areas which the trainer had not anticipated; or they may reach an accord more rapidly than he had believed possible. Trainers cannot, nor should they, interject with, "Hurry up," "You're not supposed to talk about that," or "Slow down."

One suggestion for predetermining the time required for the roleplay follows. Conduct a dry run of the intended roleplay with a knowledgeable colleague. Time yourselves. After the roleplay, analyze the additional time extensions which other roleplayers would be likely to require. Here a tape recorder will be especially useful. An analysis based solely on participative recollections is apt to overlook items within the roleplay which might demand added time. Remember also that reading a roleplay dialogue after transcription or "thinking through" what the roleplayer might say will not reflect the probable time needed. Speaking rates and thinking rates are not identical. Also, pauses in the dialogue use up time which must be taken into account.

If the roleplayers complete their assignments prior to the estimated time needed, the trainer then has the option of expanding the learning into the additional available time by the use of role reversal or through rotating other roleplayers through the protagonist's role.

Organizing Training Group into Roleplay Teams

The functioning of a Level One open roleplay was demonstrated on p. 89 f f. However, there will be questions about the arrangement of the teams, each consisting of a protagonist and an antogonist. But first, a reminder: these terms must be avoided in the conference room; they have been invented as a convenience for professionals applying roleplaying in many diversified settings.

Prior to considering the specifics of team arrangements, trainers should have studied the composition of their trainee population. Unless special compelling reasons exist, the trainer will so arrange the teams that each consists of strangers. Fellow employees in the same office back on the job or superior/subordinates should be assigned to different teams.

When meeting for the first time for a training session, trainees tend to sit alongside associates or friends. As he moves into roleplaying, the instructor has several elective approaches open to break up this natural, self-assigned seating. The easiest and most direct choice is to apply a numbering system. Each trainee is labeled 1, 2, 3 or 4 and so on, depending on the group size. Next, like numbers are paired, the trainees shifting within the room to join their new partners. The room had been previously arranged in a conference setting. Every other trainee is then assigned a role, developed from a case which the group has just completed.

Assume, for instance, that the case study concerned an employee relations problem between Tony (the line manager) and Jim (the employee). Every other trainee in the rearranged room becomes Tony. Each of the other trainees becones Jim. Because Jim has entered Tony's office to discuss the problem, every Jim in the room stands and turns to face his boss (Tony). This action is directed by the trainer to ensure an identification by the trainees with their roles and an understanding of what each is to do next. At this juncture (with the Tonys seated; each Jim standing and facing his Tony), the trainer proceeds to give the final instructions for the concurrent open roleplay. His remarks may be something like this:

Now, gentlemen, this is where we're at: Jim has come into Tony's office. There has been a problem of which you're all aware. Each Jim here, please shake hands with Tony (which the trainees should proceed to do). You're alone with Tony, your boss, in his office, and the two of you are starting afresh to work at this problem.

Since it's likely to be a bit noisy here, with all the other folks working along on the same problem, please put yourselves together so that you can hear one another without difficulty. Again, ignore *everyone* except your own partner. Any questions before we all begin?

The two trainees should be encouraged to get close together—without any artificial barriers, such as tables or desks.

Normally these instructions are sufficient to launch the concurrent open roleplay. If questions are raised, the trainer will clear these up for everyone's benefit before the concurrent roleplaying begins.

Roleplayer Breaks the Action

The single roleplayer, instead of adhering to role, turns away from the other roleplayer and faces the trainer or group and says: "This is what I would say."

Somehow, this trainee has missed the message. He wants to talk about what he might do instead of doing it. This fundamental misunderstanding may be genuine in that the trainee has really failed to comprehend the requirements of roleplaying. Such a mistaken notion, on the other hand, may indicate a fear of being unsuccessful as a roleplayer before one's peers. The trainer, ever-so-gently and supportively, reminds the trainee to talk to the other roleplayer *in the first person.* The trainer might say: "Bill, assume that you are here with Joe (the other roleplayer). Forget, if you will, about us. And don't tell us *how* you would respond. Respond to Joe, here and now, just as you would back on the job. Don't tell us what you would say. Say it!"

Sometimes, the roleplayer stops the action, either to restudy his role or to seek clarification on how to proceed.

When this occurs, trainers quickly will appreciate the importance for thoroughly briefing the roleplayers. The break in the action has most often been caused by the trainer's hurried delineation of the roleplay situation. He knows the case, and it may be one that he has used successfully many time before. What he has overlooked is that the roleplay calls for *repetition* and *reinforcement,* and this is not unlike what is demanded in Job Instruction (JIT).

When the roleplayer stops the action for clarification despite a reasonable briefing, and if clarification given openly will not destroy the remaining roleplay action, the trainer should step in and say: "Parenthetically, what Bill is asking is such and such." Here, the trainer is speaking both to Bill and to the group. He then proceeds to reexplain to Bill and to the group so that the roleplaying may continue.

If the trainer's *open* response to Bill's query will seriously damage the remaining roleplay, he should stop the action momentarily and provide the requested information to Bill, out of the hearing range of the other roleplayer. Perhaps this is not an especially desirable solution to our problem. However, it is the better alternative. The other, removing Bill as the roleplayer and rotating a different roleplayer in his place, may appear more expeditious, but Bill loses face. He was forced out because he missed some key factor within his role.

Male into Female?

What should be done with a roleplay calling for a female role, when working with a group that includes no females?

The assignment of roles is normally made, not on the basis of sex, but on the basis of other factors, including where the individuals are seated and how the trainer decides to introduce the roleplaying materials. There is no harm and often much empathy to be gained in males playing female roles or women being assigned to men's roles. The trainer sets the tone of the roleplay, making it clear that the male adopting the female role should empathize with it, doing the best that he can within the role. It is, however, undesirable to attempt an imitation of the other sex's speech and gestures or to make the roleplaying appear absurd.

Double-duty given names for the roleplayers, such as Clare, Robin, Joe (for Joseph or Josephine), Lee, Sandy, Terry or Chris, are helpful devices to further the role transition.

Not True to Life?

How does the trainer respond to the participant who openly insists that the roleplay "isn't true to life"?

Depending on the stage of development within the roleplay exercise, the most direct approach for the trainer to take is to ask the participant to explain how it would become "true to life" and then to roleplay it with him starting all over again, or the trainer may ask for a volunteer to fulfill this special chore.

An alternative response is to concede:

Sure, this isn't true to life—but within the confines of this conference room, let's see how we can work to duplicate the "real thing." We're all here to learn. By insisting that this isn't precisely true to the way things happen back on the job, we're claiming that simulating the "real thing" is worthless. What the astronauts have learned in years of practice, as an example, is hardly worthless even though they were in the earth's environment. The real thing for them was behavior on the moon. Nonetheless, if they had not practiced on earth, the moon experience would have been almost impossible.

Observers: What Do They Do?

When a roleplay is scheduled during which observers will be present, the trainer should be certain of his objectives. The observers will want to understand their function. Is it to record and to provide feedback on what they will observe? What are they to look for? How critical are they supposed to be?

Roleplay observational sheets will be extremely helpful as guides for the observers and for ease of collecting data during the postenactment discussion. If the roleplay is a covert one, the sheets should contain specific instructions on what the observer should be looking for and how his data is to be recorded.

A formalized system of noting action increases the value of the observers. Each is required to focus attention on those special factors which the trainer considers important. By concentrating observations where required, in terms of session objectives, extraneous and irrelevant input is reduced. During the discussion period, the trainer collects the observer data, writing this information on the board or flipchart. This represents the range of observations by all recorders. Such feedback, given a positive, empathetic commentary by the trainer, serves to influence trainee behavior both for the roleplayer and the observers. The observer record form is intended not as an individual rating sheet but rather as a device which encourages group support for *desirable* behavior. Avoid, therefore, viewing these records as weapons, to undermine or belittle individual roleplay effectiveness. Encourage self-criticism and self-awareness and any reasonable approach that furthers these goals.

Trainers intending to have observers systematically report on what they've seen may prepare a single form for that purpose to be used by all observers. It should be simple, and the roleplay objectives must be reflected in the factors sought for feedback (see pp. 118, 183 and 184 for examples).

An alternative method is to construct several special purpose observer sheets. For instance, the total trainee group may be divided into the roleplayers plus two or three kinds of observers. One group may simply record who does the most talking or who introduces and argues for each ma-

Observer Record

Name of Roleplayers

Factors	#1	#2	#3	#4	#5
Spoke first					
Asked leading questions					
Interrupted					
In first half of roleplay, did most talking					
In second half of roleplay, did most talking					
Attempted to sell a point of view					
Argued					
Displayed flexibility					
Made progress					
Lost ground					

Solution developed: yes ☐ no ☐
Describe:
Comments:

Figure 6.1. This example of Observer Record contains many of the factors common to most observer records. It is shown here solely as a sample.

jor point. Another group will be charged with ascertaining roleplay impact on *feelings* of the roleplayers; how the observers thought roleplayers reacted (apprehension, fear, concern, pleasure, disgust, annoyance, hostility, etc.) and the *causes* of such reactions. Figure 6.1 is an example of an observer record.

When trainees are acting as standbys, waiting to be interchanged with one of the roleplayers, they should not be provided with observational sheets. The two assignments are in conflict and may be seriously distracting. This view is based on the fact that two distinct mind-sets are needed. The first, that of observer, tends to be passive and even impersonal or detached. The second, that of standby, is active. Here the trainee watches and listens to the roleplay while preparing his own approach, as if he were there in the other's place. It is difficult to be analytical under such circumstances. Another way of stating this is to concede that the trust levels between roleplayers and observers are analogous to those between ball players and umpires. But, between standbys and roleplayers, trust levels are encouraged to be open so that as the trust level within the total group moves up, the standby trainees will be available to rotate through the roles.

Odd Man Out

When initiating a concurrent roleplay where two-man teams are a prerequisite, what does a trainer do when the team pairing does not come out even? The most desirable solution to this problem is to attempt to control the number of trainees so that the trainer does end up with an even-numbered group. If this is not possible, the individual who is not matched with a partner is given a special assignment as an observer. The simplest observer task that he might perform would be to record who did the greater share of the talking. In most protagonist-antagonist roleplays, the protagonist should do most of the *listening*. The special observer circulates among the concurrent roleplayers, after receiving a short explanation of his assignment by the trainer. He is provided with the opportunity to report on his findings during the group discussion period.

In Concurrent Roleplay, Team Fails
To Get Down to Business

The author has observed trainers who, after initiating their groups into a concurrent roleplay, walk out of the room for a cup of coffee! This is indicative of an attitude that says "Once you've got the trainees talking, most of your work is finished."

The trainer's responsibility is to keep his eyes and ears open as the individual teams roleplay concurrently. Occasionally, he will find two individuals who fail to cooperate. He should move to these trainees quickly and ask them firmly to please commence their roleplay without delay since they will be involved in a subsequent discussion, describing the completed protagonist-antagonist actions.

Usually when a team has failed to commence the roleplay, it is because the two roleplayers were unable to understand their initial instructions, or there may have been a disagreement between the two trainees as to who was supposed to do what. This may occur despite the most specific instructions by the trainer before the exercise began. After the trainer has reexplained the assignment to the trainees, they should begin their roleplay without delay. The concept of a concurrent roleplay means that all teams begin action simultaneously. When the trainer stops the action, there will usually be some variation in team progress. The team that begins far behind the others or does not start at all will cause unnecessary problems for the trainer and for the other participants.

Assignment of Roles: Trainer or Casting Director?

How are trainees to be selected for their roles? Should the trainer hand-pick individuals for particular role assignments, or should he seek volunteers?

Role assignments are contingent on the sessions's *objectives*. Why was roleplaying selected as a method? The decision to use roleplaying as a teaching method should be tied to the objective which the trainer seeks to attain. If the purpose of the exercise is to *warm up* the trainees for a more complex learning activity, then the trainer would want to use a concurrent roleplay, which means that everyone might participate. When *focusing* on an issue where the group members observe the action, the trainer will seek volunteers from within the group. If the trainer knows his group, he may select the roleplayers. However, volunteers to commence an action are generally preferable over hand-picked leads.

As the roleplay proceeds, the trainer will request group members watching the action to rotate through the same roles. This accomplishes two things: (a) it broadens the learning experience, and (b) it offers the group more than a single illustration of how to handle the issue.

Some behavioral objectives and accompanying methods of roleplay selection to be considered for each are summarized in Table 6.1.

Table 6.1. Behavioral Objectives and Methods of Roleplay	
Objective	Selection
At completion of roleplaying exercise, participants will have accepted roleplay as a method, preparatory to involvement in more fundamental objectives of course.	Concurrent roleplay (everyone participates).
After completion of roleplay, roleplayers and observers engage in discussion on the principles illustrated by this experience.	Concurrent roleplay. Also, use of volunteers.
After completion of roleplay, roleplayers and observers engage in discussion relating to success or failure of roleplayers as they handle assigned problem.	Roleplayers are volunteers or selected by trainer from "stronger" participants. Group members may be asked to rotate through roles.
Participants actively seek, at conclusion of roleplay, direct feedback on their effectiveness as roleplayers.	Roleplayers are volunteers.
At completion of roleplay, observers will have viewed a complete process or method of handling a particular situation.	Select sharpest participants as roleplayers, or use outsiders, as experts, to illustrate the process.

Low Speaker in a Single Roleplay

Roleplaying is intended to simulate true-to-life occurrences. Imagine, therefore, the roleplayer whose voice is low and soft and whose statements and responses are not easily heard by the observers. The other roleplayer, seated or standing next to him, is able to converse readily and may even lower his voice to match that of his partner. What does the trainer do?

Prior to the start of a roleplaying exercise such as this, where a single roleplay is observed by the rest of the class, the trainer reminds the roleplayers that they should speak loud enough so that they can be heard throughout the room. The role setting, naturally, should be quiet and free from distractions. Frequently in big cities outside traffic noise may create an annoying problem, and even if the roleplayers raise their voices, the observers are unable to hear every word.

Here, the trainer has two choices. He may break in and request that the roleplayers speak still louder. Usually this is not desirable; it destroys the naturalness of the exercise. A better approach is to ask or motion the observers to move in and gather around the roleplayers so that they are able to hear the dialogue. The roleplayers, deeply engrossed in their problem, are unlikely to be effected by this change in trainee seating. The trainees will be able to hear what is taking place, and the subsequent analysis will be based on more reliable understanding. Trainers, therefore, must be careful to watch if trainees are straining to pick up the language of the roleplaying.

Roleplay Is Drifting; No Evident Progress

What options are open to the trainer when the roleplay develops into a repetitious dialogue with neither roleplayer budging from his fixed position? The same ground seems to be covered over and over again. The roleplayers become uneasy; the observers are restless. The trainer must be carefully atuned to the progress of every roleplay. The roleplay commences, develops, and should reach a climax after a reasonable amount of forward movement by the parties. There is an optimum point within any given roleplay exercise where further progress, while feasible, is probably unproductive insofar as learning is concerned. At this point, and here the trainer may have to act intuitively, the action should be cut.

When a roleplay fails to develop after a reasonable period, something is wrong. One or both of the roleplayers are clearly inhibiting the dialogue's progress toward the climax. The trainer, at this point, has the choice of proceeding along the following paths.

1. The trainer may cut the roleplay temporarily. He asks one or both roleplayers to step down. Replacement roleplayers are reassigned to the same role. The former roleplayers become observers, and the dialogue begins afresh. Hopefully, this time more progress is evident.
2. The trainer may cut the roleplay temporarily. However, instead of dismissing the roleplayers, he asks each openly—and before the rest of the group—why no progress seems to be made. Each roleplayer is encouraged to talk freely. Each may restate his role; each may discuss why he believes an impasse has occurred. The trainer has a responsibility to facilitate forward movement by the roleplayers themselves. He should, however, discourage advice from the observers to the roleplayers on what they should say.
3. The trainer may simply ask the two roleplayers to reverse their roles, and recommence their conversation.

Finally, the trainer must recognize that successful results are apt to be highly relative. No magic formula exists which will resolve every deadlocked situation. Trainers considering the introduction of roleplaying into their sessions may fear failure. Some back out, saying, "It's too risky for me." These are poor trainers. Hoping to teach *others* problem analysis and decision making and how to resolve conflict in human relations, they themselves present a rather poor example. Low profile trainers, unwilling to chance innovative methods because they fear failure, are in the wrong business. The greatest experts in roleplaying have, at times, been unsuccessful.

Advanced Methods

Roleplaying is comparable to driving an automobile. Most people are able to learn how to drive. Not everyone, however, is equipped to handle heavy, high-speed superhighway road conditions. All would agree that it is unwise for the new licensee to move his vehicle into the most difficult of road conditions simply to prove that he is unafraid. While displaying bravery, he may also reveal his lack of common sense. Similarly, nearly every trainer should be able to conduct an open roleplay exercise. However, while trainees are learning how to learn, the trainer is, at the same time, learning (through experience) how to apply a complex learning mechanism.

In a comparable vein, the trainer inexperienced in advanced phases of roleplaying might consider himself to be gutsy when introducing complex techniques with which he has little familiarity. The most sensitive of human conditions is involved in roleplaying: exposing one's behavior before others. It is, therefore, critical that the trainer understand *what* it is he is doing, *why* he is doing it and *what* he hopes to accomplish (see footnote on p. 127).

While roleplaying is not a precise discipline, a number of technical terms have crept into the process. The following discussion attempts to explain the meanings of key methodological terms used in advanced roleplaying and how these are applied.

Alter Ego

An *alter ego* describes the trainee who accompanies a protagonist or antagonist out of the room during the briefing process involving covert materials. He listens in on the same briefing as the roleplayer to whom he is assigned. The roleplay may function with either one or two alter egos, each being assigned to a protagonist and antagonist. During the roleplaying, the alter ego, is seated near his roleplayer, *maintaining his silence*. He is,

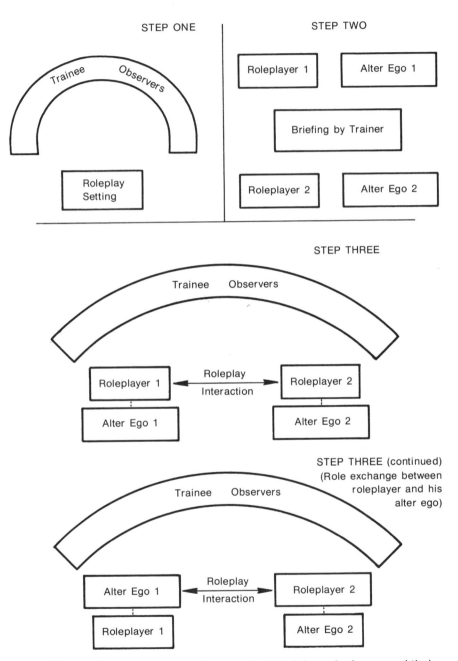

Figure 6.2. Seating arrangements for roleplays involving roleplayers and their alter egos.

however, permitted to pass notes or to whisper advice to his roleplayer. In one sense, the alter ego serves as a sort of silent partner or consultant to the roleplayer to whom assigned. The rationale for incorporating an alter ego into a roleplay is to facilitate and support the action—to bring out into the open thoughts which the roleplayers might miss or forget during an interchange. The alter ego's function should be carefully limited. He goes through channels. He does not interject himself into the midst of a roleplay; he works through his roleplayer. Occasionally, at a given point within the roleplay when the action appears to drag, the alter ego may seek permission from his roleplayer to take his place, continuing the roleplay in place of the principal roleplayer.

During the briefing the trainer must explain the alter ego's responsibilities and the limits of his authority. When switching places with the roleplayer, for instance, the alter ego first gains his roleplayer's approval for such action. He must not shoulder his way into the process if the roleplayer feels that he should continue, even if the alter ego is convinced the roleplayer is "goofing the action." The alter ego's views may be voiced *after* the roleplay has terminated and after the principal roleplayers have stated their positions as to the manner in which the roleplay operated.

In *Step 1* of Figure 6.2 the classroom facility has been arranged so that the roleplayers may be observed by the trainees. In *Step 2,* the roleplayers and their alter egos (here illustrated as one alter ego assigned to each roleplayer) are being briefed by the trainer. Each side is briefed separately. The roleplayer and his alter ego must not overhear the briefing which the other roleplayer and his alter ego receives. It must be remembered that the briefing also includes the study of covert materials describing the role.

In *Step 3,* a suggested seating arrangement is shown for the roleplayers and their alter egos. Generally, the latter sits in back or slightly to the side of their roleplayers, as seen by the trainee observers.

Auxiliary Ego

In Greenberg's *Psychodrama and Audience Change**, the reader may find a comprehensive explanation of auxiliary ego as this term is applied in therapy. When this term is used in a training and development roleplay, the designated meaning has been circumscribed to a narrower range of interpersonal activities. This has been done deliberately. Without having acquired

*Ira A, Greenberg, *Psychodrama and Audience Change*

highly specialized instruction given by experts†, trainers attempting to use therapeutic-like techniques within the roleplay will get themselves into serious trouble. Methodologies used in therapy for emotionally disturbed people should not be transported into an apparently "healthly" group of trainees by the trainer—not unless he has a sound foundation in what it is he is doing and unless the course objectives call for such an approach.

In this concept of the auxiliary ego is envisioned a *reinforcing* figure for either the protagonist or antagonist, or both. Ideally, the auxiliary ego is used *after* the trainees have observed and worked with an alter ego.

The auxiliary ego speaks out, voicing aloud the feeling and attitudes of his roleplayer who is, for the moment, silent. The auxiliary ego will participate when the roleplay seem to drag or is off on a tangent or when one of the roleplayers seems to be stuck and in unable to express what it is he would like to say.

The auxiliary ego does not comment on what his roleplayer is or is not doing or how effective he is. For instance, during a heated exchange, he would not pat his roleplayer on the back and say, "Why don't you really tell him off?"

To be an effective auxiliary ego is hardly an easy chore. Auxiliary egos who do not reflect accurately the feelings of the individual with whom they are participating may upset the momentum of the roleplaying situation. Occasionally, the trainer himself may assume the responsibility of acting as an auxiliary ego.

Doubling

This means, in effect, talking to yourself with the aid of someone (perhaps the trainer) who serves as a nondirective verbal reflector. The concept of doubling is to be found in the work of Carl Rogers. An effective explanation of the nondirective approach may be found in a filmed lecture by Dr. Rogers entitled "Some Personal Learnings about Interpersonal Relations.*

Cutting the Action

After a roleplay exercise has been launched and the roleplayers are

†Courses in roleplaying are provided on a regular basis in New York City by the Metropolitan District Office, School of Industrial and Labor Relations, Cornell University. Roleplaying training, directed toward therapeutic goals, is given at the Moreno Institute, Beacon, New York.

*Produced by Academic Communications Facility, UCLA. Running time: 33 minutes.

progressing reasonably well, the trainer should restrain his natural tendency to expedite matters by leading a discussion prematurely. The group's attention will be on the roleplay, not on the trainer.*

The best rule for trainers to follow is to keep quiet and listen, even if the roleplay's forward momentum fails to follow his predetermined estimate. Cutting the action, by having the trainer break in, will normally occur only when the roleplay has peaked and the major difficulties have been resolved or when it is clearly drifting and there is no evident progress. Otherwise, the trainer should remain silent at the rear of the room.

The action is cut with a low key gesture. The trainer is not a Hollywood director. He does not call out "CUT THE ACTION!" Instead, he may simply stand, walk to front and say, "Fine, Let's stop here." His next move is to turn to the protagonist (who has carried the burden with roleplay) and inquire: "Bill, how do you think it went?" or "Bill and Joe, before we review this case, you'll want to comment on how you felt it progressed. Bill, your comments first."

The sequence for transition from roleplay to group discussion goes like this:

1. Roleplay.
2. Cut action.
3. Permit protagonist to comment.
4. Permit antagonist to comment
5. Move into group discussion and analysis

Applause for Roleplayers?

After the completion of a single roleplay, the group members may applaud the efforts of the trainees who served as protagonist and antagonist. Is this acceptable? Should the trainer cut it off? What are the guidelines, if any?

Sincere, spontaneous applause by observers for a sound effort is acceptable. Applause is not encouraged, however, for an acting performance. And comments by one of the parties such as, "Don't applaud. Just throw money," are not to be invited. This type of statement reflects an attitude which impedes the learning by mocking the setting and the process. Trainers should not initiate applause. They will, of course, provide positive reinforcement to

---

*See useful discussion relative to the instructor's personal needs in Allen A. Zoll, *Dynamic Management Education.*

an effective roleplay. Such reinforcement—unlike applause directed at a single actor—is given as well to the other learners.

Revealing the Secrets of the Roleplayers

Unlike what occurs during an open roleplay, there are secrets held in reserve by both roleplayers at the termination of a covert roleplay. Does the trainer direct them to reveal all? If so, at what point should this be done?

Prior to the completion of every covert roleplay discussion, the trainer should be cognizant of the fact that each roleplayer would like to be privy to the assignment given the other roleplayer. Not knowing all the facts bothers most people. Observers also are interested in learning the specifics of each assignment.

The most desirable point for such revelation is prior to the conclusion of the entire roleplay discussion. The disclosure of information provides the trainer with a lead-in to a summarization of the case. He has the opportunity to explain the rationale for structuring the role in the manner each was arranged. This then gives the entire group a practical opening for a discussion of the case details and the principles which it illustrated.

Occasionally, the hidden data is made known when the protagonist and antagonist are permitted "to take themselves off the hook" just before the general group discussion commences.

After all has been revealed and if sufficient time is available, the entire role situation may be reversed, proceeding along the lines of an open roleplay. Generally, each roleplayer reveals his own inside information by reading his assigned role upon request by the trainer.

Tape-Recording the Session

When, if at all, should roleplaying sessions be taped? What about video tape recordings?

Recording capabilities today are far different than they were a few years ago. The flexibility of recording instruments provides the trainer with many imaginative and intriguing possibilities when planning a roleplaying exercise.

It is clear that trainers should definitely use some type of playback device, preferably video, if *process* roleplaying is taking place. The trainee must acquire as accurate a feedback of his individual roleplay as is feasible. VTR cannot be surpassed by any group verbal recitation of how effective the trainee was or where he was off target. Summary comments by observers are less likely to be accepted by trainees for behavior modification than the very personal look at how one actually performed.

Individual coaching of the process roleplay, tied to a replay using VTR equipment, may be arranged. This is separate and distinct from the group discussion of the same exercise. For instance, the trainer takes his group members through the warm-up, followed by individual roleplays, each of which is video taped.

The trainer schedules each trainee to a private viewing of his practice roleplay, this being done during an open period between the formal group sessions. These highly individualized coaching sessions, covering trainee strengths and weaknesses, will be followed by the review or summary lesson for all participants.

In all other types of roleplaying, recording equipment may be introduced when the trainer senses that the group's trust level is high enough to tolerate such devices and if the recording contributes to the learning. The trainer will be in the best position to judge. Another related point here concerns trainees who bring their own portable cassette tape recorders into the session. The *trainer* is in charge of the session and must control the decisions whether to allow this equipment to be used.

Two major cautions or concerns must be observed in using any type of recording equipment. The first concern is the acceptance of recording equipment by the trainees. This does not mean, of course, that the trainer must obtain their permission to record, but it is questionable whether recordings should be planned without the knowledge of the trainees. If trainers plan to record they should explain why this is to be done. They should also provide assurance as to the confidentiality of such recordings. This rule must *never* be broken. Revealing to a trainee's superior, through a recording, the work of a trainee in a learning session will most assuredly serve to destroy the trainer's usefulness and the total impact of the course.

The other caution about recording involves the time required to rehear or reobserve the roleplay. The added time necessary may make tape-recording prohibitive in terms of meeting the objectives of the session. In effect, to get the entire picture the trainer might have to repeat large segments of the roleplay. If it can be done within the time allocation for the course, it is well and good. However, this time must be allotted within the lesson plan. Otherwise, the roleplay work, extended by the recording review, will reduce the time apportioned for other topics and thus effect objectives.

How to Direct a Role Reversal

Role reversals are undertaken to increase empathy on the part of all participants and to provide an improved perceptive appreciation of the problems of "the other guy." Assume that a roleplay has been completed between team partners. Such a roleplay may have been either a concurrent roleplay or a single roleplay with observers. The trainer then requests that the participants physically change places, explaining: "Let's see how this might have worked if we each had had a different role assignment. Let's begin all over again from the beginning. Each of you understands that you are now assuming the role of the other person. Are there any questions? Okay, let's start from the very beginning!"

Since a simple, straightforward approach has been taken in switching trainees from one role to another, it is unnecessary to provide complicated explanations as to the rationale for such a role reversal. In the postenactment discussion, each trainee will generally enunciate the altered attitudes which he had acquired as a result of the reversal—the "before and after" viewpoints and what impact these might provide back on the job.

Roleplay into Case Study: A Problem in Reporting the Facts*

Since the conversion of a case study into a roleplay has been explained, what value might there be in a reversal process? Would it be worthwhile to start with a roleplay exercise and convert this into case material? There are training circumstances where such a transference would be of lasting value to the trainees. For instance, in situations where trainees are being taught factual reporting and the importance of objectivity, the reversal process offers some fascinating possibilites.

Two trainee volunteers, knowledgeable with roleplay methodology, agree to roleplay a covert roleplay before the trainee group. This group has been divided into two-man teams.

The volunteers roleplay the situation through to a terminal point, at which time the trainer cuts the action. No discussion takes place. Instead, each two-man team then works to construct the case study, as each observed the situation. The case study format is followed. Each case will contain the introductory data, including essential background data presented by the roleplayers.

*See also, "So What's the Story," p. 109.

Next, the problem, real or alleged, will be stated. Predicaments or roadblocks to a solution, as seen by the teams, are shown at this point. Finally, questions for discussion purposes are developed by each team, touching on the most important factors within the case as the team observed it.

At this point, the trainer requests each team to read aloud their newly constructed cases and the accompanying questions. The *differences* in case facts (English grammar is not a vital consideration) are compared and analyzed. Why did one group see a particular aspect of the roleplay differently than another? To what extent are the trainees' past experiences influencing factors on the way live actions are perceived? These are but two suggested areas for consideration within this learning exercise.

7. Writing
Covert Roleplays

Covert roleplays are, as has been demonstrated, a logical extension of case study building. All cases are not suitable or practical for conversion into roleplays. A study, however, of effective roleplays tells us which elements within cases are likely to contribute to successful end products. For the most part, situations of human interaction are sought where each roleplayer sees the issues from his viewpoint and where disagreement, hostility, disaccord and conflict are apt to be the natural consequences of such differing perceptions.

Identifying Basic Ingredients of Covert Roleplays

The principles of clear writing will not be reviewed at this point. Those who intend to write roleplays are expected to know and to apply such principles. Here the emphasis will be on those unique or special considerations required when covert roles are written and assembled.

In part, the following discussion is based on critical roleplay factors, identified by Wallace Wohlking, senior extension associate, Metropolitan District Office of the New York State School of Industrial and Labor Relations, Cornell University.* Mr. Wohlking noted that in order to be

*Reproduced by special permission from the November, 1966, *Training and Development Journal* (copyright 1966 by the American Society for Training and Development, Inc.)

useful as a teaching device, the covert roleplay must achieve the following.

Provide Comprehensibility

The trainee must be able to understand his assigned role. Therefore, write in simple, straightforward language.

Provide Ready Identifiability for the Trainee

If the suit of clothes is poorly cut, the wearer is likely to be troubled or uneasy. Similarly, the roleplayer should feel comfortable with his assigned role. Without going through mental transpositions, he should be able to relate to the assigned role.

The role assignment must allow the trainee to identify easily with the role. Identifying with the role must come quickly; therefore, the role construction must facilitate this process. Beware of strong language. Words with an emotional meaning may inadvertently reduce the identifiability sought. Guth* illustrates this point by classifying selected words as "complementary," "derogatory" and "neutral." Using this respective order, the *law officer* becomes either a *cop* or a *policeman*.

The writer must use the *second person* when establishing identity in the first sentence or two. As an example: "You are Cathy Bourke. You are employed as a principal stenographer in the. . . ." Never present a role in the third person form.

Remember to match the information within the roles with the trainees and their needs.

Provide Maneuverability

Wohlking suggests that the roleplay writer stay away from "moralistic descriptions of behavior." Avoid also pejorative adjectives which appear to cue the roleplayer's outlook so as to effect his identifiability. Eliminate, therefore, such terms as stupid, wiseacre, selfish, shiftless and so on. Thus, the role must be written in such a way that the trainee is not locked into a specific mode of behavior that he is able to exercise and display individual thinking in the manner in which he takes on his role assignment.

*For other examples, see H.P. Guth, *Words and Ideas,* p.237.

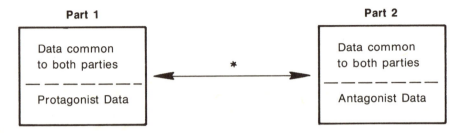

*Although the data is common, the manner in which
it is recited within each part is likely to vary.

Figure 7.1. Covert roleplay with dual roles and no introductory statement.

Provide a Focus

This means that the role situation zeros in on the essential issues; that unimportant or extraneous items are excluded. Trivia, although seeming to make the role more "human," ought to be cut away. For example: The roleplayer's marital status is of no interest unless such status provides a focal point for the case situation.

Now the way covert roles are put together can be demonstrated. *Three* basic forms are shown. This has been done by diagramming the role formats (Figures 7.1, 7.2 and 7.3), together with comments on essential ingredients which each role form contains, if it is to be acceptable.

Covert Roleplay: Dual Roles, No Introductory Statement (Figure 7.1)

1. Data within each part must encourage interaction with the other part.
2. Data must dovetail and not contain contradictions as to basic facts. This is extremely important. The following illustrates this point: *Roleplayer A was hired right out of college.* If this is significant enough to be included as information for A, then Roleplayer B should also be made aware of this fact. If not, why include it?
3. Role write-up is stated in direct and easily understood language. Assimilation of role data by reader is facilitated so that the average role may be read in less than seven minutes.

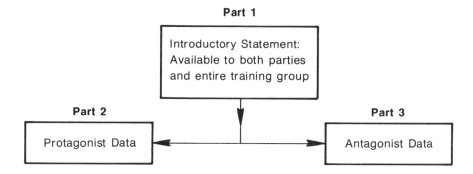

Figure 7.2. Covert roleplay with dual roles and introductory statement.

Covert Roleplay: Dual Roles, with Introductory Statement (Figure 7.2)

1. Part 1 sets the scene and contains all common, factual information of a noncontroversial nature. Do not repeat information in Parts 2 or 3 which has been stated in Part 1. Remember that one purpose of Part 1 is to inform the observers of the facts so that the roleplay is intelligible to onlookers.
2. Comments made under "Covert Roleplay: Dual Roles, No Introductory Statement" apply here as well.

Covert Roleplay: Three or More Roles, with Introductory Statement (Figure 7.3)

Comments are the same as noted for other covert roleplays. Also, remember that conformity in role data must not only be ensured between protagonist and antagonist but also *among* the antagonists as well. The following example highlights this point:

Roleplayer C is a close friend of Roleplayer D. They always take their lunches together. Roleplayer E must be advised, somehow, of this fact, if it is critical to the exercise. Otherwise, the roleplay is unrealistic and untrue to life. In addition, Roleplayer E will be confused during the exercise.

This example leads us to a final point in connection with the covert roleplay having two or more antagonists. The adversary situation which is present in a simple covert case involving a protagonist and antagonist may be missing

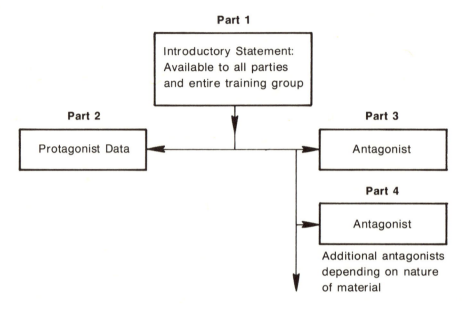

Figure 7.3. Covert roleplay with introductory statement and three or more roles.

completely when two or more antagonists are present. Obviously, this will depend on the inventiveness of the writer in terms of the objectives which he has set for the roleplay. The antagonists created within this type of situation may not be aligned against the protagonist; they may be having their problems with each other.* Certain antagonists will be looking to the protagonist for support against other antagonists. Some may have no set position at all; they may appear to be completely indifferent to the problem in the case. Often, that is the way it is in simulating a true-to-life situation. Consequently, the writer must think imaginatively to avoid structuring the roleplay in which all antagonists have roles which require them to gang up on the protagonist.

Words of Power for Roleplaying

If the parties were in agreement, no real use for the roleplay would exist. The roleplay's immediate objective is the attainment of a reasonable accord

*For an illustration of this type of situation, see the "Case of the Punch Press Painters" on p. 143.

between the parties. The long-term, more meaningful objective is learning how to reach such an accord. Therefore, for the writer of role materials, isolating words possessing special significance in situations of disaccord would seem to be desirable. The following list contains selected words which serve as catalysts for many a covert roleplay. As the reader examines these words, he will—or should—do some internal brainstorming, considering situations which each suggest—situations which lend themselves to roleplaying. Individual words advance individual ideas. In suitable combination, such words advance the development of exciting and challenging exercises.

Put another way, as the roles are written, proportionate amounts of true-to life "toil and trouble" are melded into the roleplay cauldron. The level of difficulty must depend on the trainer's objectives for the case, which in turn must rest on the abilities of the trainee group to handle such mixtures.

The words and their usages described are hardly all inclusive; they are intended as idea starters for roleplay development.

Antipathy: An outlook toward persons or things, this may be perceptual. It means essentially the same as *aversion,* as in an aversion to change. The antipathy of managers to newly installed methods is likely to be most disconcerting to the systems analysts.

Anxiety: This is a feeling of apprehension or concern about what might happen in the future. Employees frequently have a sense of deep anxiety when rumors circulate concerning the possiblity of cutbacks in the organization. Others, sometimes managers, are *anxious* about reassignments, labor problems or working with new bosses.

Attitude: An orientation of the mind toward work, fellow workers, the firm, women, minorities and so on, *ad infinitum.* Attitudes are an integral feature of roleplay exercises, particularly when each roleplayer thinks that his attitude is the same as that held by his associates about a particular issue. In fact, they are often at different ends of the spectrum. This makes for useful roleplay action.

Audacity: Sometimes audacity is tied to arrogant dismissal of the risks when launching something new. Audacity provides the opposite of *caution.* Audacious bosses may have cautious subordinates, and vice versa.

Competition: This is a "healthy" condition of life when displayed between private businesses. Competition developing between associates in the same system striving for identical personal goals is likely to be frightening or it may generate anger.

Conflict: A contest (open or hidden) engendered by opposing views between and among the parties constitutes a conflict. Wohlking* cites six types of conflict useful for structuring covert roleplays: conflicting internal emotions and motives, conflicting allegiances, perceptual differences, divergent goals, competition and structured interaction.

Controversial: Something that is debatable or open to argument is controversial. For the low profile manager, controversial issues create emotional problems too numerous to mention here. For roleplay development, however, these cover a wide latitude of ideas: minority employees, members of women's liberation groups, long hair, unions, pollution, drugs, etc.

Disagreement: A difference of opinion is displayed. Shall the organization expand? Manager A says, "No." Disagreements spring up over goals or objectives, extent of discipline, assignments, selection and placement, training and so on.

Disharmony: The system is out of tune; the managers are not following the same notations. *Discord* is both a cause and a result of disharmony. Disorder and disorganization are consequences of disharmonious interpersonal relations.

Distrust: Somewhat more than a simple lack of confidence is involved. Basic communications are badly disrupted when trust levels have reached the point where one supervisor no longer trusts one of his associates.

Emotions: Man is a highly emotional creature who struggles mightily to hide his emotions: joy, sorrow, fear, hatred. He doesn't want to be seen as soft or weak.

Friction: Rubbing two sticks together vigorously creates heat, and if rubbed together long and hard enough, a spark may ignite the accompanying tinder. Abrasive topics are apt to lead to friction between roleplayers. How successful will the roleplayers be in avoiding the spark?

Hostility: A deep unfriendliness between people, hostility is usually the result of previous experiences or a fear of the consequences being developed by one party or another.

Indifference: Apathy or unconcern about situations, indifference may indicate mediocrity, at least in the eyes of the viewer. Indifference may lead, for example, to an apparently mediocre performance. Morale, motivation and employee appraisal come to mind in connection with this word.

Opposition: Persons in opposition actively refuse particular positions, ideas, proposals and plans. Most agree that one has to be more than just a

---

*Wallace Wohlking, "Guide to Writing Role Playing Cases" (unpublished).

part of the opposition. To be effective, an opponent must propose countervailing ideas of his own.

Tension: Relating to strain, stress or nervousness, frequently between parties, tension originates as a result of excessive job pressures, problems at home, difficulties with work or with employees. For some, alcohol helps relieve tension. Employee counseling needs may be tied to this word.

8. Complex Learning Exercises

Complex exercises provide for the planned participation of three or more trainees giving their attention to a structured problem. The one-to-one protagonist-antagonist interchange of the simple roleplay becomes expanded by the number of possible interactions among all participants. Group encounters within the real world are apt to offer clues to the type of complex exercises which would highlight vividly the objectives of a training session. For instance, a problem between two budding junior executives about priorities on accepting dictation, as set by the supervisor of a steno pool, may signal several key suggestions to the alert and perceptive writer of learning exercises. In complex exercises there may be a protagonist-antagonist relationship, but the number of antagonists (with their different points of view) will inevitably result in either supportive action among the antagonists or selective kinds of conflict. Handling complex exercises is a challenging and demanding assignment. Extremely careful preparation with attention to the sensitivities of the group members and to the *real* objectives of the session is *always* required. While it is often easy "to get going" in such situations (setting the scene, selecting the participants and staging the action), this represents *only the beginning of the action.* Complete awareness of all of the implications within the exercise is a must for the trainer. The use of complex exercises in conference leadership training is examined, and what to do if a learning exercise fails to take hold is analyzed.

Two's Company; Three's a Challenging Roleplay

Articles and publications dealing with roleplay exercises tend to describe these solely as dyads. But a married man, after having become involved in a "discussion" with his wife, along with the active assistance of one of the children, can readily recall that the verbal action can become pretty complex. The larger the number of people in a group, the greater the possibilities, insofar as the patterns of group interaction. A three-man roleplay, for example, involves a triad. Two of the roleplayers may take a passive role, two may gang up on the third or there may be an equal level of participation among all the roleplayers.

An objective in many roleplaying exercises is to teach the trainee how to cope with a stress situation. Customarily, it is the protagonist who is on the spot. However, in the roleplay entitled "On the Way to Pasture," the protagonist is not always easy to identify. The true protagonist is Joe Fields, the vice president of JCN. It is he who has the authority and the ultimate responsibility to make the necessary decisions concerning the two other individuals in the case.

This case is included because it offers an unusual and effective bridge between a simple roleplay and the more complex type of learning exercise. The class is divided into small group units of three (or six or nine). Each small group is asked to develop a written role for Bill or Wes or Joe. Each role must be compatible with the printed case data. The groups are not permitted to introduce surprise items within the roles. Examples of acceptable roles which might be developed are shown on p. 142. These are provided for the benefit of the trainer solely as a guide.

A spokesman for each group then reads the completed role. This is done to reinsure that there are no surprise factors within any of the roles and that each role conforms to the general structure of the written case. Any inconsistencies are quickly reconciled by the trainer before the entire class. Trainees divide and proceed into a three-man concurrent roleplay.

After the concurrent roleplay, the trainer may direct that this is reenacted by three volunteers before the entire class, followed by a critique, discussion and summarization.

On the Way to Pasture

The JCN Corporation has a fine retirement system for its senior executives. In Bill Madden we observe an interesting example of the senior manager who, after 35 years of service, is close to mandatory retirement. The fact is that Bill will be out in about four and a half months. His golfing buddies at the JCN Country Club have been kidding him about having joined the Preretirement Club. Although he takes this kidding good naturedly, Bill has really been rather unhappy lately. It's not that he is unprepared for retirement. That's not it. What has been troubling him is the fact that he is almost completely being bypassed by his boss.

Joe Fields, vice president in charge of the manual typewriter division, has been acting lately as if Bill had already left. Memos, copies of letters and confidential communications are being sent to Bill's number one boy, Wes Stewart. At first, Wes felt a little awkward about this situation and would bring this material in for discussion with Bill. Lately, however, Wes has been acting pretty much the same way as Fields—as if Bill were no longer around. It's obvious that Wes and Joe Fields have been meeting together, making vital decisions about matters directly concerning Bill's area of responsibility (the design department). Bill has spoken to Joe Fields twice about this situation, pointing out that he is still aboard and that he would like to be kept informed as to what's going on. Joe's response has been a good natured kidding about "not getting into a sweat" about problems which are going to be someone else's to resolve. Examples of roles which the groups might prepare and use for concurrent roleplay follow.

Wes: You feel rather awkward about this business: No one is trying to bypass Bill *deliberately*. It's just that Joe has indicated that you'll probably be taking over when Bill leaves, and he wants you now to take an *active* role in the day-to-day operations of the department. You would like to keep Bill informed, but what are you supposed to do when Joe calls personally on all kinds of things which in the past he would have taken up through Bill? Bill is evidently taking this bypassing rather hard. He's a tyrant who always kept an eagle eye on every detail. Frankly, you'll be glad when this upcoming meeting with him and Joe is over.

Bill: You've been with JCN for 35 years—and that's a long time! You consider your present treatment to be unprecedented. Senior managers have always kept a tight control of their own area of responsibility up to the day of retirement. Joe is handling this very badly, and you can't understand Wes Stewart's attitude. He knows the chain of command. There's a lot of mistakes likely to be made, and no one is consulting you. You've asked for this meeting with Joe and Wes, and maybe it will serve to clear up where you stand.

Joe: Bill Madden is a perfect example of a McGregor X-oriented manager.* He's autocratic, unbending and unwilling to change. We have been waiting a long time for Bill's departure. There are a number of important changes which I hope to make as soon as Bill is out. Meanwhile, I am trying to determine if Wes has enough internal drive, stamina and initiative to be able to take over when Bill leaves. I am concerned that Wes has been brainwashed by Bill into a passive, low profile type of manager. And that is exactly what we don't need more of around here! I know that Bill is displeased with being bypassed,

---

*Douglas McGregor, *The Human Side of Enterprise* (New York: McGraw-Hill Book Company, Inc., 1960).

which is why I agreed to the upcoming meeting. On the other hand, if I don't get a chance to give Wes a chance to display some independence before Bill leaves, I'm afraid I might be stuck with him with almost no tryout period. I must have an opportunity to see whether this fellow can make it on his own.

Conflict between Antagonists

A complex roleplay, including two antagonists seemingly displaying conflict and hostility towards each other, represents an opportunity for all parties, particularly for the protagonist. The roleplay materials which follow are based on the case study shown on p. 63. Rewritten as a complex roleplay, the trainer may elect to use it as a *concurrent* roleplay, involving his entire training group, or he may choose to have volunteers enact the case before the other trainees, who would then serve as observers.

The protagonist is Al Adams, the superintendent of the Precision Company. The two antagonists are Bill Barrett and Clayton Collins, foremen of their respective shifts. A meeting has been called by Adams to resolve the problem described within the case material.

Realistically, a meeting such as this one called by Adams would probably not be convened on the spur of the moment. Logically, there would be an interim period between the calling of the meeting and its start. Perhaps a day or two might elapse. Therefore, the roleplayers in a training session selected for this assignment may well be given reasonable time to study their roles, to consider all implications and to develop positions which they would take at the upcoming meeting. The extent of time allowed by the trainer would depend on the schedule for training; it could be given as an overnight study assignment. An even longer period is feasible when weekly training sessions are scheduled. This type of approach contributes to the realism of the roleplay. It also adds to the probability that the problem will be solved. When this time interval is made available, the trainer warns the roleplayers that they are not to discuss their roles with the other trainees during the intervening period.

The Punch Press Painters: An Exercise in Roleplaying

Background Data for Observers

The Precision Punch Press Products Company manufacturers punch presses for the domestic and international market. This is a medium size firm operating on a dual shift. One of the final steps in manufacturing, prior to packing and shipment, is the painting of assembled punch presses.

To the punch press operator the color scheme is important. It improves the visibility of the parts during operating periods, reducing the possibility of accidents. The workers employed as painters during the day are generally young men, and it has been their practice to use masking tape when performing the job in order to line up the different color markings neatly and clearly.

The evening painters are older men who are quite meticulous in their work and who prefer the freehand method of putting on lines between colors.

The completed work of each shift is apparent to the other when the men show up for their respective shifts.

The day painters gripe about the "sloppy," uneven work of the evening painters and suggest that the evening painters use masking tape to get their lines straight. These suggestions have been made orally to the foreman on several occasions.

The evening painters, on the other hand, complain bitterly about the tape used by the day painters. They point out that prior to packing, the tape must be removed. And if the paint has not dried properly when the tape is pulled off, its removal results in bits of the paint being pulled off the steel. At times, each shift must touch up the work of the other just prior to packing.

The friction between these two groups has reached a point where something must be done. Excessive periods of time are being devoted to criticism, and the competition which at one time seemed "healthy" is now getting out of hand.

Al Adams is the plant superintendent. The foreman of the day crew is Bill Bennett; the foreman of the evening crew, Clayton Collins. Bennett's crew has five men; Collins has four. The day crew turns out slightly more work. Both men are present and are about to meet with Adams to discuss their problem.

Role for Al Adams

1. Read background data sheet provided observers (see above).
2. You have called this meeting to analyze and resolve all aspects of the problem. Production is being affected by the continued conflict between these two groups of painters. Bennett and Collins are here now. The conduct of the meeting is your responsibility,

Role for Clayton Collins

You are Clayton Collins, foreman of a four-man crew *employed evenings* for the Precision Punch Press Products Company. Each of your men is a capable, dependable employee. You believe, and your men agree with you, that the appearance of the finished product before it is packed and shipped is critical to the way a product is accepted by the customer. From a technical viewpoint, there is no doubt that your firm produces a topnotch punch press. You hate to see such punch presses, presumably the best in the industry, produced which don't look as nice as they should. Everyone realizes that the color scheme is important to the punch press operator. Color improves the distinctness of the parts during operating periods and reduces the possibility of accidents. It has been the practice of your crew to do a careful finishing job by freehand drawing on the finished press. This is done with great care to line out the different color markings neatly and clearly.

The problem is not with your men but rather with the painters who work the day shift. These men are a bit younger than the fellows in your crew. Their foreman, Bill Bennett,* has been opposed to the fine, freehand work done by your men. He insists on using masking tape! He claims that this ensures that the job, when completed, will have straight lines between the colors. Therefore, Bennett's men stick yards of tape onto the jobs to apply the lines between the colors. Since the unfinished work of the day painters must be completed by members of your crew and because their work is often applied in a careless fashion, it is necessary that your men redo a fair portion of the work supposedly finished during the day. All masking tape must be removed before packing and shipping.

You have discussed this situation at least three times with Bennett. You have urged him to abandon the use of masking tape, but so far his attitude has been unchanging. Your crew, when pulling the tape off of completed jobs done by his men, often find that the paint has seeped under the tape. As they remove the tape—which is a sticky mess, they cannot avoid tearing the paint. This makes the job look ragged. This extra work, which calls for a fair amount of touch-up, is reducing your crew's output.

All this unnecessary friction between your crew and Bennett has evidently caused your boss, Al Adams (the plant Super), to call a meeting to discuss "all aspects of the situation." You enter Al's office.

Role for Bill Bennett

You are Bill Bennett, foreman of a five-man paint crew *employed days* for the Precision Punch Press Products Company. Each one of your men is a capable, dependable employee. You believe, and your men agree with you, that the appearance of the finished product, before it is packed and shipped, is critical to the way a product is accepted by the customer. From a technical viewpoint, there is no doubt that your firm produces a topnotch punch press. You hate to see such punch presses, presumably the best in the industry, produced which don't look as nice as they should. Everyone realizes that the color scheme is important to the punch press operator. Color improves the distinction of the parts during operating periods and reduces the possibility of accidents. It has been the practice of your crew to use masking tape when performing the painting job. This is done to line up the different color markings neatly and clearly.

The problem is not with your men but rather with the painters who work the evenings shift. These are men who are a bit older than the fellows in your crew.

---

*Five men, plus Bennett, in day crew. They turn out slightly more work than your crew.

Their foreman, Clayton Collins,* has been opposed to the use of masking tape. He claims that this makes the job too mechanical and that a good painter should be able to draw straight lines between the colors. Since the unfinished work of the evening painters must be completed by members of your crew before packing and and because their work is often uneven or sloppy, it is necessary that your men redo a fair portion of the work supposedly finished at night. This sometimes causes your crew to fall behind schedule.

You have discussed this situation at least three times with Collins. You have urged him to have his men try masking tape, but so far his attitude has been unchanging. Recently, his crew has been pulling tape off completed jobs done by your men before the paint had completely dried.† As everyone knows, this has the effect of tearing the paint and making the job look ragged. Collins claims that touch-up work required, after the tape was removed, is reducing his crew's output.

As far as you're concerned, this is hogwash. If the evening painters would permit the paint to dry before removing the tape, there would be no need to retouch.

All of this unnecessary friction between your crew and Collins has evidently caused you boss, Al Adams (the plant Super), to call a meeting to discuss "all aspects of the situation." You enter Al's office.

Comments on Problems Presented by This Roleplay

In certain work situations, the day-to-day contact between a manager and his subordinates may be highly superficial. Unless a highly significant problem develops, the manager and his foreman often have few real contacts. Planning, analysis, study of work operations and the other so-called managerial responsibilities are not applied because of lack of time, an indifference or the assumption that "everything is O.K.; why make waves?"

In this case, Adams has permitted two separate work systems to grow, develop and become institutionalized within each work group. Separate work methods, perhaps supported and originated by Bennett and Collins, have been functioning without any real attention being given by the plant superintendent as to the impact on work flow.

There are other obvious problems, such as requisitioning the masking tape, a fact which may be inferred from the role data. It is clear that one group, the day painters, uses tape, an item which costs a fair amount of money. For instance, a 60-yard role of standard one-inch masking tape is worth about $1.70

*Four men, plus Collins, in evening crew. They turn out slightly less work than your crew.
†All tape must be removed before packing and shipping.

wholesale.* Masking tape is also a useful household item—one easily borrowed by employees for household jobs or outside painting activities.

The painters operating without tape may or may not take more time to do their work. This is not known. No standards have been developed concerning the time a crew should require to complete the painting of a punch press.

Some of the questions which might well be raised are the following:

1. The time required to apply the tape.
2. The time required to remove the tape.
3. The cost of the tape.
4. Assuming that a painter is able to follow a straight line, put on perhaps with a marking instrument, which method is indeed the faster? Is the cost of the tape offset by the payment for the additional handwork?
5. What standards are acceptable insofar as straight lines are concerned?
6. How long should it take to complete painting a press?

Each of these questions, and perhaps others, should be considered by the superintendent before this problem is resolved.

Possible solutions to this case include:

1. Standardize on either all freehand painting or all masking tape utilization.
2. Unfinished work to be completed by the crew starting the job. This involves the matter of storage space for the uncompleted work during the day or evening period (which may not be feasible).
3. Each shift must complete its own work during the shift period when work is started. (This may not be feasible.)
4. A special touch-up man should be assigned to handle all uncompleted jobs.

Which one is to be your choice?

There are times when the boss must deliver a decision which is certain to displease some of his subordinates temporarily. In all probability, extensive arguing may be anticipated, no matter what Adams does—even if his decision were to leave the problem alone. Unlike the example presented in the case of "Who's Cold and Who's Warm," these punch press painters are employed at different hours in two separate groups. Thus, from a practical

---

*Knowledge of exact cost is not vital. Alert participants would recognize, however, that there is a real cost involved.

viewpoint, it would not be feasible to bring these two groups of men together for the purpose of finding a solution to the problem.

Based on the data given, it seems probable that dropping the use of the masking tape would be Adams' best choice. Evidently the evening painters are able to produce about as much work as the day painters—work which *is* acceptable for shipment. The day painters should be trained to draw freehand lines; the masking tape should be eliminated; equitable production standards should be developed, treating both crews as a single unit.

How This Roleplay Was Written

For the reader's benefit the steps followed in creating the roleplays in the "Case of the Punch Press Painters" have been summarized. Initially, available case study materials were reviewed to determine which met intended objectives—in this situation, an illustration of a conflcit requiring a solution between antagonists. The protagonist carries the authority and the responsibility to achieve such a solution.

The case had to be *suitable* (i.e., short enough, appealing to the general reader, and feasible for conversion into a roleplay).

The "Case of the Punch Press Painters" met these requirements.

The case was then reproduced. Names were selected for the principal roleplayers.* The role of the day painters' foreman was written, based directly on the case material. Very little basic rewriting was necessary. The reader may wish to compare the language in the original case (see p. 63) with the required rewrite effort.

Next, after this role had been typed and edited, a copy was made. The role of the foreman of the evening painters was then ready to be produced. Working with the copy, names were changed as needed, and the facts effecting the evening painters were inserted. Those concerning the day painters were removed.

Both roles were then reread to ensure the complete dovetailing of information. Finally, the role data necessary for the protagonist was included. Most of the material in the original case, with the addition of the names of the roleplayers, was believed to be adequate.

For the benefit of the observers, a few minor revisions were made, completing the job.

---

*When more than two roles are required, it may be helpful to use an alphabetical approach to name selection. The trainer is thus assisted in identifying the parts.

Conference Leadership

Courses in conference leadership frequently use a form of roleplaying. Each trainee is expected to "lead" a conference during the term of the course. The other trainees assume the roles of the conferees or serve as observers. The problem solving conference is generally the most difficult to conduct, and a typical complex roleplay, involving a manager or supervisor leading a conference of members of his own staff offers a profitable illustration of the complex roleplay in action.

In the case which follows, "Who's Cold and Who's Warm," the supervisor is cast in the role of conducting a problem solving conference with the members of her staff in attendance. The staff members are the antagonists; the supervisor, the protagonist. The burden is on her to achieve the objectives of the conference. In this particular case the objective means achieving a *group* solution to a problem which affects all members of the steno pool.

Depending on the size of the trainee group, the available time and the course organization, the trainer may use this material either as:

1. A single roleplay: one protagonist and eight antagonists provide the role enactment, with the rest of the trainees observing. This is followed by an analysis and summarization lead by the trainer.
2. A concurrent roleplay: the entire class is divided into nine person teams. All extra trainees are observers. After roleplays are completed, analysis and summarization are lead by trainer.

Caution

Trainees assigned complex materials, such as "Who's Cold and Who's Warm," must have working experience with simple forms of roleplaying. Trainers who intend to introduce complex roleplays, as in conference leadership training, should first ensure that the trainees are experienced with what roleplaying is and how it works. One protagonist facing six or more antagonists is an extremely threatening condition. It may be doubtful whether any real learning takes place when the trainee is literally scared to death of making a fool of himself in front of peers. The author once observed a prominent proponent and instructor of roleplaying techniques throw a trainee into a complex roleplay completely unprepared for the consequences. The outcome was embarrassing for the trainee and for most of the group—and the learning level of the man on the spot (and several empathetic others) probably dropped to a below zero level.

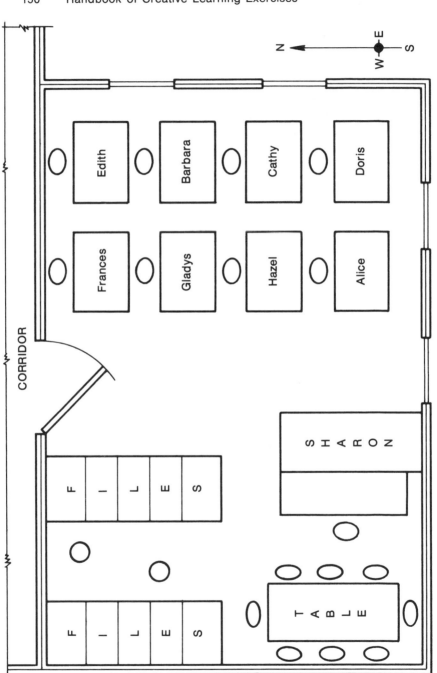

Figure 8.1. Arrangement of steno pool and file section.

Who's Cold and Who's Warm?

This exercise is primarily intended for use in conference leadership training. Nine participants are selected by the trainer for each roleplay group.

Sharon: The supervisor of the steno pool and file section.
       Age 29, married, 8 years service.
Alice: Senior steno. Takes Sharon's place when she is out.
       Age 26, single, 3-½ years service.
Barbara: Steno. 3-½ years service. Age 24, single.
Cathy: Steno. 3 years service. Age 24, single (engaged).
Doris: Steno. 2-½ years service. Age 23, married.
Edith: Steno. 7 years service. Age 34, single.
Frances: Steno. 2 years service. Age 23.
Gladys: Steno. 1-½ years service. Age 22.
Hazel: Steno. 8 months service. Age 21.

General Information for All Participants and Observers

The following situation occurred during a very warm August after vacation period has ended.

The steno pool and file section of the organization is located in the southeast section of the building on the ninth floor (see Figure 8.1). This spot was selected about four years ago when the organization moved here. At the time it was a real improvement over the dark, dingy quarters occupied in another part of the city. All of the girls, with the exception of Sharon (who is the pool supervisor) and Edith, have joined the pool during the past four years. All girls are good or superior in their performance. Edith is the oldest person in the pool; Hazel, the youngest. A telephone is on Sharon's desk with a bridge to Alice's desk.

All girls are expected to file and maintain the file unit, which is used by other sections of the organization. However, the girls with the least amount of service are usually expected to do most of this work. Generally speaking, desk assignments have been made on the basis of seniority. This is an unofficial practice which was established and followed in the previous location.

Ventilation is a vexing problem because it seems that half of the girls would like to have the windows open while the other half would like them closed. There is no possible way to move any of these girls to any other part of the building, and there is no air conditioning* or fans in this office. The only possible way to get fresh air or to cool the office is to open the windows. This is the problem which confronts Sharon.

---

*Air conditioning is impossible because of electrical load capacity of building.

Role for Sharon

You have a real problem: the girls are constantly complaining about being either hot or cold or having to sit in a draft or in a dead spot, with no air. Complaining has reached the point where production is being affected. You have discussed this problem with your boss and have received his blessing and support for any plan which you can come up with to solve this problem *within the confines of the steno pool and file section.*

As you view the situation, Barbara wants to have the windows closed whereas Gladys would like to see them open. Frances is always complaining about the draft. The same general circumstances, but perhaps not as severe, exists in relation to Cathy and Hazel and Doris and Alice.

As far as you have been able to tell, the girls have gotten along fairly well together until this heat problem messed things up. Hazel and Gladys seem fairly close and usually prefer to take their lunch together.

Your boss has agreed to purchase draft deflectors if this will help, but this action will be taken only as a last resort. You personally know how long it takes to get a requisition through the organization. It will be late October before these would be installed.

Having recently attended a training course in conference leadership, you are determined to "involve" the girls in getting this problem solved.

Role for Alice

As the No. 2 girl in the pool, you have often thought that you should have a corner desk. While Sharon wants you opposite her (because she believes in keeping an eye on the file area), you would be much happier if you had another spot. (Edith's would be fine!)

Insofar as being hot and cold, you view this constant harping as part of the normal complaining system which has been raised by every group of girls with whom you have ever worked. Cathy, in your view, is absolutely unreasonable. She wants a window spot but does not want the fresh air that comes in *through the window.*

Role for Barbara

You have a very nice spot next to the window, and the view is fine. The trouble is that Gladys and Frances insist that they are hot and want the window open much too high. This blows the papers about and makes you very uncomfortable.

This constant complaining (and even opening the window when you go out to the ladies' room) is getting you down. Yesterday you had a squabble with Gladys about the window, and consequently, she isn't talking to you today.

Role for Cathy

Your eyes are not too good and you require a window spot. You would like Edith's spot, but everyone knows how touchy she is. You enjoy fresh air but certainly not a gale. You have been taught that drafts are bad at any time of the year. Over the past year while sitting next to the window, you have had too many colds because some people have insisted that the window be kept open.

Role for Doris

All day long the girls complain, complain, complain! Cathy raises a fuss when you open the window high, and when you do (to accommodate Alice or Hazel), you are caught in the cross ventilation. You believe that air conditioning is the best way to solve this problem.

The light and view are great but you have just about "had it" in terms of this window problem.

Role for Edith

It is no secret that you probably have the best location in the office, and you also know that Alice would like to have your spot if she could. You have good light, ventilation and little draft and want to hold on to what you have. Most of this complaining really comes from the young girls. They just have to recognize that they have to wait their turn to get any window spot, since this is done on the basis of seniority.

Yesterday Gladys opened the windows between your desk and Barbara's (while Barbara was out in the next room). You didn't mind because it *was* very warm, but when Barbara came back, she slammed the window down, and you could see the "sparks fly" between her and Gladys.

Role for Frances

You are caught between the door and the window. If the door is open (which Alice does not particularly care for) your desk is caught in an awful draft. On the other hand, if the door is shut (which is most of the time because Sharon and Alice don't want to have any of the men looking in), then it means that you are in a dead spot. You'd like a bit more air and are reasonable enough to understand that the present arrangement could probably be improved. There must be a way to rearrange things so that everyone might be happier—at least for a while!

Role for Gladys

As you view it, Barbara is very self-centered. She should try sitting in your place for awhile, and she will understand what this is all about. Why can't we get an exhaust fan to get air *out* of the office, through the windows, instead of the other way around? Ideally, air conditioning is the answer, but you know that the organization will never go for this.

Yesterday while Barbara was out in the ladies' room, you opened the window (which belongs to Edith as much as it belongs to Barbara). When Barbara came back, she got real nasty, and you are not talking to her now. Your closest friend in the pool is Hazel, and she feels the way you do about this matter. Both of you are about ready to quit if this problem isn't straightened out soon.

Role for Hazel

As the low gal on the totem pole, your views do not seem to count much. It does get pretty warm, and if Cathy wasn't so stubborn or selfish, she would let you open the window a bit more. Doris is much more reasonable. If it wasn't for the fact that you are in the file section so much of the time (and it *really* gets warm there), you would tell Cathy off about her attitude.

Gladys feels the same way you do; she had a run-in with Barbara yesterday about getting more fresh air. Gladys has been arguing that you and her should threaten to leave if this business isn't resolved to your satisfaction.

Case Discussion

The involvement of group members in gaining an acceptable solution to a problem such as this one is highly desirable. While it is true that Sharon, as the supervisor, could most certainly develop and impose a response to the ventilation problem herself, the participation of the individuals directly concerned with the outcome would make the solution much more acceptable. Not infrequently, lower level employees will say, "Don't ask me; I'm not being paid to make those decisions." But when they are adversely effected by the outcome of these decisions, they will then complain, "Nobody asked me."

Obviously, solid participation is desirable, not for its own sake but because of the stake that each participator has in the end result.

When reviewing a problem such as this, the trainer will certainly have a chalkboard or a flip chart at hand. Members of the problem solving group may visualize more easily the office layout and join actively in evaluating the effectiveness of the proposed solution. Several possible answers to this particular problem can be achieved. Two are shown in Figures 8.2 and 8.3.

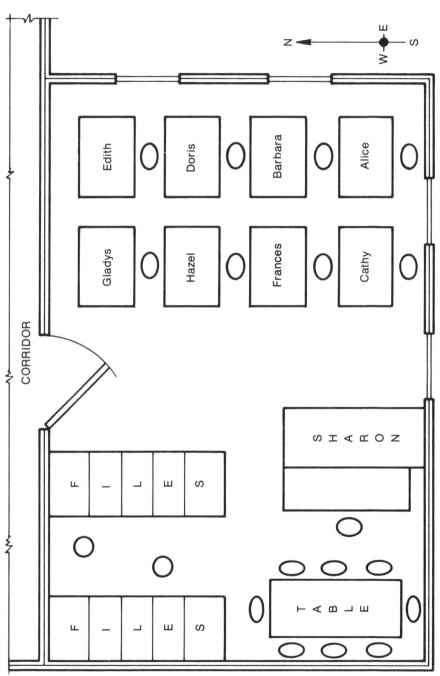

Figure 8.2. Possible solution for rearrangement of steno pool.

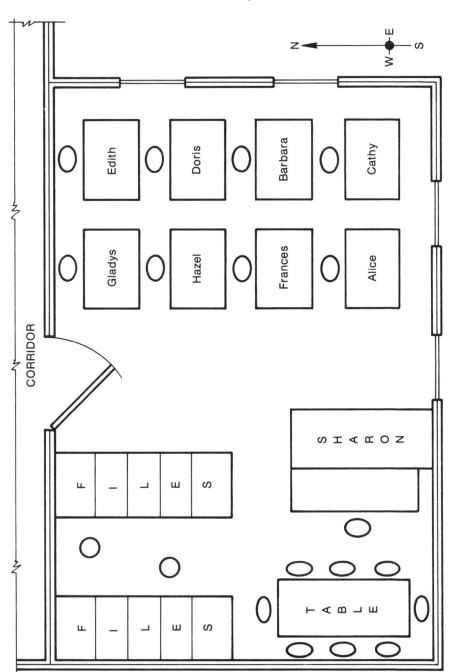

Figure 8.3. Another possible solution for seating arrangement of steno pool.

The principles of successful conference leadership will not be covered in this chapter. Several excellent publications noted in the bibliography treat this topic at length. Needless to say, the reader is urged to consult these books when determining how to apply a complex roleplay in a conference leadership training program.

Using Complex Exercises
in Conference Leadership Training

Training in conference leadership usually requires that the trainee simulate the role of a real conference leader. After the instructor has covered the principles of how to prepare and conduct a conference, each trainee, in turn, practices as a conference leader, putting into action the newly imparted skills. Sometimes a trainee will practice leading a conference which deals with a broad, in-house topic—such as the functioning of a blood donor program. Employing this kind of topic provides an excellent subject area for more than one trainee. However, the trainer may run out of ideas for such generalized topics with which all trainees can empathize. Also, it is boring to use the same topic for more than two or three practice leaders. Hence, adopting specific complex exercises, such as "Who's Cold and Who's Warm," is desirable.

When a complex exercise is used in conference leadership training, it is helpful that the trainee acting as the leader be given suitable preparation before beginning the assignment. In real life conferences there are generally two types of leaders.

The *impartial* leader who may have little formal or definite knowledge of who is who within the group and which members may have ulterior objectives. This leader's job is to serve as an identifier of problems, a synthetizer and a summarizer. In effect, the impartial leader is an outsider to the group, and he can maintain his group role only through (a) his formal status within the organization (such as executive assistant to the president) and (b) his ability to come across to the members and to relate to the group as a whole. If he lacks the latter skill, the group is likely to ignore or bypass him.

The *partial* or biased leader who has a definite interest in the outcome of the conference. For instance, the manager who calls a meeting of his staff to get the facts or to solve a problem (assuming that he really is committed to obtain an unpremeditated solution) is not impartial because (a) he knows his staff and the strengths, weaknesses and attitudes of individual members, and (b) he is also aware or cognizant of his group's sociometric patterns.

Complex learning designed for conference leadership training generally typifies the second type leader. Therefore, in the case of the trainee assuming the latter role, he is permitted to read (but not to retain) the written roles assigned to each of the other participants. He may make notes, but these should not be used once the session begins. This is desirable to encourage a feeling of reality among all the conferees.

In a real life conference or meeting, the participants normally chat with one another before the session starts. People sit next to one another on the basis of mutual interest or friendship patterns. After all trainees have studied their roles and before the practice session begins, they should be encouraged to "loosen up." They should be allowed to chat for about five minutes about any subject while the trainee designated as the leader is permitted to scan their roles.

What to Do If The Exercise Is Unsuccessful?

Failure of a training exercise—whether it is case study, a roleplay or a complex exercise—can be sensed. The signals are there—near the beginning or during the exercise itself: confusion among the trainees; nervous laughter, perhaps; trainees asking questions of each other; an awkward silence. After an exercise has ended, hints of nonsuccess may be found in direct, candid questions from trainees, such as, "What was the real purpose of all this that we just went through?" "I don't see how this relates to. . . ." "You know, Mr._____, we're a bit puzzled by the time we just spent on °°°°."An absolute indifference among the trainees about the results may also indicate failure.

There are many reasons why a training exercise may be unsuccessful. Perhaps the trainees received a faulty pretraining briefing, or they may have received no briefing at all. When no briefings are provided on the job about the course to which the trainees have been assigned, rumors about the purposes of the training are likely to have a harmful effect. Trainees may bring a sense of personal hostility into the course and to the entire idea of training itself. ("Am I being punished for some inadequacy on the job?") This hostility may vent itself within an exercise requiring the trainees' active participation.

Secondly, the philosophy being taught by the exercise may be at direct variance with that which the trainees have been taught and believe in. Exercises often fail because the trainees will find it difficult to bridge the relevance of the exercise to the needs of the job. This is sometimes transferred, in the minds of the trainees, in terms of an expenditure of time and as a kind of hidden cost-benefit analysis. ("What am I doing here? I should be back at my job where the work is piling up.")

Exercises may be unsuccessful because of faulty fundamental assumptions about the trainees which the trainer had in his mind when he planned the program.

If an exercise fails, what should the trainer do? What are his options? He can elect to do nothing with the trainees themselves as a group. If the course in which the exercise was used is part of a series in which other trainees are to participate, he must collect more information than he presently has. The trainer may find it desirable to talk to the trainees as individuals, to meet with some of their superiors and to reevaluate the exercise itself. These are all open options. More facts must be gathered before recycling another training sequence.

He can level with the trainee group at the time the exercise failed. He can tell the trainees honestly what the objectives of course were and how the exercise fitted into the course pattern; what was intended; why it was included; how he planned to apply it; what outcomes were anticipated. This should lead toward a frank discussion with one's trainees about the exercise *per se*. Did it fail because of its internal form or because it had no link to anything which the trainees could relate to back on the job? This distinction is vital. In one case, a mechanical failure is noted; in the other, a seeming failure of mission.

A mechanical failure may mean that the exercise instructions were faulty; that some operating directives were confused or misunderstood. The trainer should explain to the group what was intended. He should concede the error and then move into the substantive discussion—after the group has understood how the breakdown effected the desired end results.

Exercises which fail because they appear as irrelevant or as contradictory to the trainees' view of company policy present the trainer with a different challenge. The trainer should restate to the trainees the course objectives and discuss these in detail. He must be certain that these truly reflect that which management had agreed should be a reasonable outcome of the training. Next, he must lead the discussion toward the exercise itself—how it fitted into the scheme of things in terms of meeting the objectives and why it was included. Differences of opinions as to fundamental program goals, for example, are likely to surface during such discussions. This is a sound procedure and will be immensely beneficial, both for the trainer and for management interested in feedback on the course results.

Protagonist Lacks Authority

The following exercise has been devised for use by individuals who work with volunteer groups, over whom a protagonist would hold no direct authority. Originally, it was written as a problem for a college-level course in leadership and group dynamics.

Although one person convened the meeting, which provides the setting for the exercise, that person possesses no power to compel any action by those attending. To achieve his objectives, he must rely on persuasion, compromise and logic. Further, he will have to recognize that he holds no direct *authority* over his colleagues within the meeting. Thus, the *responsibility* for the success or failure of the group activity, whatever it may be, must be generated and *shared* by each participant. No one has been forced to attend; therefore, it can be assumed that more than a passing interest exists in the subject of the meeting. However, it cannot be assumed that all the participants' personal goals necessarily coincide and are completely harmonious. Rather, it is likely that several people will have special axes to grind. These will probably be seen as selfish, crass or self-seeking by the "others." Sometimes, these "others" hold enough power to block or completely wreck worthwhile group endeavors.

In the group setting, the individual actions become transformed into dynamic interactions between and among all the group members. "The Central City Memorial Auditorium" exercise is concerned with how the participants interact, their reasonableness in stating their own positions, listening to others, working for suitable compromises and developing a group climate which fosters harmony rather than discord. Agreement is sought initially on factors about which agreement is easiest to find.

Progress will often be slow and difficult. It will depend on how the group atmosphere was created: open and candid or closed and hypocritical. Progress also hinges on how progress is perceived, recorded and accepted by the group. Creativity—the stimulation of thoughtfulness and inventive ideas—is vital to progress. When conflict develops between participants—how is it handled? Is it brushed aside or is it worked out in a helpful manner?

Obviously, other skills, usually found within the leader's domain, contribute to progress. These relate to the controls over participation by individual members (not too much; not too little) and the ability to focus in on the important issues with the requisite amount of direction.

The Central City Memorial Auditorium

Instructions to Trainer

This exercise is to be used as a roleplay with nine participants, plus observers. If your training group is large enough, you may elect to use this as a concurrent roleplay for two or more subgroups. The use of observers is, of course, optional. To be most effective, this exercise requires that all participants carefully study the role information. It is, therefore, completely acceptable that such information be provided on an overnight, take-home assignment basis. Each participant receives a copy of the background information, has individual role and the letter from Eugene Plummer inviting him to the meeting.

For this exercise, name cards with the names of the roleplayers are to be placed on a separate table. The participants should be encouraged to pick these up and be permitted to seat themselves with roleplay friends as they desire. They should *not* be forced to sit in assigned seats.

The time required to complete this exercise will vary from about an hour and a half to two hours or more. The participants may take a break but should not discuss the role situation during the downtime period.

No single, ideal solution exists for this case. The roleplayers may agree on a single multipurpose facility which is acceptable to all personal, vested interests, or they may simply agree to disagree and schedule a future meeting. The important issues are not specifically what the group accomplished, but rather *how* the group proceeded, what the communication patterns within the group were and the degree of leadership exercised by the various group members.

General Background Information

Central City (and its environs) is a community of some 375,000. Over the past 40 years it has experienced a slow but steady growth pattern, and it is typical of many urban areas throughout the country. The Community Development Association (CDA) was created 25 years ago as a voluntary civic group. It was organized by prominent local citizens to encourage "planned growth" within the Central City area. Today CDA is well accepted as part of the power structure within Central City.

Over two years ago, CDA launched a campaign for a convention hall or auditorium because Central City had no facility capable of holding more than 2,000 people, and these failed to provide adequate parking.

The campaign for the new hall seemed to be lagging until the death (three months ago) of J.J. Jarman, a wealthy manufacturer and life-long resident of Central City. Jarman's last will and testament provided a choice parcel of ten acres near the new crosstown arterial highway, plus a sum of $2.5 million in cash for building purposes. Jarman's donation of land and money was contingent on two factors being accepted by CDA (which had been named as principal trustee of the proposed project):

1. The name of the building must be "The Central City Memorial Auditorium" (with the work "memorial" to be construed as a "living memorial" to the

deceased veterans of Central City.

2. The citizens of Central City contributed an additional 4.5 million—the approximate amount required to *initiate* construction. The remainder, about 5.5 million, could be financed through loans, which would be repaid through funds earned by the users of the new facility.

Eugene Plummer, a local attorney, is the chairman of CDA. He seeks quick action to proceed with planning for this project.

Therefore, after consultation with the executive committee of CDA, approval has been given to Plummer's proposal to create a separate auditorium fund-raising group within the framework of CDA. All people invited to the meeting are CDA members. Besides Plummer, Philip Alexander and John Bright are also CDA Executive Committee members. All invitees are known to be strongly supportive of the necessity for an auditorium in Central City. The group has already been referred to in the *Press* as the Ad Hoc Committee on the new Memorial Auditorium, and a lead editorial in the *Press* gave much support to the upcoming meeting.

Attending the meeting are the following:

Eugene (Gene) Plummer, CDA chairman
Philip (Phil) Alexander, president of the Greater Central City Chamber of Commerce
John Bright, president of the Central City Hotel and Motel Owner's Association
Louis (Lou) Philmont, executive assistant to the Mayor (Joseph Morgan)
Dr. Wainwright Jackson, president of Central City University (a private, non-denominational school)
Lawrence (Larry) Casey, president of the Central City National Bank
Mrs. Willson Graham, president of the Central City Symphony Society
Julian (Julie) Harper, chairman of the Central City Athletic Association
H. Clarence Mecklin, Publisher of *The Central City Press*

Additional Background Data

The interests of all the above parties should be *fairly* obvious. For the sake of clarity, Lou Philmont (and his boss, Mayor Morgan) are active *Republicans*. The next election for Mayor will be held in about three years.

Julie Harper, besides being heavily involved with sports, is also the *Democratic* leader in Central City.

Gene Plummer is a junior partner in the prestigious law firm of Vance, Brown, Brown and Plummer. It has been rumored that Gene has political ambitions, although he has not expressed party allegiance at this time.

Mrs. Graham is said to be quite well-to-do.

Eugene Plummer

This meeting has been called at your request; however, this does not mean that you will go after the chairmanship (although you will take it, if the group insists). Actually, you would prefer to have Mrs. Graham assume this responsibility because you realize that five or six of her symphony society members have enough money (and, hopefully, commitment) to put the drive well *over the top*. Your main plan for tonight's meeting involves:

1. Obtaining a *group* commitment for the auditorium.
2. *Defining the objectives* for which the auditorium will be used. The members of the committee must agree on the principal purposes for which the Memorial Auditorium will be available. An architect must "appreciate" these needs before he can develop a plan which will be meaningful.
3. Determining preliminary plans for fund raising. This is the most important because 4.5 million dollars must be pledged before Jarman's contribution becomes effective.

In private life, you are the junior partner of Vance, Brown, Brown and Plummer, a well-know law firm in Central City. You became interested in CDA about 2½ years ago and you would like to make this project a success. Some people have assumed that you may have political ambitions, but this is *not* true—at the moment, at least. Both Julie Harper, whom you respect, and Mayor Morgan, about whom you have some doubts, have been anxious to get your support. As an attorney, you recognize the value of political connections. For the time being, however, you are not planning on making a fixed commitment to either party. Your deep commitment to the concept of a Central City Memorial Auditorium is based, perhaps, on your idealism. Such a living, usable monument to the deceased veterans is far better than some remote piece of statuary. Besides, you liked J.J. Jarman as a client and as a friend, and you would like to see this project developed to completion.

Lawrence Casey

You represent the largest financial institution in Central City. You also are well aware of the "power structure" in Central City:

1. *Mrs. Graham* is extremely wealthy, with at least $15 million. Several of the members in the Central City Symphony Society are also *very* affluent.

However, she does *not* pass her money out to charities very easily. She must be convinced of their value.

2. *Lou Philmont* is a bright politician who represents the Republican power in Central City. He's a good man—a personal friend and golfing buddy.
3. *Julie Harper* is an old-line politician. He is the Democratic Chairman of Central City but spends most of his time in connection with promoting baseball, boxing and basketball.
4. *Gene Plummer* is an up-and-coming young attorney who most certainly has political ambitions.
5. The rest of these people here represent their own special interests, as indeed, you do. You would like to see your bank handle any mortgages or related funding which may be required to erect the building.

Dr. Wainwright Jackson

This is a *vital* project as far as the University is concerned. Here is how you see it:

1. You would like to see a decent, multipurpose facility, but one which would be available to the Central City Symphony, which now uses your gymnasium.
2. You are all for encouraging the arts, but *not* at the expense of college varsity basketball!
3. With a new auditorium facility, you could "kill three birds with one stone": Get the Central City Symphony out of your gym and hence "beef up" your basketball schedule to include some really big name teams. You would have a place for the drama and music students to perform when the Central City Symphony wasn't using the place. Lastly, you'd unload all the convention and meeting requests for the use of the University by Phil Alexander for the benefit of the local businessmen in Central City.
4. You are prepared to offer placing the new facility under the control and direction of the School of Dramatic and Performing Arts of Central City University. The University would provide one-half of all maintenance, handle personnel costs for building upkeep, and so forth, and request *no* public aid for its annual budget—*if* your terms are accepted.

The Central City Symphony would be given full opportunity to perform, and a schedule could be worked out to meet everyone's objectives—of that you are sure!

Mrs. Wilson Graham

You are *delighted* to be involved in this project. It has been your personal dream (and, that of your membership) to be able some day to provide a *decent* concert hall for the Central City Symphony. The gymnasium at Central City University, where the concerts are now being held, is absolutely impossible, acoustically. Furthermore, Dr. Jackson (president of Central City University) has been rather "anxious" to have your organization move elsewhere. He wants the facility for basketball. Imagine! What has higher education come to? Basketball is more important these days than a fine concert of Bach or Beethoven.

With a new concert hall, you might well induce the New York Philharmonic Orchestra and the Philadelphia Orchestra to perform at Central City while on tour. Even the Metropolitan Opera Company might make it! You know that Clarence Mecklin feels the same way you do about this, and you're pleased to see that Mr. Plummer had the good sense to invite Clarence and yourself.

You have discussed this matter with your Symphony Society Board of Directors before coming to this meeting. They have noted their full support, and several key members have stated that they would contribute a total of at least $1,000,000 if the plans meet with their approval. You would personally be prepared to provide a million yourself, in memory of your dear (departed) husband. Your personal fortune is in excess of 18 million, and your attorney has pointed out the advantages of this kind of contribution. But nothing will be given unless this project works out the way it should!

Philip Alexander

You have been an active CDA member and are now on the Executive Committee of that group. It is largely through your initiative that the present meeting has been convened.

Two weeks ago, the Greater Central City Chamber of Commerce's board of directors passed a resolution giving *full endorsement* to the new Central City Memorial Auditorium. This facility has been needed for years; only the expense of construction has held it up. Perhaps it is stating the obvious to note that the convention hall would bring in a lot of business, and *this* is what your people want. They will support the needed fund-raising effort, and you estimate that your members would probably contribute about $350,000.

During the past few years, the so-called student activities at Central City University have given that place a bad name, and the groups which once used the university during the off-season now will have nothing to do with that place. One of your friends in the Legion claims that the University has been infiltrated by Commies—and he's probably right!

Personally, you view this new project as a great challenge; if an auditorium, or convention hall is built, this will be a big boost to local business. Political conventions, statewide meetings of the Legion, Masons, or Knights of Columbus would bring in a lot of dollars. The merchants would be happy—and if they're happy, you're happy!

Louis Philmont

As Executive Assistant to Mayor Morgan—and as an aspirant for the job of mayor yourself someday—you can readily see the value of completing this project for Central City. Both you and your boss are most keen on getting the state Republican organization to meet in Central City for the state convention. A lot of political strength can be acquired by having the sessions in Central City, and you *want this done* while "your man" is still in office. His term has three more years to run; therefore, this project has *got to move.*

You are prepared to throw the full support of the local Republican organization behind the fund-raising drive—provided this project moves the way you want it to move! You are not displeased to see that Julie Harper has apparently decided to get involved—even if he is a Democratic "wheel." If this auditorium is built during the regime of Mayor Morgan, the *Republicans* will claim the major credit for accomplishment! Larry Casey, one of your best friends (even though he beats you at golf once in a while), agrees with your judgment. Obviously, you're pleased that Larry is on this committee. Gene plummer's position is, of course, that of the typical do-gooder. As far as you know, he has no stated political ambitions. You are aware that Plummer's law firm is handling the Jarman estate—which may explain his motivation in this project.

Julian Harper

As Chairman of the Central City Athletic Association (boxing, basketball, minor league baseball) and as the acknowledged Democratic leader in Central City, you've decided that there is much more to be gained than lost by supporting the fund-raising drive. With the right kind of auditorium, you have been guaranteed that the Universal Basketball League will grant a franchise to Central City. Furthermore, with a first-rate auditorium you can get the top draws in boxing, wrestling and even ice hockey. It would also be a real "feather in your cap" if you could get the state Democratic convention to Central City. This would ultimately improve your leverage within the Party.

In order to make your plans successful, you will push hard for a facility which has plenty of height and is oval-shaped, where the spectators sit around the outside. A movable stage can be set up for party gatherings and other similar events. A close friend is an architect, and he has advised you that he "will be happy" to provide advise upon request.

You view Philmont's interest in this project with some suspicion. As the Mayor's chief "flunky," he must have some axe to grind; otherwise, he would not be here.

Gene Plummer is a sharp young attorney whom you personally admire. He would make a fine candidate for mayor.

John Bright

You have been an active CDA member and are now on the Executive Committee of that group. It is largely through your initiative that the present meeting has been convened. Obviously, you are pleased to participate in this meeting because your members in the Hotel and Motel Owner's Association want action on the auditorium. The auditorium will mean that Central City will be able to host *large* conventions—which it is unable to do now—and this means money in the pockets of your people. In turn, your members are prepared to support, financially, the funding of the project. While no firm commitments have been made, you would guess that your membership should be able to contribute at least $100,000 (and maybe more). Two of your important members have stated that if the Democratic and Republican state conventions could be held in Central City, they "would go all out" in providing help.

H. Clarence Mecklin

You appreciate Gene Plummer's thoughtfulness in asking you to become involved in the auditorium project. While you never thought much of old man Jarman when he was alive, this idea is one that you can buy. Central City needs more culture. When the auditorium is completed, the Central City Symphony will have a better place to perform. Its present site, Central City University's gym, is pretty awful.

You imagine that the real reason you have been asked to work on this project is because of its "public nature" in Central City. Obviously, your paper can do a great deal, of a positive nature, to promote the success of the program, especially as far as fund-raising is concerned. You have no preconceived notions about the memorial auditorium, except that it should be great for Central City, and, hence, it may help sell more copies of the *Press*.

Politically, your paper is more or less nonpartisan on local issues. In state and national affairs, you tend to support Republican causes.

Letter from Eugene Plummer
to Committee Members

(Each assigned roleplayer should receive personalized copy together with special role data and general background information.)

Dear _____:

I am confirming our telephone call concerning the upcoming meeting on _____, at the _____, dealing with the proposed Central City Memorial

Auditorium. Be assured that I am most appreciative of your willingness to participate in this tremendously important project for Central City. A suitable auditorium will do so many things for our community. I know that you will bring to the meeting many excellent ideas on how we should proceed with out planning.

At our first meeting I hope that we shall be able to define the major objectives for which the auditorium should be used. Each of us will have our own points of view, naturally. I know I can depend on you to help work out the various possibilities for the use of a facility which will meet many different kinds of needs. I also trust that we can agree before we start talking to an architect. We must, as a committee, have our own ideas pretty well thought through beforehand.

Another important purpose of this meeting will be to develop preliminary plans for suitable fund raising. You are aware that according to the bequest in Mr. Jarman's will, about four and a half million dollars must be pledged before the bequest itself becomes available to us.

With every good wish!

Sincerely,
Gene

Instructions for Observers (Sample Questions for Discussion Period)

Who initiated discussion?

How were problems stated?

Did everyone agree with statement of problem? Explain.

Did everyone understand problems? Explain.

Enumerate (1 through 9) *order* of participants as they expressed their own special points of view:

Eugene Plummer _____ Philip Alexander _____ John Bright _____
Louis Philmont _____ Dr. W. Jackson _____ Lawrence Casey _____
Mrs. W. Graham _____ Julian Harper _____ H.C. Mecklin _____

Did individuals' proposals seem *reasonable* or *emotional*? Explain.

Who seemed to be in conflict with whom? Explain.

Were these conflicts heightened or lessened as discussion progressed? Explain.

Who served as the compromiser? Was he or she accepted in this role? Explain.

To what extent did the group members reach accommodation or possible solution?

Do you feel that group members *really* understood each other? Explain.

Rewriting the Case

When two or three or four people gather to rewrite or revise material which is in need of polishing, the potential for a practical group learning experience exists because the achievement of a common product—such as a piece of writing—requires consensus. Individuals tend to chart diverse paths toward what they perceive as the "proper" group outcome. Most often the rewrite job concerns a news release, an important business letter for a wide audience or a memorandum, representing several viewpoints for higher authorities. A case study has been employed here as a sample. However, the written material used is only a vehicle to get at the *interaction* of people in a small group.

This exercise may also be applied to enrich and to enliven courses in written communications where the objectives focus on the language skills rather than on the interpersonal relations. Since these goals are very different, the instructor using this exercise as part of a course in report writing must be careful to stick to his subject and to avoid the interpersonal examinations which would develop naturally in a setting designed to develop personal perceptions of self and to build trust.

How to Use the Exercise

In Written Communications Training

Training in written communications is intended to teach how to simplify the sender's message. Its ultimate objective is to ease and facilitate the receiver's reading. Improved written output calls for the acquisition of new skills and, often, new attitudes. How we speak and how we write reflects fundamental, personal attributes and feelings about our finished product. This particular exercise is suggested as one method of assisting in the instructional process. In most written communication courses, the teacher's approach tends to rely on the lecture or the lecture-discussion. Our aim, through the use of this exercise, is an enlivened learning atmosphere. Trainee involvement will be strengthened by deliberately encouraging *competition* between small groups within the class.

A piece of writing in rough draft form was selected and then reduced to an acceptable piece which transmits essentially the same basic message but with fewer words. The case study example was chosen simply because this is a book about training, and the case itself may be helpful to the reader. The instructor employing this method will be free to specify what kind of written material he wishes to use. The idea is to begin with material which demands reworking. It should be excessively long and wordy, or it may be obscure in part and contain horribly constructed sentences and similar ingredients usually found in poor writing.

On p. 176 the case is presented as it was originally written (by a trainee in a college-level course in supervisory practices) along with its improved format. The length has been cut from 250 to 120 words without a substantial change in its message. This condensation, planned and completed ahead of the class session, serves the teaching method: to place small groups of trainees (maximum of four) in a competitive workshop setting. It is suggested that this exercise be introduced following a lecture or lecture-discussion covering the subject of brevity, sentence arrangement (such as confusing interruptions, awkward coordination or use of the passive) and paragraphing.

Each group simultaneously receives copies of the material requiring revision. Enough copies are provided so that each trainee has his own to study. Since the exercise stresses learning through intergroup competition, each group is free to organize itself anyway that it chooses. The instructor fixes a time limit, which depends on the type of material being rewritten. The example shown on p. 176 would call for about 20 minutes of work by a group of four. A group of two or three will naturally require somewhat less time. The instructor also sets a goal in terms of the number of words to be eliminated without a substantial revision of meaning. In fact, a clarification of the communication's meaning is sought through a reduction in verbiage.

If it is feasible, each group's completed product is typed and transferred to a transparency for the overhead projector. This may be done during the break period. The model rewrite will also be available on a transparency. While it is not the only way that the rewrite can be done, it is sufficiently definitive to be used to compare and judge which group succeeded in doing superior work. The instructor's commentary covering the principles of good writing, while weighing one product against another, will emphasize (and praise) the positive accomplishments of each group.

During the discussion period, the instructor will encourage the trainees to respond to the following types of questions.

General

How much detail does the completed material need to be functional?
How would you outline the case?
Should the background be stated first and then the problem presented?
Or vice versa?

*Words**

How many words are needed to do the job? What kinds are best? How
much does the potential audience control your decision?
What biases toward the problem and its author arise because of the words
chosen to present it?
Can slang or other substandard usage have a place? Why? With what
effect?
Under what circumstances would formal, scholarly usage be appropriate?
Why?

Sentences

Should the structure and length of sentences be varied for interest or would
uniformity assure greater clarity?
Do the order of sentences and the placement of phrases and clauses within
sentences determine the emphasis trainees see in the problem?
To what extent? How much do order, subordination and qualification really matter in this case?
To what extent do grammatical corrections control the presentation of the
material and the outcome of the training exercise? What is lost or gained if a sentence is grammatically incomplete, if subjects and verbs do
not agree in number and if dangling modifiers or pronouns without
clear antecedents are let stand?

Paragraphs

Can the material be best presented (both for logic and attractive

---

*See Robert Gunning, *How to Take the Fog Out of Writing* (Chicago: Dartnell Corp., 1964),
and Will Strunk, *Elements of Style,* E.B. White, ed. (New York: The Macmillan Company,
1959).

appearance) in a single paragraph? Or would several paragraphs be better?

If several paragraphs are used, does each makes its own point and then stop?

Are transitions between and within paragraphs easy-to-follow aids to clarity?

Working for a Common Goal

Here the objective is very different from that contemplated directly above. This rewrite exercise serves as a means to an end: how individual trainees act and react when they are required to work on a project as a team. Fostering more accurate self-perception—that is the principal objective.

Step 1. All trainees receive copies of the original rough draft material. They are told to read the instructions attached to the draft, to follow these carefully but not to discuss their assignment with anyone. Half of the trainees receive the following instruction.

> Read the following material carefully. As you can readily see, it is much too long. Actually, it contains exactly 250 words. Your task is to reduce it—*without a substantial change of message*—to 195 words (*no less than that*). If you find that you cannot hit 195 exactly, you may go up to 200. You are not, however, to reduce it below 195.

> Prepare your finished product in five copies and bring these with you since you will be working as a team on a final draft. Work by yourself. Please do not ask anyone for help. Of course, you are free to use the dictionary. Good luck!

The other half of the trainees receive identical instructions except that they are told to reduce their finished product to *150* words, with a similar five-word upward spread.

Step 2. When the trainees reconvene, which may be a day or a week later, according to the training schedule, divide them into teams of four trainees. Half of each team will have worked to reduce the writing to 195 words; the other half, to 150 words. The teams are then given the following instructions:

> Working as a team, you are to reduce the draft material originally given you to 120 words, or less, without a substantial change in the message. You are to use the completed efforts which each of you have written. Exchange copies so that everyone has a set of the work done by all team members. Your team's finished

TEAM # _____	YES	NO	NO OPINION
1. As a whole, I was satisfied with the results of our work.			
2. This exercise was a waste of time.			
3. We could have done a better job. Explain.			
4. Everyone else on my team will state that they were satisfied with the results of our work.			
5. Generally, the group accomplished its goal.			
6. People tend to be sensitive about how they write. If YES, explain.			
7. Our team's effort was superior to anything we might have done individually.			
8. If you agree with the above, explain why we don't use such team efforts elsewhere.			
9. We needed more time. If YES, explain how extra time would have been used.			
10. We would have done a better job if our team membership were restructured.			
11. I didn't get to participate the way I would have liked. Explain.			
12. I learned something as a result of this exercise. Describe.			

Figure 8.4. Questionnaire on group effort.

Table 8.1. Characteristics Which Contribute to Achievement of Group Goal	
Flexible	Pursues ideas
Listens	Encourages other views
Gives attention to others	Synthesizes
Patient	Sincere
Perceptive	Straightforward
	(does not beat
	around the bush)
Open-minded	Outspoken
Cooperative	Logical
Show enthusiasm	Appreciative
Displays interest	Helpful and supportive
in others' ideas	
Imaginative	Displays humor
Sparks ideas	Persuasive
Stimulates and motivates	Confident
Curious	Convincing
Facilitates	

product will be evaluated as to its clarity, brevity and accurate message. You have 45 minutes to complete this assignment.

After the teams complete their chores, permit closure. Go through to the completion of the assigned exercise: reducing the written product. Each team reports briefly on how well the original material's message held together while its body was being condensed. Perhaps the trainer may wish to collect the completed group work.

Avoid leaving the impression that they have been manipulated. Then, move the discussion toward an analysis of the way that the groups functioned. We are seeking to bring into focus for the trainees the *process* rather than the end product. One way of doing this fairly quickly is to request that each trainee complete a questionnaire, relating to how he saw the group effort. (see Figure 8.4)

An examination of the responses may be tabulated on the board. All trainees will observe the results, sparking some intensive, gut-level deliberations. The trainer has the option at that point of moving the group toward a consideration of the Johari Window concepts.*

Another variation open to the trainer would be to direct the discussion in accord with the following commentary and the accompanying materials.

Personal attributes displayed in a group serve to "type" individuals. No

*Joseph Luft, *Of Human Interaction* (Palo Alto, California: National Press Books, 1969).

Table 8.2. Characteristics Which Detract from Achievement of Group Goal

1. Indifferent (I couldn't care less.)
2. Uninvolved (I don't want to get into the act.)
3. Wants to be neutral (I'm a completely impartial person.)
4. Self-effacing (I'm really not very bright.)
5. Uninterested (This doesn't turn me on at all.)
6. Inattentive (This sure is a nice day. Oh, what did you say?)
7. Bored (What the devil am I doing here?)
8. Patronizing (I suppose I must lower myself to their level.)
9. Pompous (Who says I'm stuffy?)
10. Elitist in attitude (My ideas are correct because I am me.)
11. Arrogant (Who do these jerks think they are?)
12. Negative outlook (It won't work, so why try it?)
13. Know-it-all (What would you like to know? I'm an expert on everything.)
14. Cocky (Go ahead. I know I will be proven right.)
15. Conceited (I love me.)
16. Domineering (I'm the boss; now listen to me.)
17. Litigious (There's nothing better than a good debate for its own sake.)
18. Contentious (Put up or shut up.)
19. Argues excessively (Yes, but . . .)
20. Concedes with ill grace (So you are right for once.)
21. Stubborn (I'm not giving up.)
22. Resists making revisions (My pride of authorship is as solid as yours is.)
23. Impatient (Come on; come on; let's get moving. We have wasted too much time already.)
24. Rigid (I'm not switching.)
25. Shows temper (Who gave you the right to control me?)
26. Sarcastic (Yes, you've finally come up with a winner this time.)

neutral ground is available for the person within a group once the group goal has been set. Those who fail to support the group are, in fact, detracting from the group's potential.

Two broad listings of positive and negative characteristics are provided in Tables 8.1 and 8.2. These are available as discussion starters and as self-perception awakeners. The trainer's ingenuity is challenged to find ways to capitalize on these listings in a creative and productive way. Because it is easier to identify nonpositive patterns, each of these has been illustrated with a parenthetical observation. The group should be encouraged to work at doing the same for the supportive actions.

One Final Word

During a group activity the behaviors required will vary according to the stage of the activity. Desirable behaviors at the inception of an activity may be completely undesirable at a later point. For instance, attempting to encourage the summarization of what has been covered while a group is in the process of developing additional new ideas will detract from the attainment of the group goal. The trainer should comment on this during the discussion dealing with broad trainee characteristics.

Rewriting the Case

Original Version

The company was bidding on a new job, but before they could submit an official quotation to the Early Enterprise Corporation, for whom they would be doing the work, they had to make certain that it could be done on their present equipment, which was questionable. Determining the feasibility of production on their present equipment called for the design of a special fixture to be used in a mock test to simulate an operation that would have to be done when producing this new item for Early. The Engineering Department designed the fixture, and the three machine shop mechanics commenced its building. But the engineer who conceived this fixture design and who was responsible for the preparation of blueprints to be used by the machine shop mechanics didn't have enough time to furnish all the details on the blueprints, and, having in mind the exact configuration of certain parts, he would work on the finishing touches himself to produce the precise shape of the part which was essential for doing satisfactorily the operations required in connection with the testing of their equipment for the production of this new item for Early.

One fine day, in the middle of his work, he was interrupted by the shop superintendent, who told him that he had just been handed a grievance by the union steward, claiming the engineer was doing the job of the mechanics and was therefore cutting down the overtime of the shop mechanics, thereby making the union people most unhappy.

Revised Version

Before bidding on a new job, the company had to be sure its present equipment could handle the work. To determine this, a special fixture was needed for a mock test to simulate a production step.

The Engineering Department designed the fixture, and the machine shop mechanics began to build it. But the engineer responsible, lacking enough time to furnish all details on the blueprint, worked on finishing touches himself, so that the fixture would be precisely the shape required.

One day the shop superintendent interrupted the engineer at his work to tell him that the union steward had just filed a grievance claiming the engineer was doing the mechanics' work, thus cutting down their overtime and aggravating the union.

Leaderless Group Discussion

The use of court case material may offer several significant advantages in *leaderless* group discussion exercises. The realism of the case and the ease with which the participants empathize with the parties involved helps to move the discussion and provides many useful opportunities for interpersonal confrontation. For example, in a case concerning an auto accident, most people would have a good working appreciation of how and why collisions might occur. Driving habits and attitudes toward driving are readily understood by any typical jury.

The jury case is also well suited for mixed training groups. The influence of the on-the-job role and status of individual trainees will be lessened during the "deliberations." Similarly, training groups composed of men and women may be less inhibited in their intragroup communications.

The "Case of the Concrete Stairs" is based on a real-life adversary proceeding, but as the motion picture script writer would say, "Any resemblance to persons living or dead is purely coincidental," insofar as the details of this case are concerned.

The jury system is well founded in Anglo-Saxon legal traditions, and it is applied in both civil and criminal law. Its effectiveness has long been debated: is it *fair* to expect nonexperts to sit in judgment and render decisions *as a group* on complex problems about which they have no first-hand information until they are assembled? Further, jurors rarely, if ever, know each other *before* being impaneled. Hence, as strangers they *must* interrelate with one another, communicating about situations whose outcome will have a very profound impact on the parties in the case.

In the criminal case a person's freedom for years—or perhaps his very life—is at stake. In civil cases where monetary damages are levied, one party may gain (or lose) vast sums of money. Yet, for all its seeming weaknesses, the jury system is still the most equitable and reasonable format devised to resolve controversy between opposing parties.

Theoretically at least, the key to the success of the jury system as a *method* rests on the impartiality of the jury members. Because of this, attorneys seek to ensure, insofar as it may be feasible, that *each* juror has no previous knowledge of the case or built-in biases or preconceived notions "about cases such as these." In civil cases jurors are frequently questioned about their employment; whether they have any "feelings about large awards" to aggrieved parties; whether they own stock or have an interest in insurance companies; and, if the case involves an automobile collision situation, they drive a car.

The judge—who is essentially an umpire interpreting and applying the law—will permit questions about insurance only during the selection of the jurors. The question has pertinency because large numbers of people carry liability insurance coverage against claims for damages. Where the parties cannot agree on who was at fault in a given situation, the resulting dispute may go to trial for settlement. Because some people consider that jury awards may be excessively generous and that such awards result in higher premiums, their views may well result in a prejudgment of the case.* Hence, this question is permissible during jury selection process by the counsel for the aggrieved party.

After the selection process, the case is heard. No note-taking is permitted, although the stenographic record of testimony may be requested for clarification by the jurors *after* they have commenced their deliberations. Normally, the jury must rely on its *collective memory* of the testimony in reaching a decision.

The interactions among the jurors affords many beneficial lessons in how humans communicate with one another in a group. This is, of course, the primary purpose for using the "Case of the Concrete Stairs." A secondary instructional feature to be observed is how the group decision-making process operates. This includes how the group organizes itself, how individuals may demand and seek answers to problems well before the facts have been assembled and analyzed. Personality traits may be noted, involving such qualities as patience, caution, argumentativeness, impatience and analytical ability. Certainly, if used properly, the case will provide a productive learning experience for the participants and for the observers.

The Case of the Concrete Stairs

Instructions to the Trainer

Three factors must be considered during the preparation process: the size and nature of the group, the locale for training and the amount of time available to the jury group and for the subsequent evaluation session.

The "Case of the Concrete Stairs" requires a total group of at least ten. The

*No-fault automobile insurance has drawn its support from individuals holding these views.

ideal maximum would be about 18, although up to 25 trainees could be accommodated. The case is well suited for use in group training courses in supervision, in management (where the so-called "human relations" approach is emphasized), in communications skills or as a microlab exercise as part of an organizational development activity.

The training location must be quiet, free from interruptions and large enough to handle the "jurors" and the observers (if these are available). The total time required for the case will vary to some extent, depending on the number of trainees in the total group (jurors and observers). Normally, *at least* two hours should be allotted, although three hours may be required for larger groups where observers' contributions will be solicited and discussed during the evaluation process. The arrangement of the participants in the exercise would be the following:

1. Those selected as jurors will be seated in an oval facing each other. Tables should *not* be used. Jurors should be assigned numbers and will hold these numbers (or they may be pinned on clothing) for the benefit of the observers.
2. The observers will be seated behind the jury members. Each observer will be assigned to record that data which the trainer considers desirable in terms of the session's objectives.

Members of the training group who might be attorneys should *not* sit as jurors; they may serve as observers, however.

A careful reading of the case by the trainer is a must! If the trainer does not understand the details of the case, the discussion by the jurors may not be fully appreciated and the subsequent evaluation will not be fully productive.

The trainer will select the trainees to serve as jurors and will seat them in the oval. Any number of trainees *over* 12 will act as observers and sit in back of the jurors. The following statement will be read aloud by the trainer at this point.

You are to imagine that you are in the chambers of a Supreme Court in a New York State Courthouse. The Supreme Court hears adversary proceedings in civil law cases. Some of you have been selected as jurors; others will have the unusual privilege of "sitting in" on the deliberations of the jury as *observers*. If you are an observer, please do *not* comment in any way while the jury is deliberating. You will be given instruction sheets indicating your assigned roles while the jury is working. As for the members of the jury, read the case carefully. Do not ask for any assistance or additional information. *All* the information available is included therein. You should be aware that you would not be able to ask any information which was not presented to you if this were a *real* courtroom situation and if you were a *real* juror. You would be *forced* to act only on what you saw and heard.

At this point the trainer will distribute the "Case of the Concrete Stairs" (See: p. 186) to the jurors *and* observers. Approximately 10 to 12 minutes should be sufficient for reading the case, After the trainer is assured that all jurors have read the case, he will read the following statement to the jury (slowly and deliberately).

This is Justice Muste speaking. May I thank you for the attention which you have given to this case up to now. It is your responsibility, as a juror, to consider all the testimony and evidence presented. You will want to review and discuss this testimony and evidence *carefully* with your fellow jurors.

Take your time and do not reach your decision in a hasty, trifling or frivolous fashion. Two parties' rights are at stake! Accord to each the same fair and evenhanded treatment which you would want if you were in a similar controversy and were being judged by others. Voice your own opinion and do not be swept along to a decision simply because it seems like a good idea.

It may seem that certain testimony presented by one party is in conflict with that offered by the other. You are, of course, to decide in such instances which party you would believe.

In connection with the law of negligence, let me say this: if the plaintiff is in any part negligent in contributing to the cause of the injury, he cannot recover damages. The yardstick for considering contributory negligence would be based on what a "reasonable person" might do under similar circumstances. You should also note that our laws require a landlord to maintain one's rental property in a safe condition for his tenants.

No jury foreman will be required in this case. Ordinarily—in a real-life jury—the first juror selected becomes the foreman, although he may relinquish this assignment if he does not wish to serve in this capacity.

The deliberations of *this* jury will result in either a finding for the plaintiff or a finding of no cause for action. If you find for the plaintiff, you *must fix* a dollar figure for appropriate compensation.

I shall hope that your decision will be achieved *unanimously*. You may, however, reach an acceptable decision if ten out of twelve jurors are in agreement.*

You may now commence your deliberations

At this point jurors go to work on case. The trainer and observers should be *busi-*

---

*Note to trainer: if only ten or eleven participants are used as jurors, require that nine be in agreement.

The Case of the Concrete Stairs

Participant's Task Sheet #1

Directions: Circle either Y or N according to whether you agree or disagree with statement. If uncertain, circle ?.	Y	N	?
1. Every group requires a leader.	Y	N	?
2. Most people tend to allow a few people to dominate a discussion unless they have a vested interest in the outcome.	Y	N	?
3. It's far better to listen than to talk.	Y	N	?
4. In groups containing men and women, the women tend to "take over."	Y	N	?
5. In groups containing men and women, the men tend to "take over."	Y	N	?
6. People who talk too much tend to be boring.	Y	N	?
7. It's almost impossible to reach a group decision unless a strong leader takes control.	Y	N	?
8. Decisions are apt to be of better quality when all group members pitch in and participate.	Y	N	?
9. Without a leader, group members have a real problem in communicating effectively to each other.	Y	N	?
10. Every discussion group requires a leader.	Y	N	?

Figure 8.5. Participant Task Sheet #1.

The Case of the Concrete Stairs			
Participant's Task Sheet #2			
Directions: Circle Y for YES; N for NO; ? if uncertain of your responses.	Y	N	?
1. Based solely on what you read, did you reach a personal decision on this case?	Y	N	?
2. Were you satisfied with the way the jury handled the case.?	Y	N	?
3. Did the group decision agree with your initial decision?	Y	N	?
4. Did the group (as an entity) influence your decision?	Y	N	?
5. Is it useful to volunteer information in a group session?	Y	N	?
6. It's best to "lie back" and let others do the talking.	Y	N	?
7. Most people are apt to be prejudiced when considering a case such as this.	Y	N	?
8. A few people are apt to be prejudiced when handling a case such as this.	Y	N	?
9. If I were in an automobile accident, I would never permit my attorney to take my case to jury trial.	Y	N	?
10. I was unable to decide who was telling the truth.	Y	N	?
11. The jury system is about as fair a method of solving disputes as can be devised.	Y	N	?
12. Some people will not speak their minds or voice their opinions unless prodded.	Y	N	?
13. A strong-willed individual can unduly influence a group.	Y	N	?
14. Problems which demand a "logical" approach in their solution are best handled on an individual basis, rather than by a group.	Y	N	?
15. People should not be influenced by others who are extremely articulate or persuasive.	Y	N	?

Figure 8.6. Participant Task Sheet #2.

The Case of the Concrete Stairs

Observer's Task Sheet #1

Directions: Circle Y for YES; N for NO.	Y	N	Comments
1. Seating of jurors effected the discussion.	Y	N	
2. As a whole, logic seemed to rule in this group.	Y	N	
3. There were few, if any, problems in interpersonal communications.	Y	N	
4. Jurors seemed to say what they meant to say.	Y	N	
5. There seemed to be acceptance of a reasoning process in reaching the solution.	Y	N	
6. Some jurors seemed to make a bid for leadership in group.	Y	N	
7. Some jurors seemed to be communicating at two levels.	Y	N	
8. At times, the group tended to separate into subgroups.	Y	N	
9. The men jurors dominated the women (if applicable).	Y	N	
10. Some jurors did not seem to be listening carefully.	Y	N	

Figure 8.7. Observer's Task Sheet #1.

	1	2	3	4	5	6	7	8	9	10	11	12
The Case of the Concrete Stairs **Observer's Task Sheet #2**												
Juror #												
1. Number of times speaking.												
2. Tended to make original points in discussion.												
3. Tended to acquiesce.												
4. Tended to make counter arguments.												
5. Tended to summarize.												
6. Tended to be analytical.												
7. Which jurors tended to join forces (draw connecting lines).												
8. Tended to assume leadership.												
9. First proposed a decision.												
10. Clearly had difficulty expressing himself.												

Figure 8.8. Observer's Task Sheet #2.

ly engaged in watching and listening as the jury process goes forward. The jury should be permitted to deliberate until it either reaches a decision or feels that it is hopelessly deadlocked and cannot possibly decide the case. It is permissible—if the training schedule permits—for the trainer to call for a coffee break if such a deadlock occurs. As the judge, he cautions all jurors and observers *not* to discuss the case while they are out on a break.

In this case, the trainer is provided with several options on how to approach the evaluation of the work performed by the jurors.

Two *participant task sheets* are available and should be applied as follows:

1. In the training group where *communication* is a significant skill which the trainer has set as an objective for improvement. Task Sheet #1 (Figure 8.5) should be completed in a *previous* class session and the results tabulated and analyzed. It must *not* be used shortly before the start of this training case. However, Task Sheet #1 may be administered *after* the group training activity as a post-test for both jurors and observers. The trainer will have the results of the pretest (given in the previous session) available, and the comparisons will be valuable in the discussion session. Of course, Task Sheet #1 will have value—depending upon the objectives set by the trainer—in discussion areas other than communications training. Leadership styles, the extent of influence exerted by the group on the decision-making process or the processes of group dynamics would all be valid topics for which this task sheet could assist the trainer in evaluating changes in trainee attitudes and in the discussion process which would follow the exercise.

2. Task Sheet #2 (Figure 8.6) is intended for use immediately after the conclusion of the jury's work. Ordinarily it should *not* be necessary to employ both task sheets. Task Sheet #2 is to be given to the trainees who have served as jurors. Like Task Sheet #1, it is designed to reveal attitudes and prejudices of individuals in a group environment. For example, the question—Did the group influence your decision?—will be productive in evaluating the extent of group pressure required to change views or opinions. The trainer must determine, based on available time and the nature of his training group, which task sheet will be most advantageous.

In training groups which are larger than twelve, observers will be available to watch the jury in action. As nonparticipants they will be able to concentrate their attentions on the group *processes*. The trainer must ensure that they clearly understand this role and do not comment (or make facial expressions of delight or disgust) as the deliberations proceed. As passive—but alert—observers, they will be bringing a degree of impartiality to the discussion and evaluation which follows the jury's actions.

Two observers task sheets are available:

1. Observer Task Sheet #1 (Figure 8.7) will be used if the number of observers is four or less. This sheet calls for yes-no responses and comments which should relate to specific incidents noted by the observers. The observers will be watching the *entire* jury and reporting on *all* jurors.
2. Where the training group is large (over sixteen), the trainer will have the option of using *both* observer task sheets. Two or more, depending on the size of the total trainee group, can use Observer Task Sheet #1. At least four additional observers must be available to handle Observer Task Sheet #2 (Figure 8.8) effectively. The trainer will allocate two or three jurors to each observer, who will "keep tabs" on his assigned jurors. Certain questions on Observer Task Sheet #2 may be deleted, depending upon the objectives set by the trainer and the nature of the group. The trainer must take care to read the observer task sheets carefully and decide which items may be inappropriate for discussion purposes.

Principal Characters

Louis Green, the victim. Not very bright and somewhat akin to Jackie Gleason's "The Poor Soul." (The Plaintiff)

Mabel Green, his wife. Somewhat sharper and undoubtedly the brains of the family.

Mrs. Logan, the landlady. No youngster and well set in her ways. (The Defendant)

Mrs. O'Hara, a friend and former neighbor of the Greens. She lived in Unit #3 during the time that the Greens lived in Unit #2. (See Figure 8.9)

Mr. Dowdy, attorney for the Greens.

Mr. Formidable, attorney for Mrs. Logan.

Dr. Kronkite, witness for Louis Green.

Hon. Justice Muste, the Judge (and your trainer).

The case which follows is based on a real-life adversary proceeding in the Supreme Court in New York State. Many cases such as these which are scheduled to go to trial and settled out of court *before* they are presented to a jury. This case, however, went "all the way" (to quote the lawyers), and all the appropriate arguments were presented and heard (apparently) by jury.* The following data covers, in essence, the main arguments heard over a period of 4-½ days' time.†

Based on this information, which is excerpted below, indicate *what the essential problem is* and *how you would vote, if you were on the jury*.

January 18, 1964, fell on a Sunday. At approximately 5:30 a.m., Louis Green walked out of his downstairs flat, which he rented from Mrs. Logan, who lived

---

*The jury must rely on its "collective memory" in reaching a decision.
†With much time out for delays due to conflict in the court calendar.

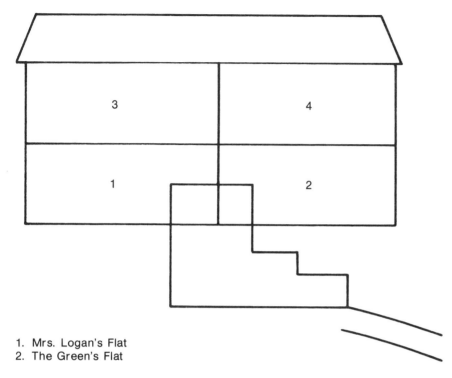

1. Mrs. Logan's Flat
2. The Green's Flat

Figure 8.9. Diagram of downstairs flat.

across the hall, and walked out onto the front stoop heading to work (see Figure 8.9). Green worked as an orderly in the Good Shepherd Hospital.* In order to get to work, Green (who did not own an automobile) had to catch a bus approximately one half mile from his home. He proceeded across the short porch, stepped onto the top step of a flight of concrete stairs leading onto the walk (five steps) and slipped down this flight of stairs.

Green landed in a puddle of icy water underneath the eaves of the house. He claimed that he hurt his back in the process. His cries attracted the attention of his wife, Mabel, who was pregnant at the time. She came out, saw his predicament and realized that her husband was unable to move. An ambulance was secured from the Good Shepherd Hospital. After about 20 minutes, the ambulance finally arrived, having considerable difficulty getting in the drive due to the icy conditions of the road and sidewalk. One of the ambulance attendants slipped on the walk as he was carrying the stretcher to pick up Green, who was still in icy water under the eaves.

*He earned $68 per week.

In the hospital, Green was x-rayed and remained under doctor's care for a period of about ten days before being released. After release, he wore a back brace for approximately six months. He admits that he is now fully recovered.

Green came into court claiming money damages against Mrs. Logan on the ground that she had not maintained the front stairs properly. Green claimed that Mrs. Logan had allowed the snow and ice to accumulate over a period of ten days to two weeks prior to January 18, 1964. Green claimed that the snow and ice had become "hard and lumpy." He further claimed that he had talked with Mrs. Logan to gain her permission to clean the stairs and walk on two occasions before the date of the accident, the last time on January 17, 1964. He claimed he had done this because of his concern for his pregnant wife.

Green stated that Mrs. Logan had not permitted him to touch the stairs because she said that this might harm the concrete if he were to chip the ice. She also would not, according to Green, allow anyone to put salt on the stairs since this would also ruin the concrete. There was no guardrail on the stairs.

Green's testimony was corroborated to a large extent by his wife, Mabel, who made a good impression on the jury.

A former neighbor, Mrs. O'Hara, was brought in as a "surprise witness." She claimed to have heard about Green's request to Mrs. Logan to clean the stairs. However, in the cross-examination of Mrs. O'Hara, Mr. Formidable, attorney for Mrs. Logan, succeeded in getting Mrs. O'Hara to admit that she was no friend of Mrs. Logan, and that, in fact, she had sued Mrs. Logan herself for another cause. Her testimony was, therefore, largely discredited.

Green's injuries were described by Dr. Kronkite: bad back injury with no permanent complication. Total medical expenses amounted to about $300, plus loss of salary.

Dr. Kronkite's testimony was not contested by Mr. Formidable since the latter did not deny the injury. It was Formidable's contention that the fall was Green's own fault in not taking proper precautions in going down the stairs. Formidable also claimed that Green was in a hurry to catch his bus to the hospital and should have gotten out earlier in that kind of weather.

Mrs. Logan is a woman in her late seventies. It is obvious that she is a very proud and strong-willed individual. There is no doubt that she kept her apartment (flats) in good condition, especially in view of the fact that the rental was only $35 per month. This was brought out by the questions asked of her by Mr. Formidable. She denied any knowledge of any conversation with either Mr. Green or Mrs. Green concerning the cleaning of the stairs or walk before the date of the accident.

It was her contention that there was no need to clean the stairs or walks since the stairs and walk were clear. Since the freezing rain had not begun until about 2:00 on the morning of the accident, it was her contention that this was something on which she could have done nothing. The freezing rain was conceded by both parties. Mr. Formidable pointed out to the jury that the freezing rain was a "general condition . . . all over the City of_____" and that Mrs. Logan could not be held responsible for such an event starting very late during the night.

Mr. Dowdy, attorney for the Greens, produced weather bureau records which showed that it had precipitated several times during the week prior to the accident and that two days before the accident it had snowed about one half inch.

Under cross-examination by Mr. Dowdy, Mrs. Logan stated that she was able to take care of the walk and sidewalk by herself and that she did not need the help of her tenants in keeping the place clean; that this was *her* responsibility. She also stuck to her denial of any conversation with the Greens about cleaning the walk the day before the accident.

Layout of Mrs. Logan's Four-flat unit is illustrated Figure 8.9.

To What Extent Was Justice Done in This Case?

While it is improbable that no two juries will arrive at an identical conclusion, trainees may be curious in learning the "real-life" solution to this case. The following summarizes the collective thinking of the original jury and its verdict.

The fact is that the plaintiff, Mr. Green, did fall and was injured. We have no doubt in our minds that there had been a freezing rain early that morning, as was conceded by both parties. We surmise that the concrete stairs were completely unprotected as there is no indication that the porch had a roof extending over the stairs. Also, there is no mention of a rain spout which presumably would have carried some of the water away from the stairs or would have prevented an excessive amount from accumulating on the stairs.

There was no railing on the stairs.

We are discounting the records about precipitation several times during the week prior to the day of the accident since, in our minds, this had no immediate bearing on the accident itself. The fact that there was a freezing rain very early that morning would be sufficient, without prior precipitation, for one to assume that the stairs would be icy and slippery. We are discounting the conversation that the plaintiff, Mr. Green, claims to have had with the defendant, Mrs. Logan. His seeking permission to clear the stairs the day before would not have prevented the ice from forming early that morning. We are also disallowing the neighbor's testimony as prejudiced.

Mrs. Logan, the defendant, stated that she did not require help from the tenants in keeping the place clean; that was her responsibility. The defendant's attorney, Mr. Formidable, pointed out that the freezing rain was a "general condition" and that Mrs. Logan could not be held responsible for such an event which started very late during the night. With these things in mind, we must reach the conclusion that there is no proof of negligence on the part of the plaintiff, Mr. Green. Short of having slid down the stairs on his derriere, there is little that he could have done to prevent the fall. While it is claimed that he was hurrying to catch his bus and should have started earlier because of the icy conditions, there is no proof that he was, in fact, hurrying. As to his starting out earlier because of icy conditions, the freezing rain had begun late in the night so he most likely would not be aware of conditions until he arose that morning. He could not use a railing to support himself in descending since the stairs had no railing. He could not have used salt on the stairs since he was not permitted to do this. Thus, we found for the plaintiff, Mr. Green. He was injured through no fault of his own.

The original jury awarded Green approximately $1800, which was intended to cover all expenses, including attorney's fees. Inflation would make this worth about $3000 in 1973.

Additional Information for Trainer

The purpose of this case is *not* to discuss the laws of negligence. However, trainees will seek, during the postenactment discussion, an explanation of what negligence implies.

Contributory negligence means any want of ordinary care on the part of the person injured. It is stated in the summary that contributory negligence in this case would be based on what a "reasonable person" would do under similar circumstances. A "reasonable person" could be defined as rational, clear-headed and reasoning; having the faculty of reason; governed by reason. Ordinary care is that degree of care which persons of ordinary care and prudence are accustomed to use and employ. "Ordinary negligence" lies in the field of inadvertence (heedlessness). Reasonable care is such a degree of care, precaution or diligence as may fairly and properly be expected. Reasonable care means *not* extraordinary care but such care as an ordinarily prudent person would exercise under the conditions existing at the time.

The weight of judicial opinion is that the attempt to divide negligence, or its opposite due care, into degrees will often lead to confusion and uncertainty. The distinction in degrees of care is unscientific and impracticable as the law furnishes no definition of these terms which can be applied in practice.

Resume Exercise

To what extent does the education and experience of a new potential employee accurately reflect the manpower needs of an organization? How are these needs seen (by managers and supervisors) when confronted with a real candidate? Normally, of course, the selection and placement of new employees is a specialized staff function. Consequently, the line manager tends to be faced with a *fait accompli* when the new employee is referred to his unit. Even when the manager has the option for a screening interview, the chances are good that irreversible decisions have already been made topside. The interview becomes a social formality.

Line managers, *as individuals*, will perceive the organization for which they work in many different ways. If given a suitable forum, their understandings, opinions, prejudices and intuitive feelings may be reflected in a variety of responses. Despite popular claims of organizational homogeneity,* people in organizations will certainly reflect highly diverse views and attitudes. The larger the organization, the greater such diversity.

When managers with such apparently divergent outlooks are forced to achieve consensus on *what* questions they would ask of a new college recruit and *why* they consider these questions to be significant, we have the touchstone for our exercise. Ideally, the managers (the trainees) should all be members of the same organization and be at about the same level of power or rank. Managerial attitudes will be examined through application of this exercise, and in the hands of a skillful trainer, the exercise will also be aimed at a more accurate trainee self image, *within the context of the work environment.*

Reacting to the Resume

How the Exercise Operates

The trainer shall have prepared one or more hypothetical resumes, which a *new college-level* applicant would have submitted along with his formal application for employment. Each resume will contain data on education, employment (paid and unpaid), extracurricular activities, hobbies and other interests. *Variables* within the fictional resume will relate specifically to items which will be apt to engender personal feelings among the trainees. A sample resume, along with suggested variables, is shown in Figures 8.10 and 8.11.

The selection and arrangement of the variables will depend on the trainer's understandings of the organization and the trainees participating in the exercise. First of all, like or compatible variables must be drawn together. For instance, it would make little sense to include affiliations with both the New Democratic Coalition and volunteer work for Senator James Buckley of New York. Secondly, there will be other variables that the imaginative trainer can introduce which undoubtedly will be more effective in helping to polarize the trainee groups than those shown on p. 193.

*William H. Whyte, *The Organization Man* (New York: Simon and Schuster, Inc., 1956).

RESUME

Stephen P. Hemphill*
9828 Westmere Boulevard
Clearview, New Jersey 01875

Single (Born 3/3/   )
SSN: 069-12-8308

Telephone: (517) 439-4247

Elementary School: Clearview, New Jersey

High School: Clearview High School (19   )
        National Merit Semifinalist

College: Tufts University
        A.B. Degree (19   ) (Cum Laude)
        Double Major in Business Administration and Economics

Employment History:
        Two summers (while in high school) packer and checker at Shoppe and
        Save Markets, Clearview, New Jersey.

        Gas station attendant, North Paramus, New Jersey (part-time,
        vacations).

        (While in college) construction laborer: one summer, H & S Home
        Builders, Plainview, New Jersey.

        Timekeeper, two summers for same firm.

---

*If trainer decides that female resume is required, make changes in name and in employ-
ment as may be necessary.

Figure 8.10. Resume of Stephen P. Hemphill.

The trainees are organized into small groups of three or four (no leaders to be designated) and have received these instructions.

The objective of this exercise is to decide *as a group* which questions an interviewer should *plan* on asking the individual whose name appears on the resume.

1. Chapter vice president—New Democratic Coalition	2. Chapter vice president—Young Americans for Freedom
3. Worked as volunteer in Buckley campaign for Senate in New York State	4. Worked as volunteer in Wallace campaign for President
5. Worked as volunteer in McGovern campaign for President	6. Spent junior year studying at University of Vienna (Austria); wide travel throughout Europe, including Eastern Europe
7. Worked in Newark ghetto teaching black youth basic consumer economics	8. Volunteer researcher for Ralph Nader on cost-profit ratios in auto industry
9. Two years ROTC (resigned in junior year)	10. Hobbies: guitar and folk singing
11. Hobbies: backpacking and spelunking	12. Member: Sierra Club
13. Member: Zero Population Growth	14. Member: National Rifle Association
15. Member: golfing team	16. Member: football team
17. Member: investment club	18. President: Business and Government Club
19. Associate Editor, Student Weekly Press	20. Organizer: College chapter of Friends for a Democratic Rhodesia
21. Treasurer: college chapter of Gay Liberation Movement	22. Member: Black Student Alliance
23. Member: Theater Group, Greater Boston College Association	24. Member: Guerilla Theater Movement
25. President: Intervarsity Christian Fellowship (an evangelical, fundamentalist movement)	26. Resident advisor, Black Cultural Center
27. Counselor to Help (local volunteer drug addiction clinic)	28. College representative for "Ramparts" magazine
29. Chapter president of National Organization for Women (NOW)	30. Member: League of Women Voters
31. Member: Daughters of the American Revolution (DAR)	32. Organizer: Shirley Chisholm campaign for president

Figure 8.11. Variables for Resume. Select four or five compatible variables to be added to basic resume document for typing, duplication and distribution to trainees (where appropriate, substitute for summer employment).

This person is a strong candidate for an entry-level professional job in your organization. (Resume copies are handed out to all members for study and to make notes.)

Each question must be stated in writing. Every question must be rated—from most important to least important. The *rationale* for each question, in terms of organizational needs, should also be noted by the group. This will be used during the followup discussion period. Finally, assume that the individual (whose name is on the resume) were to ask you (as a group) what the advantages are to joining the organization. In other words, why should someone *want* to work for your outfit? Insofar as practical, decisions relating to all aspects of this exercise shall be reached through a consensus of group members.

Other Suggestions on How to Use Exercise

"Reacting to the Resume" is intended as an organizational development exercise—one which may be put into practice at several different levels. First of all, it may be applied by the trainer as a diagnostic mechanism. It will open up the trainee's thinking: a self-appraisal of personal attitudes towards this hypothetical outsider about to be thrust into one's unit. The trainer will also have his perceptions awakened. What manner of people are these with whom he is working? Is *this* how they feel? Why are they asking these kinds of questions? Why these doubts?

Secondly, at the later stages of organizational development, there is an opportunity to explore what kinds of new employees should be added to the organization. Trainees who have developed to the point where they are more in touch with their special organizational culture and are aware of the urgency for change will experience through the exercise the need for plans to implement such changes.

Another result should be the sharing of both common and unique reactions. This is because the exercise serves to expose deep-seated trainee values. The skillful trainer should be able to get the trainees to reveal the real reasons for their positions toward certain information within the resume. This feature of the exercise contributes to trust-building.

In a slightly different vein, this exercise may be adapted for use by personnel people to root out deeply held personal biases toward potential employees who can provide beneficial inputs for the organization.

Finally, for an exhaustive and interesting analysis of the special problems presented to organizations by employees of today's generation, the reader is urged to consult David Nadler's *The Now Employee.** Treated here in a very readable fashion are many of the issues likely to be generated by this exercise. Trainers will find several ready rewards in tying together Nadler's observations in *The NOW Employee* during the post exercise discussion of "Reacting to the Resume."

Exercise Objectives and Suggested Questions

One objective of the exercise is to examine the organizational *image* in terms of people being hired.

What image does the organization project?† How does the image become altered by people?

To what degree does management have a role in setting the image or in altering it?

In what way does an organization change in response to societal pressures? (We know that resistance to change is in inherent factor within systems. We also know that absolute resistance to change may lead to stagnation.) How is organizational renewal enhanced by a greater openness in attitude towards the acquisition of "new blood"?

Other questions

Are we recycling our errors by perpetuating outmoded attitudes as reflected in the people being hired?

What is the attitude of the organization toward women as managers? Is this attitude valid? Should it be changed?

What are our current attitudes toward the recruitment of minority personnel?

When new employees are sought, what are we looking for? (Discuss "low profile" people versus others.)

*David A. Nadler, *The NOW Employee* (Houston: Gulf Publishing Company, 1971).
†Roger Harrison, "Understanding Your Organization's Character," *Harvard Business Review* 50, no. 3.

Does the organization—as an entity—give greater attention to people or things? (This will lead toward a discussion of the *Managerial Grid** as applied to the work system.)

Trainees' perception of this: How important or significant is involvement in controversial or sensitive issues while in college?

Will the new employee rock the boat?

Does the organizational "boat" need rocking? If so, why?

Is the new employee likely to *embarrass* the organization or harm it financially? Explain.

How much *uniformity* is desirable within the organization?†

How is uniformity acquired?

In what way is uniformity ensured or enforced?

Suggestions for Using and Developing Complex Learning Exercises

Just as the learner learns how to learn, proceeding from case studies through various stages to more complicated roleplays, so the writer of such exercises should be equipped to move from simple to intricate materials. Consequently, one should not attempt the development of a complex exercise without first having achieved reasonable success with cases and simple covert roleplays. This is not to say that when the trainer perceives a real-life situation which may be captured as a complex exercise, he should not take pen in hand and get it down for future application. Unfortunately, the *matching* of real-life events (i.e., describing what happened as a sort of potential object lesson) with the objectives of a course is often impossible. Lacking a specially written exercise to meet the needs of his trainees, the trainer may fail to do what he knows should be done. The unenterprising trainer will introduce a ready-made exercise, perhaps not on target, but one which is "fairly close"

*Robert R. Blake and Jane S. Mouton, *The Managerial Grid* (Houston: Gulf Publishing Company, 1964).
†Reader should be familiar with lyrics in "How to Succeed in Business without Really Trying" by Frank Loesser. See, especially, the song, "The Company Way."

and one that trainees are "sure to enjoy." This is hardly an acceptable solution.*

Creating a complex exercise is, in and of itself, a problem in creative problem-solving. Creativity can be enhanced in everyone. A process for augmenting human creativeness is described in *Supplementary Guide*, a publication of The Creative Education Foundation† (Chase Hall, State University College, 1300 Elmwood Avenue, Buffalo, New York 14222).

One issue must be discussed before beginning the complex exercise. This, in the broadest sense, concerns the needs of the trainees. Exactly how does one capitalize on their needs when classroom efforts are structured. We decide, for instance, that the trainees will accept more readily what we have in mind if they are involved in the learning. This is something trainers know intuitively. What we are not certain of, however, is what *level* of matching is optimal between the contents an exercise and the trainees' back-on-the-job requirements. But we are aware of the application of general learning principles, which have been treated in Chapter 1. These are recapped in the form of questions.

1. Are the trainees ready, through past experiences, to tackle an exercise with more than a reasonable probability of success?
2. Will the trainees readily perceive the connection between the purpose of an exercise and the realities of their organizational existence?
3. Is there a reasonable assurance that the results of their work on a suitable exercise will provide a transference to the work environment?
4. Will the inclusion of the exercise within the framework of the total course complement the other proposed learning? In other words, will we have a completely balanced and compatible instructional package?
5. Has sufficient time been set aside for an exercise?

Points 1, 2 and 3 concern the trainees and their "exercise readiness."

---

*The evaluation of any creative learning exercise is difficult, and it becomes even more confused when interesting and even exciting, but off-target materials are used. See chapter on "Evaluating Employee Development", by H.M. Engel, in Kenneth T. Byers, ed., *Employee Training and Development in the Public Service* (Chicago: Public Personnel Association, 1970).

†This organization was founded by Alex F. Osborn, See *Applied Imagination* (New York: Charles Scribner's Sons, 1963). *See also* publications by Sidney J. Parnes. Information on publications, some of which are available gratis, may be obtained by writing the Creative Education Foundation.

Points 4 and 5 relate to the course design and course management. If the answer to these five questions is "yes," work can be begun.

Creating a Complex Learning Exercise

1. State the *purposes* or *objectives* of the exercise. This is done primarily to maintain a focus, as we brainstorm for ideas to achieve our purposes.
2. State the *operational perimeters* of the instructional setting. This includes "reminder-type" data on group size, maximum training time available, the nature of group (strangers versus family) and similar facts which fix the outside limits of this exercise.
3. Arbitrarily, *fix a numerical goal* for exercise ideas. Usually eight to ten is sufficient for most purposes.
4. A small, intimate group tends to yield the quickest results in *brainstorming*. Accordingly, we should seek the assistance of a colleague or an associate in generating the forced growth of exercise ideas. Points 1 and 2 are explained to our helpers. Have available a blackboard or flip chart for listing ideas. No ideas should be rejected, no matter how outlandishly remote. Encourage the amendment and amalgamation of one concept with another. For example, a rereading of case study file records may kindle dormant thoughts through the building of one idea on another.

As you brainstorm, put yourself in the place of the trainees. What are they looking for? Why are they participating in training? What do they hope to get out of the sessions?

Allow a reasonable amount of time to elapse after ideas have been accumulated. Sleep overnight on ideas; new ones will spring up during the interim period. The *form* of the idea for the exercise is your goal. Once you have that worked out, writing the specific details become similar to clothing a mannequin in a store window. The writing process is that which has been discussed elsewhere under case study and roleplay construction.

Simulation and Business Games

In the broadest sense, every training method which provides for trainee involvement and participation represents a form of simulation. Many varieties of roleplays clearly intend to simulate a back-on-the-job situation. Unfortunately, the word *simulation* has been tagged with a rather special meaning. It has today become largely a euphemism for a business game. Management will accept the word "simulation;" it is less likely to tolerate the word "game." Therefore a business game is sold and adopted as a simulation exercise.

Complex learning exercises are those containing some or all of the features of covert roleplaying for three or more participants. Such learning exercises tend to focus in, insofar as objectives are concerned, on the human elements involved. We have more than a passing curiosity with the individual behavior, the group behavior and the interface between such behaviors and the fixed organizational systems. Within complex learning exercises, rules of procedure tend to be *open* and *flexible*, permitting and even encouraging the trainees to bring into the exercise experiences from their jobs or their homes. During the post exercise analysis, such experiences may add to the trainees' introspective analysis of what they "did right or wrong."

In simulation, on the other hand, we are confronted with *rules*, procedures and a typical "gaming" ingredient: *competition*. The popular Parker Brothers' game, Monopoly, represents a well-known illustration of a simulation exercise. The game's objective is to accumulate real estate, to collect rents, to destroy competition and, ultimately, to achieve a monopoly.

Sophisticated simulation exercises apply the use of the computer in solving problems. At General Electric's executive development center at Crotonville, New York, computer terminals are readily available to the trainees when they are working at their simulation problems, many of which have strong mathematical components.

A recent study of simulation by Marullo and Cribbin* produced the following observation.

> On the cost question, the technique's critics say that simulations—unlike the incident process, in-basket technique, case study, or even the video tape approach—often require special rooms for each team of participants, calculating machines, computer terminals and possibly even an intercommunication system. Also, the critics question the amount of knowledge that is transferred from the simulation situation to the work environment. The participants, they say, may become so involved with winning—or at least achieving the best results—that they lose sight of the true purpose of the simulation.

This study also revealed that simulation methods were not used by a majority of the largest corporations in the country and that many viewed

---

*Jerome Marullo and James J. Cribbin, "Whatever Happened to Management Simulation," *Management Review* 61, no. 5.

simulation as inappropriate since it tended to stress "the technical and mechanistic aspects" of the organization.

9. The In-Basket

Imagine a situation where a supervisor or manager enters into a new assignment and has received little or no in-depth briefing about the assignment beforehand. Having been "thrown-in" with very little preparation, he is required to *act on his own* without the assistance of *anyone* in the organization. The individual who held the position previously has left suddenly—either through promotion or death.

His secretary is not available, and he must rely on his own wits to determine exactly what must be done with the in-basket items facing him. The factor of time is a key ingredient within this kind of situation. Unreal? Artificial or contrived? Perhaps these descriptions may seem appropriate but many participants of in-basket exercises might argue otherwise after having gone through such an exercise.

The in-basket is, as its title indicates, a group of materials found in an in-basket by a supervisor or manager who has just been moved into a position with which he has had little previous connection. He must dig through these papers to determine exactly what has to be done within the available time. Decision-making is one of the essential ingredients within the in-basket exercise. This chapter explores when the in-basket is likely to be most effective, where materials can be obtained for in-basket exercises and how such materials should be employed. The in-basket differs from case studies and roleplaying in one important aspect. The individual trainee works by himself, charting his own path through the maze of materials in the in-basket. After the completion of the individual tasks, the scene is usually set for group discussions on how the in-basket decisions made by the individuals compare with one another. Consequently, the in-basket may lead into case discussions or even into open roleplaying.

Using In-Basket Training

Invented originally as a device for manager selection,* the in-basket was modified—as to its purposes—and converted into a learning exercise. Some candid observations about the typical in-basket exercise are noted in order that trainers consider the appropriateness of this method in terms of their instructional objectives.

Trainees participate under *stress conditions*. As a rule, they work at the exercise by themselves, studying and reacting to complex interlocking written materials. Ideally, each trainee should have a desk where he is able to spread out the material within the in-basket packet, read, analyze and act on it. Clearly, the trainee's reading speed may become an important factor when applying this method.

As they struggle with their individual packets, some trainees look over at other trainnes to see how far along they are. For some, this may spark a flashback to school days when they were struggling with a tough quiz. As they sweated over a series of especially difficult questions, there always seemed to be one or two "brains" who had it all wrapped up! The psychological value of such unplanned competition among adults may be dubious.

The *time available* for critical decision-making is another hallmark of the in-basket exercise. Customarily, the trainer fixes some sort of deadline, which includes time for study, analysis and decision-making. The trainer must also allocate sufficient time for the group discussion and summarization. All of this must fit within the total time available for the session. Consequently, at some given point the trainer must halt the individual efforts, regardless of how much or little each trainee has accomplished.

If the factor of speed is relatively insignificant, as far as the objectives of the exercise are concerned, then the trainer may find it advantageous to permit the trainees to handle the exercise on a homework assignment basis. Lengthy, complicated in-baskets are thus analyzed and the various decisions made back in the room (if the training is part of a residential program) or at home.

*The reader interested in how to use the in-basket as a tool for picking budding executives should consult F.M. Lopez Jr., *Evaluating Executive Decision Making—The In-Basket Technique* (New York: American Management Association, AMA Research Study 75, 1966).

When compared to roleplaying, the in-basket is a passive training tool. The initial action flows through the barrel of a pen. In some ways the in-basket is akin to a series of parallel and interlocking case studies upon which each participant decides action he would take. In the in-basket exercise, the trainee develops and writes out his answers. At the same time, he notes the order in which he would do or would not do what appears to be necessary.

To some trainees, especially those at higher levels of management, a certain artificiality seems to exist in the required use of the pen. Such managers being exposed to the in-basket may admit, as they advance through the exercise, that their secretaries perform most of their dirty work. In fact, there are trainees who have seemingly lost the skill to write rapidly. For them, the transcription device or secretary has largely replaced the writing instrument.

Trainers using the in-basket are able, at least theoretically, to fix objectives with some precision, depending on the emphasis sought. An ideal outcome should have been prepared, based on the ideas which the developer of the exercise had in mind before it was assembled. In roleplaying, on the other hand, many ideal solutions are apt to develop, some of which are being heard by the trainer for the first time as he uses his exercise.

If these factors and opinions are considered as a whole, the in-basket would be recommended primarily for entry-level managerial development programs. With a few specialized exceptions, above the first level of management, the methodology required by this exercise is likely to be inhibiting and counterproductive. However, among newer additions to the managerial staff of an organization, its competitive features might well be desirable as a hidden exercise objective. Trainers equipped professionally or through experience to evaluate those trainees who are bright enough "to cut the mustard" and those who "need attention" may find the in-basket to be a profitable assessment mechanism.

Having studied both the advantages and limitations of the in-basket and having determined that for his purposes the former clearly outweighs the latter, the trainer would proceed as follows. He would construct the in-basket (or select one which conforms to needs). He would then reproduce instructions and items and sort, identify and assemble items into envelope packets. A word of caution: if in-basket items resemble the organization's normal letter or memo head, each sheet must be clearly marked as belonging to the training in-basket. Sometimes the items are so similar to the real thing that they may inadvertently slip into the interoffice mail, causing much confusion. Before packets are sealed, recheck to ensure that each is complete and that no duplicate items are present.

Trainees (having been selected and assembled in the training location) are briefed on what they are about to do. For maximum training effect, trainees should have had experiences with both case studies and roleplaying. The depth of the trainer's briefing will hinge, therefore, on the sophistication of the group. Generally, all that needs to be done is a common reading of the in-basket instructions. Questions about the organization chart, if one is included, are cleared up before everyone is told, "O.K., open up your packets and start working."

The trainees work. At a predetermined point in time, the trainer calls for a halt to the exercise. For some trainees who have not finished, this may appear to be arbitrary. If a break period can be scheduled, those completing early are permitted to leave the room, allowing the slower trainees to continue for a few extra minutes.

The discussion period will be devoted to two factors:

1. A consideration of the trainee's plan of attack
2. An assessment of the substantive materials within the in-basket and the completed decision-making

The trainee's plan of attack looks like this. Every in-basket contains four kinds of items.

1. Some items have been inserted as *distractors*. By themselves these appear important, but when stacked up against other items, they shrink in insignificance.
2. There are *isolated* items of some substance but which do not affect other items when acted upon.
3. Items having a *one-way* interface with other items are included. This means that if the trainee decides to resolve Item X in a particular way, he will automatically be affecting Item Y.
4. Items which possess a *mutual* or two-way interface are present. The action with Item W affects Item Z; conversely, Item Z affects Item W. Here the decisions made by the trainees must be mutually compatible.

Another way of assessing the trainees' plan of attack is to assign a value as to the importance of each item. Did the trainee plow methodically through the in-basket, reading each item very carefully and acting on each as he read it? Or did he scan all items, sorting out the most important, leaving the less important for the cleanup period? The effective use of available time is also part of the trainee's plan of attack and should be discussed.

The second broad factor for discussion, assessment of the in-basket's substantive materials, is nearly identical to the process described under case study methods. Open roleplay is available for testing decisions when these are in dispute. For instance, one trainee proposes a particular solution to a key in-basket problem; another trainee disagrees and opts for a different outcome. Both solutions should be roleplayed, evaluating the advantages-disadvantages of each.

An alternate method of assessing trainee effectiveness when handling the in-basket's substantive features is to determine (after all items have been completed and the total in-basket assembled) the optimal solutions for all items. Having the advantage of more time than the trainees, the trainer is able to decide, with a high degree of certainty, that one course of action is indeed preferable to another. He is also in a position to document his reasoning. This analytical data is then stored for use during the post-analysis discussion. This approach is acceptable and even beneficial, provided the trainer uses this knowledge positively. One can easily get carried away with a "look and see how smart I am" attitude when leading the discussion.

In Jaffee's *Problems in Supervision: An In-Basket Training Exercise** he has devised a multiple choice quiz in which he challenges the trainees to select the best solution (one of three choices) for each item. This method is intended primarily for the trainee who is working at the in-basket by himself at his own pace.

Developing In-Basket Materials

Most in-basket exercises commence with a broad statement of introduction to the participant, acquainting him with his new role. The essential background of the role is also provided as well as his role relations with the people cited within the in-basket itself. An organizational chart is often shown so that he can visualize where he fits within the fictional organization. Following this introductory material, a calendar is sometimes included and, then, the main ingredients of the in-basket: key letters or memos in conflict with one another, memoranda suggesting further study, extraneous and insignificant letters and related trivia. Whether these items are recognized as trivia or as of consequence will depend to a great extent on the way that the participant attacks the exercise as well as his keenness and his perceptiveness.

The writer of the in-basket exercise has a unique challenge: dovetailing the

*Cabot L. Jaffee, *Problems in Supervision: An In-Basket Training Exercise* (Reading, Massachusetts: Addison-Wesley Publishing Company, 1968).

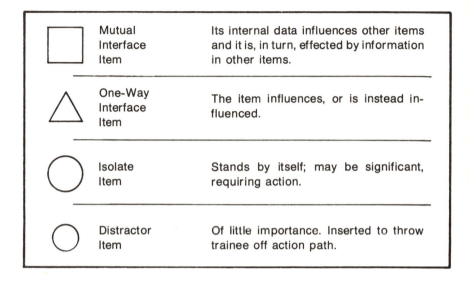

	Mutual Interface Item	Its internal data influences other items and it is, in turn, effected by information in other items.
	One-Way Interface Item	The item influences, or is instead influenced.
	Isolate Item	Stands by itself; may be significant, requiring action.
	Distractor Item	Of little importance. Inserted to throw trainee off action path.

Figure 9.1. Four symbols which identify four types of in-basket items.

objectives of the sessions with the capabilities of the training group members. For example, if the objectives of a sessions include delegation and decision-making, the writer of the in-basket exercise structures his items so that he fits the needs of the session with the language of the items.

The construction of no other form of original learning exercise seems to provide the level of job satisfaction than that emerging from the successful in-basket. For the seasoned writer of case studies, building an in-basket should be relatively easy, often providing considerable enjoyment in the process.

As has already been discerned in the review of in-basket usage, the typical in-basket exercise offers two challenges: *how* the trainee attacks the exercise and *what* he does about its internal problems. If the trainer is only concerned with the latter feature, traditional case studies would be equally effective. The carefully woven intermix of process and substance is, of course, the hallmark of the exercise. It should be remembered that an in-basket contains pieces of paper with writing; that the interrelationships of these papers are what contributes to the exercise's popularity; and that the total package must be integrated in order to meet the overall objectives. A diagram is one way of visualizing all of this (see Figure 9.1). Four basic symbols identify four types of in-basket items.

With these symbols at hand, the trainer is able to plan the in-basket writing strategy.

Fix Objectives

The in-basket's intrinsic features and its nearly limitless configurations which are open to the writer commend it for the trainer demanding a direct, interlocking relationship between objectives and methodology. An objective relating to improved communications among organizational units (stated, of course, in behavioral terms) guides the writer directly to the construction of mutual interface items. More than a single objective necessitates sufficient items to cover each. The writer must take care to establish a proper internal balance so that one group of items does not overshadow another.

Mutual Interface Items

The in-basket, "The Psychologist as an Administrator" (see Chapter 10), provides illustrations of these types of items in the "Xenofil" materials. Here are two other specific examples which demonstrate the distinction between one-way interface items and those with a mutual interface. *Language in a one-way interface item:* " . . . and so I'm asking you to contact Bill Boland, who, as you know, has been most anxious to learn our opinion about the Kirwin contract."

This becomes converted into a *mutual interface* item when the writer inserts a note in the in-basket from Bill Boland containing the following: " . . . Therefore, I've decided that the Kirwin contract should be cancelled as of September 1. I know that this may affect your plans, but given the present circumstances, there is little else to be done."

The foundation upon which the mutual interface items are built is to be found among these kinds of factors:

Changes of attitudes, opinions, etc,
Competition between parties
Complementary information/opinions
Conflicting information/opinions
Conflicting orders/directions
Differing priorities
Differing standards of values
Differing styles of management

Disagreement over . . .
Diverse ethical standards
Hostility
Incomplete information
Jealousy between parties
Misinterpretation or misunderstanding
Opposition to ideas, plans, proposals
Problems of timing
Rivalries
Suspicion and lack of trust
Undercutting
Understandings and misunderstandings

One-Way Interface Items

Although mutual interface items represent the heartland of the in-basket, the item which influences, or is in turn influenced by others, may be of near equal value in supporting the exercise's objectives. As an analogy, the mutual items are equivalent to the leading actors in a drama, whereas the one-way items provide the main supporting parts. These items should be written after the mutual interface portions have been prepared. They help flesh out the areas where, realistically, the mutual items could not fully do the job.

Isolate Items

The bright trainee who has screened the entire in-basket will quickly perceive the interconnection between and among certain items. These he will sort and commence working, according to discerned priorities. Items standing alone—not affecting any other item—may, nonetheless, call for high priority action. These are written for two reasons: to buttress objectives with materials of a broader dimension and to make the total exercise more realistic.

Distractor Items

Written last, these are, for the writer, the fun items. How will the trainee see these? Are these given equal weight with other more critical problems? Even so-called unimportant matters are apt to become transformed into something of importance when handled tactlessly.

How many items are necessary in an in-basket? In both theory and practice, an in-basket can contain a single item. Although this really is a variety of a case study, its form resembles the in-basket. Examples of mini in-baskets are included at the end of this chapter. Because the concept of the four basic types of items and the direct correlation between these and the typical in-basket exercise objectives has been accepted, the probable number of necessary items can be determined. Items should not be added simply to lengthen the in-basket and to create additional "challenges." Also sufficient time must be allotted, especially if the entire exercise is to be completed within the classroom setting. The number of distractor items should be kept low—certainly no more than three or four. For most in-baskets, the *average* of all items should not exceed about 25.

A random mixing of all items should be done before these are inserted in the exercise packet. To create a heightened level of realism, some items may be sealed in envelopes, stamped confidential or "Deliver Unopened." Such added fillips, when clerical assistance is available during the preparation process, add to the seeming genuineness of the exercise.

Instructions for Trainees

Although each trainee receives an oral explanation of the in-basket's intent before handling his individual packet of materials, the written instructions reinforce and clarify what may have been missed or misunderstood. In general, the instructions are intended to synthesize details of the assignments to be done:

1. Clear identification of the trainee's role ("You are . . .")
2. Those minimal facts which trainee must know to assume role
3. Organization charts, if these assist in clarifying role
4. A calendar, intended to assist the trainee, when many different dates are included in the items.

All completed items should be cross-checked against the instructions to ensure that trainees will comprehend the reasoning behind the total exercise. Even though the trainer has explained the rationale for the exercise, it still must stand on its own. Short sentences and short paragraphs should be used in writing the instructions because this makes reading easy. Within the in-basket's items, the style of writing should vary, as it would naturally in the correspondence and memos within a real in-basket.

Miscellaneous Suggestions

Item from Predecessor

In the exercise, "The Psychologist as an Administrator," is an illustration of the cozy, personal message from the person who held the position in which the trainee now must act decisively. Even when confronted with a deceased predecessor, it is possible to construct a type of last will and testament statement portending certain details about the parties who appear within the in-basket. How much stock is the trainee to place in this kind of confidential chit chat? Obviously some of the problems which the trainee is struggling with were caused by what the predecessor did or failed to do. Because of the diverse subjects covered within this kind of item, it is both a mutual and a one-way interface item. For instance, George Grater's observations about Xenofil and Dr. Levine, in the context of the total problem surrounding this issue, may require that Eager (the trainee) indicate the need for a follow-up telephone call to Grater for more information.

In lieu of the single broad item from one's predecessor, an in-basket may contain a series of summary statements about the people mentioned in the various memos and letters. These statements *must* be factually accurate, and unlike the letter from the predecessor, they should avoid any opinions about the strengths or weaknesses of these people.

Naming the Characters

The naming of the fictional parties was mentioned in the discussion on writing case study materials. Because of the complexities of the totally new organization with which the trainee is confronted in the in-basket, every reasonable mnemonic device should be resorted to facilitate the identification of who is who and where each fits. Alliterative names, such as Lucifer Latter, while admittedly a bit unusual, are nonetheless helpful for our purposes.

Figure 9.2 demonstrates the arrangement and number sequence of item writing for the in-basket and will help the reader to visualize the process.

Start with the most significant mutual interface item (1), tying this to the next most important mutual interface item (2). This item should then be connected to the third most important mutual interface item (3). Next, the writer has the option of hooking the third mutual interface item to a one-way interface item (4). The writing and arrangement of succeeding one-way interface items is then in order (items 5 through 8). The isolate and distractor items,

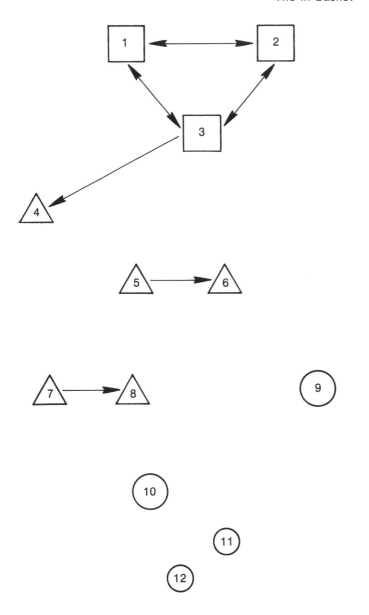

Figure 9.2. Arrangement and numeric sequence of item writing for the in-basket.

shown as 9 through 12 in the diagram, are written last. After all items are written, rearrange in a random fashion.

Mini In-Basket #1

Background Data

You are Craig Bigelow, the resident manager of the two-million square foot Montgomery Mills complex in the city of Tryon, Pennsylvania.

You have been with the firm for over 15 years. Your father and grandfather before you had been key employees in the Montgomery Corporation. Your grandfather was the inventor of a key process which made this firm what it is today. When the Corporation decided to move its main plant south some 20 months ago, you were given a choice of going along or remaining in Tryon as the resident manager of the mill. It was your decision to stay in the North to handle the firm's Tryon real estate.

Most of the plant has been empty for about a year and a half, ever since the move occurred. Your staff of about 18 consists of maintenance workers, repairmen and power plant people. Your major responsibility is to rent building space. You have, of course, very excellent relations with the mayor of Tryon, and you are a great local booster of the city. Obviously, there are many sentimental reasons for this fact. You were certainly opposed to the plant's move to the South.

So far, you have succeeded in renting about 30,000 square feet to a subsidiary of Happy Smile Baby Foods (Klip-Klap Toys). You have strong prospects for several small firms and have developed good contacts with the Commonwealth's Commerce Department. There are many other "live" possibilities, one of which may take about 200,000 square feet.

Within the structure of the Montgomery organization, you now report to the Controller, Eric Chase. As a rule, you talk to Eric about twice a week. You've visited the southern plants only once since the move took place.

Confidential letter from Frank Lucas to Craig Bigelow

(Note: Lucas is an old, trusted friend in the Montgomery Corporation. He is in charge of the polyurethane processing division. Unlike you, Lucas decided to move South.)

October 9, 1972

Dear Craig:

I'm writing you this in the strictest confidence and am asking you to destroy this after you've read it. Please don't leave it lying around.

First off: Heard from Jim Muldy [he's Eric Chase's #1 boy] that the sale of the entire M.M. complex in Tryon is going to be announced in about a week. He wasn't certain, but he thinks that *Happy Smile Baby Foods Corp.* is the probable buyer. How does that grab you?

Second, and this is *really* why I'm writing you, the "old man" is still pretty ticked off at you for not having come South. I heard him make a crack at an "executive" cocktail party night before last to the effect that you "had deliberately cut yourself off" from the firm which "had done so much for your family!" I know that's a lot of crap—and I probably stuck my neck out because I told him that the firm "wouldn't be where it is today if it weren't for your family."

In any event, the old man replied that you were welcome to all that "ice and snow"—and made another comment about your enthusiasm for winter sports.

I think that you might be in for a shafting—which is why I'm writing you. If the old buildings are sold, they'll be forcing you to come South. Right now I don't know of many openings for someone at your level. I know that with those seven kids you can't afford to be out in the cold for too long. So, I thought that as an old buddy, I'd better tip you off as to what's cooking. I'd hate to see you sever your ties with Montgomery—but you're a big boy and undoubtedly know your own mind!

Cherrio and keep smiling!

KLIP-KLAP TOYS

A Division of Happy Smile Baby Foods

Tryon, Pennsylvania

October 12, 1972

Mr. Craig Bigelow
The Montgomery Corporation
Tryon, Pennsylvania

Dear Craig:

This is to advise you that our lease, which as you know, is due to expire three months from the date of this letter, will probably not be renewed. Our plans are, at this time, yet to be defined. It may be that we shall seek a month-by-month extension, if our headquarters have failed to resolve relocation, or other decisions on which it is now working.

You will be hearing from Mr. Clifford Pritchard, Happy Smile's Rental Manager, in about a week or so, I assume. I am giving you this advance notice since our lease so requires.

I assume you'll be contacting me after you receive this.

Sincerely,

Dennis McKenzie
Plant Manager

Mini In-Basket #2

INTERNATIONAL AIR TRANSPORT CORPORATION

Memorandum (Confidential)

FROM: Mark Osborn—vice-president in charge of Industrial Relations

TO: Fred Madison—director of Organizational Development
Wednesday, March 1, 1972

Fred:

Have had to scoot down to Miami on an important union grievance matter, otherwise would have conveyed message to you in person.

As you are aware, the Chief has been getting a lot of heat lately about our executive group sensing sessions. While you and I realize that these are a vital component in our entire OD program, there are a couple of guys (and you probably know whom I am talking about) who would like, for obvious reasons, to see the whole program scuttled.

I am asking you to get your staff together and to prepare a position paper outlining the advantages of continuing on our present course. List all the benefits (and show the disadvantages as well). Produce an even-handed product—but one which, of course, supports our position.

Since we've had but three sessions to date, you'll agree that we've hardly had a chance to move toward real team building. Unless we tear down some of the distrust and conniving, I'm afraid the Chief's in for *real* trouble, and you are aware where that will leave you and me. Please have this ready for me when I get back on Friday, so that we can talk about it first thing on the morning of the 3rd.

10. Two In-Basket Exercises

This chapter consists of two traditional in-basket exercises:

1. The Branch Manager's In-Basket
2. The Psychologist as an Administrator

Both exercises may be used by lay trainee personnel. Trainees in the private sector will probably be able to identify more readily with the branch manager's problems. Professionals in the public and nonprofit sector (physicians, social workers, educators, psychologists, librarians and attorneys) may be more attracted to the second exercise.

The Branch Manager's In-Basket

Instructions for Participants

Read Carefully

You are Bill Dollar. Currently, you are the associate manager of the Firey Bush Branch of the Beltway—Metropolitan National Banks, as shown on the attached organization charts (Figures 10.1 and 10.2). You are accustomed to fill in when problems develop in other branches and have stepped in to help out at the Lingerland Branch last August. Today is Saturday, the 4th day of February, 19__. The time is 8:00 p.m. The snow has just stopped. You have just received a phone

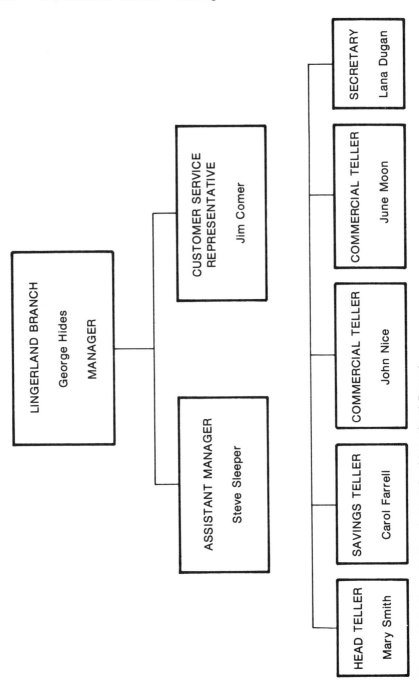

Figure 10.1. Organizational chart for Lingerland Branch.

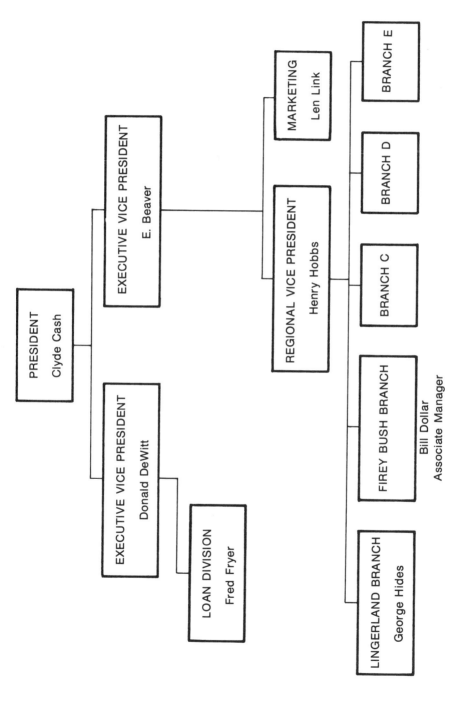

Figure 10.2. Organizational chart for Beltway-Metropolitan National Banks.

FEBRUARY						
S	M	T	W	T	F	S
			1	2	3	4
5	6	7	8	9	10	11
12	13	14	15	16	17	18
19	20	21	22	23	24	25
26	27	28				

Figure 10.3. Calendar for February.

call at home from Henry Hobbs telling you that George Hides (manager of the Lingerland branch) hurt himself shoveling snow and that you will have to manage the Lingerland branch for at least one week.

Hides has a severe disk problem—he should not have been shoveling—but the 16-inch fall evidently snowed him in. Now he is in the orthopedic unit in Central City General Hospital!

You are already scheduled to attend an important in-bank sales training seminar at the home office in Central City beginning at 10:30 a.m. Monday, the 6th. (A calendar is shown in Figure 10.3). You will return to the Lingerland branch on Wednesday morning. You have about 30 minutes on Monday morning in which to handle the problems in your basket.

Assume now that you've gotten in to your office at the Lingerland branch at 7:30 on Monday morning. The attached items are all in the in-basket. You cannot ask anyone for assistance. Work with the material on hand and be sure to record every action, whether a memo, letter, telephone call or meeting plan. Every action you wish to take should be written down, including memos to headquarters, to members of your staff, to yourself and to others. Good luck!

Data Re: Lingerland Branch Personnel

Fifty-seven-year-old *Steve Sleeper* has been with the bank for 36 years and has been assistant branch manager for seventeen years. He has a $3,000 loan limit. All clerical employees, except the customer service representative, report to him. He handles opening and closing of all types of bank accounts, such as checking, savings, safe deposit and installment loans.

Jim Comer, 25, is customer service representative, with the bank for two years, he is a graduate of bank training program. He has no loan authorization although he accepts applications. He opens and closes all types of bank accounts as the assistant manager does. He has no supervisory responsibility.

Mary Smith, head teller, oversees the entire teller operation although the tellers do not in reality report to her. She is responsible for money vault, branch proof and "sloppy work," including savings bonds, tax withholding payments, travelers checks, money orders, etc. She will assist with safe deposit access and other teller functions when business dictates.

Carol Farrell, savings teller, is responsible for all transactions on savings accounts. She accepts club payments and installment payments.

John Nice and *June Moon* are commercial tellers responsible for cashing checks, accepting checking account deposits, accepting all types of payments.

Lana Dugan, secretary, acts as a receptionist and is responsible for safe deposit access and all the typing and shorthand duties of the office.

31 January——

Dear George,

While it is still early in the year, I know that your summer positions are filled quickly. Bill Jr. is studying economics at Southern U., as we both did, and would like to work for your bank this summer. I would appreciate your giving him a challenging job in which he could learn what a banker does. Please let me know when he can come in for an interview.

Best regards to Ruth and the children.

S/ Bill

William Warton

BELTWAY-METROPOLITAN NATIONAL BANKS

Executive Offices

MEMORANDUM

TO: George Hides

FROM: Len Link

Would you please do all you can to solidify our relationship with Stainless Steel Corporation? Word has it that they expect a large contract from the government, and we would have a good opportunity to get additional balances. Their treasurer, Brooks Brokenshire, is the key to this whole operation.

_____

Director of Marketing

Box 553
Lingerland, New York 12158
31 January_____

Dear Mr. Hides,

I am getting <u>awfully</u> tired of having problems with my checking account. It seems that no matter how much money I have in my account you insist on bouncing my checks. Just the other day you bounced another.

I expect a full letter of apology or I will take my business elsewhere.

Very truly yours,

(Mrs.) Thelma Baggs

BELTWAY-METROPOLITAN NATIONAL BANKS

Executive Offices

MEMORANDUM

TO: All Officers

FROM: Leonard Link

There will be a special meeting of all officers on the 9th at 2 p.m. to bring you up to date on our advertising campaign. We want to make this Spring the best on record.

Please make every effort to attend.

BELTWAY-METROPOLITAN NATIONAL BANKS

Lingerland Branch

MEMORANDUM

3 February⸺

TO: George Hides

FROM: Lana Dugan

With the New York City banks coming into the area, I am sure one of them will offer me a job paying more than you pay. If I do not get a $10/wk raise by the end of the month, I intend to resign. Much as I appreciate working under you, I'm afraid I need the money more than the enjoyment of the work.

Lana

BELTWAY-METROPOLITAN NATIONAL BANKS

Executive Offices

MEMORANDUM

3 February———

TO: George Hides

FROM: Henry Hobbs

I am still waiting for your report of past due loans which, as you know, is due on the 25th. Please get it to me immediately.

Regional Vice President

STAINLESS STEEL CORPORATION
123 Fourth Street
Maltzberg, New York

2 February 19——

Dear George:

Thank you so much for taking the time to speak with me regarding my personal loan application for $10,000. I trust that everything is in order.

I will be out of town on the 6th and 7th but will be in to pick up the proceeds on the 8th. As you know, I am closing the deal, which we discussed in confidence, at 10:00 that morning.

Cordially,

Brooks R. Brokenshire, Jr.
Executive Vice President
 and Treasurer

BELTWAY-METROPOLITAN NATIONAL BANKS

Executive Offices
MEMORANDUM

TO: George Hides

FROM: Henry Hobbs

It has just been brought to my attention that the teller's difference record of your office is the poorest in the system.

Please formulate a plan to improve the present poor record and submit this to me by 10 February.

_____

Regional Vice President

BELTWAY-METROPOLITAN NATIONAL BANKS

Lingerland Branch

MEMORANDUM

2 February_____

TO: Mr. Hides

FROM: Carol Farrell

May I have next Friday off? I realize that it is the busiest day of the week, but it is important to me to have the time. My sister is getting married Saturday afternoon and I am the maid of honor.

Carol

MILLTOWN JAYCEES

Dear Mr. Hides,

We need you. You need us. We can both help the community. Won't you join??? Come to our next meeting to find out the details. It's to be a buffet lunch with cherry pie, in honor of Washington's birthday. The place is Mac's Den; the time 12:30 p.m., the 17th.

J. Dogooder
Membership Chairman

BELTWAY-METROPOLITAN NATIONAL BANKS

Executive Offices

MEMORANDUM

TO: George Hides

FROM: Staff Training

Mr. Stephen Sleeper has been selected to attend our supervisory training course to be held each Tuesday morning from 9:00 to 10:00 at the home office, Conference Room C, beginning 7 Feb. Please notify him accordingly. There will be ten 3-hour sessions, followed by luncheon in the officers' dining room. The attendance policy is well known to you, and we expect Mr. Sleeper to be present for all sessions.

Peter Penney
Training Director

BELTWAY-METROPOLITAN NATIONAL BANKS

Executive Offices

MEMORANDUM

3 February_____

TO: George Hides

FROM: Len Link

I have recently received several comments from customers that your advertising in the Maltzburg area is second rate. It is important that we discuss this in detail soon. Why are we still using radio station WFEB (5,000 watts) when WMAR (10,-000 watts) is now available at about the same rates?

CONFIDENTIAL

CENTRAL CREDIT BUREAU

NAME: Brooks Brokenshire, Jr.

ADDRESS: 1 Wayward Lane
          Suburbia

TRADE	DATE	HIGH	BALANCE	RATING
Jeweler	Nov.	Low 4	High 3	Slow
Furniture	Oct.	Med 3	Med 3	Poor
Clothing	July	Med 3	Low 2	As Agreed

Collection Accounts

DATE	AMOUNT	Favor of a bank	Status not satisfied
1972	$2,270		

BELTWAY-METROPOLITAN NATIONAL BANKS

Lingerland Branch

MEMORANDUM

TO: George Hides

FROM: John Nice

As you know, for the last several weeks I have had to cover the drive-in window. While I will always be a loyal employee, I would appreciate your relieving me from this duty as soon as possible. You are aware that I am very susceptible to colds, and the draft from the window is something which I should avoid. I hate to lose time off due to unnecessary illness.

2 February_____

BELTWAY-METROPOLITAN NATIONAL BANKS

Executive Offices

MEMORANDUM
(Confidential)

TO: George Hides

FROM: Donald Dewitt

For some period now we have been concerned about the evident lack of development on the part of Mr. Stephen Sleeper. He has shown almost no growth pattern in the past dozen years. As you may know, he is related by marriage to our current president, and we feel that he has received more than adequate treatment by our organization. Since the merger, three years ago, we intend clearing out the deadwood. I have recommended that Mr. Sleeper attend a supervision course (his third, I believe), and if he doesn't improve his performance, we shall be forced to ask him to resign or retire.

The Linger-A-While
Shopping Plaza

Beltway Blvd. (Exit 15)
Lingerland, N.Y.

TO: Geo. Hides

FROM: Lester Log, Building Manager

I want to respond to your call and apologize for the tardiness of our snow removal crew in clearing out the lot on Thursday. The six-inch fall on top of the four inches we had the previous Tuesday was a "bit much" for my boys. I realize that you have to be open for business at 9 a.m., and we will always try to do our best to keep the parking areas and entrances open. My annual snow removal budget is getting pretty tight, and I'm praying these days for sun instead of that white stuff!

By the way, I'll have my crew over on the morning of the 6th to fix the leaky roof. When all the snow accumulates, it forms ice—which gets under the flashing. I can appreciate your concern about the leaking in the safe deposit vault.

BELTWAY-METROPOLITAN NATIONAL BANKS

Executive Offices

MEMORANDUM

TO: All Officers

FROM: Frederick Fryer

Effective immediately we will strictly enforce all requirements in extending loans. Money is tight and we must only extend credit where we are on safe ground and certain of repayment.

F.F.

25 January———

Dear Branch Office Manager,

I have been referred to your bank by a mutual friend, Gilmore Gruff. I have just relocated to your area, and I expect to be the night bartender at the Nite Lite Bar & Grill.

Mr. Gruff told me it was easy to get small loans at your bank, and I expect to see you as soon as I move into the area. I hope you will open my account then.

Sincerely,

Joc Phife

The Psychologist as an Administrator

Instructions for Participants

Read Carefully

You are going to participate in a new type of activity. You will work as an individual on some problems of the type that must be dealt with by an individual rather than in group discussion.

You will work as if you were Edward Eager, Ph.D., the new chief psychologist at mental health's Midtown State Hospital. Midtown Hospital has a patient load of approximately 7,000, with slightly less than 2,000 employees in all categories. In your position as chief psychologist, you have replaced Dr. George Grater, who resigned recently. (Organizational charts are given in Figures 10.4 and 10.5.)

You have come from Central Rock Hospital. Your promotion came rather suddenly, since Dr. Grater left Midtown with very little notice.

You have been on the job since Thursday, May 17, 1972. This is Monday, May 21, 1972. You have returned to the office after a long meeting at the out patient clinic and must leave in one hour to catch a flight from Boston.

On Tuesday and Wednesday you are taking your ABEPP (American Board of Examiners in Professional Psychology) oral examination in Boston. On Thursday and Friday you will chair the meeting of the APA Ad Hoc Committee on Professional Standards for Psychologists in Mental Hospitals, scheduled to meet in Cambridge. This is an important meeting. Since the committee is ready to assess the results of a study it made, it must have the assessment ready to submit to the APA Board of Directors for their forthcoming meeting.

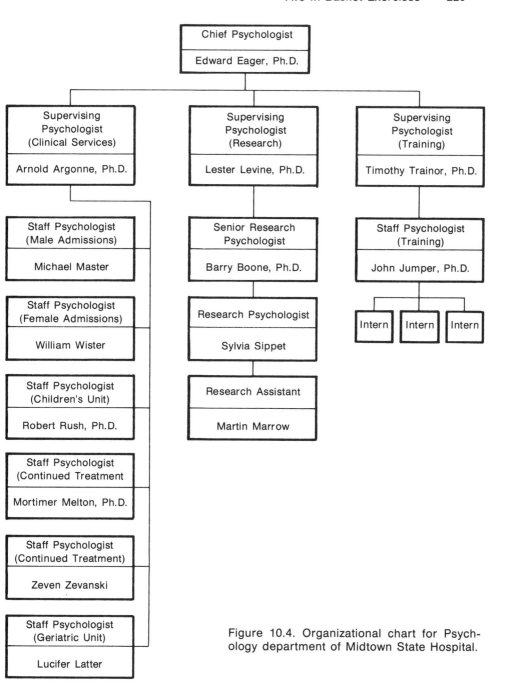

Figure 10.4. Organizational chart for Psychology department of Midtown State Hospital.

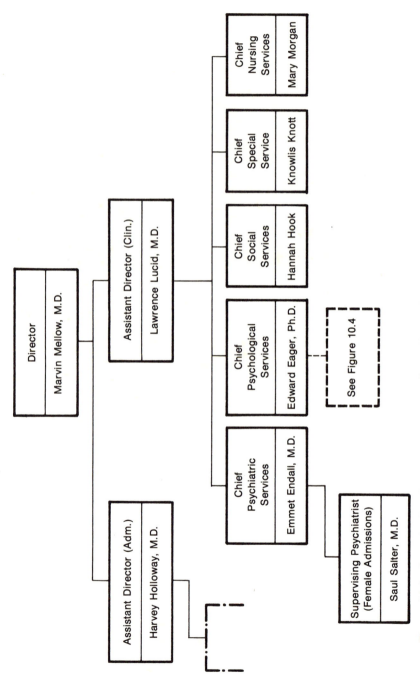

Figure 10.5. Organizational chart for Midtown State Hospital.

MAY						
S	M	T	W	T	F	S
		1	2	3	4	5
6	7	8	9	10	11	12
13	14	15	16	17	18	19
20	21	22	23	24	25	26
27	28	29	30	31		

Figure 10.6. Calendar for May.

You will return to the office on Monday, May 28.

Your regular secretary is Mrs. Tessie Timely. However, Tessie has been out with a serious operation. Her temporary replacement is Miss Kay Kaper. Since Kay is not regularly assigned to your office, she is not very familiar with the routines of the psychology department.

The enclosed materials were left in the in-basket on your desk by Miss Kaper. You are to go through the entire packet of materials and take whatever action you deem appropriate on each item. Every action you wish to take should be written down, including memos to your secretary, memos to yourself and others. Draft or write letters where appropriate; write notes to yourself. Write out any plans or agenda for meetings or conferences you would want to call. You may write notes directly on the pieces of correspondence you are dealing with or may attach notes by means of the paper clips provided.

Be sure to record every action, whether a memo, letter, telephone call or meeting plan.

You are to use your own experience as the basis for your actions in assuming the role of Edward Eager. Please try to place yourself in Eager's place for the next hour. Although the situation is somewhat artificial in point of time, the problems are typical and real and should be given your serious attention.

REMEMBER!

The day is Monday, May 21, (a calendar is shown in Figure 10.6). Time—7:00 p.m. Write down every action you take on any item. You cannot call on anyone for assistance. The switchboard is out of order.

The director and assistant directors of the hospital are off the grounds attending an evening meeting.

You must work with the material at hand. You will be out of the office from 8:00 o'clock tonight until Monday, May 28.

You cannot take any of the material with you on your trip.

GOOD LUCK!

AIR MAIL—PERSONAL AND CONFIDENTIAL—DELIVER UNOPENED

Edward Eager, PhD.
Chief Psychologist
Midtown State Hospital
Midtown, Illinois

Dear Ed:

Had I known that you would succeed me at Midtown, I would have filled you in personally, but it was only after I arrived here on the Coast that I heard about your coming.

I hope my sudden departure doesn't leave you in too much of a box, but I had to take advantage of this opportunity, which seemed to me to be a once-in-a-lifetime offer.

I know that you'll like Midtown and I am sure that you will find the hospital staff and psychology department staff all good people to work with, with only minor exceptions.

Dr. Mellow is an excellent boss. He is progressive and is willing to utilize all the professional resources in the hospital to the fullest extent. One thing you have to watch, though, is his tendency to be overly broad and general. He may give his blessing to things without sufficiently evaluating their specific organizational consequences. Dr. Lucid, however, supplies what Dr. Mellow lacks in this regard. He is a highly competent, organized and efficient person. It is not too difficult to accept his rather authoritarian and rigid insistence on protocol because of his complete integrity and dedication and competence. Be sure, though, to comply with any requests or decrees which he makes. Accepting this, you'll find him a fine person to work with. Dr. Halloway is a rather weak person who derives his solace and strength by rigidly adhering to the book. He knows the Mental Health Department well and is somewhat of an expert in policy, procedures, merit system law, etc. If you relate to him carefully and don't let him overwhelm you, he can be helpful. Although he probably can't hurt you, he can make things highly unpleasant as regards your dealings with the department under him.

That about covers the situation outside the psychology department. Oh yes, I should mention Hannah Hook, my old "friend." I really feel I understand her, and I did learn to accept her. She's an old-timer and for the most part well meaning. However, she still can't think of psychology as a fully grown profession in its own right. Actually, way back it used to be under her wing. She watches us closely and may tattle if she sees something she doesn't like—e.g., presumed flouting of the hospital regulations or working hours by psychologists, etc. Just stand your ground with her, and you'll come out fine.

One other person deserves mention, although you probably won't cross paths with him much—Dr. Salter. The only thing I can think of to say is that he's a real "odd-ball." Everybody recognizes this and tolerates him. Actually, he's very well versed in dynamic psychiatry, but he tends to go off the deep end, and his methods may be very unconventional to say the least.

The psychology staff is really a good gang. There is a lot of strength. All of the supervising psychologists are competent, dependable and motivated. Below this level there are weak spots, but nothing unusual.

Arnie A. has been helpful, doing a good job in Clinical Services. Occasionally, he's been a swell backstop, although Dr. Mellow has never really appreciated his efforts. (This is probably why he didn't get the nod for my job.) Tim—you know well.

One man, Bill Wister, must be mentioned, however. Bill reminds me a little of Dr. Salter—only he's better organized. It all came to a head shortly before I left, so I really couldn't work out the problem to my own satisfaction. I received reports from reliable sources that Bill was "behaving improperly" with female patients. Just what this means, I don't know. I attempted to discuss it with Bill, but never really did determine the facts. I would judge that his behavior was probably not what we would consider "typical" for a professional. Anyway, our discussion became heated, and I warned him that he could be ousted, despite his permanent status. This brought him up so short and he almost pleaded with me. The outcome was that I would study the matter while he was at the psychoanalytic meetings (after which he is going to take two weeks vacation time). Unfortunately, I had to leave for the Coast sooner than I expected and I don't know anything more than I've told you. However, since he'll not return until the 28th, you'll have ample time to investigate the matter and decide what to do.

Oh yes, another item. Les Levine, who is an unusually well-rounded researcher, has a proposal for a drug project. He's negotiating with some drug company for the funds to go ahead. Usually his research is of the highest quality, but I just can't see this one (nor can others with whom I've discussed the project). Really, I think it won't look good for psychology if he carries this one off. I think he has been taken in by the drug company representative (Les tends to be a little bit naive in expecting others to have the same strong sense of integrity he has).

Anyway, I think I may have given Les the impression that I approved of the project, not wanting to take away any of his authority and hoping he'd see the light. Maybe you can have a nice, long, leisurely talk with him—watch it, though, he's sensitive! Losing him would be a severe loss in the department.

I hope I haven't given the impression that there are any real troubles. Actually, things run along pretty smoothly. You almost have to invent problems.

Have fun!

See you at A.P.A. in September.

Best wishes for success.

Sincerely,

George G.

The Weekly Clarion
Midtown, Illinois
May 18, 1972

Dr. Edward Eager
Chief Psychologist
Midtown State Hospital
Midtown, Illinois

Dear Dr. Eager:

As editor of The Weekly Clarion, I would like to welcome you to our community. I am sure that you will find Midtown a fine community to live in.

As is customary when a person in a position such as yours comes to town, we like to cover the event with an article about the person and his background. The deadline for next Friday's edition of the Clarion is Wednesday. I will be most appreciative if you will send me a detailed account of your professional background, together with a recent photograph. We would also like to include something about you personally so that the folks in town can get to know you.

We are saving ample space for you so don't be too modest in your account of yourself.

Sincerely,

Jebb Jason
Editor

M E M O R A N D U M

May 18, 1972

TO: Dr. Eager

FROM: Dr. Endall

SUBJECT: Xenofil

I am responding to your department's request for my evaluation of this drug. We find it very promising indeed. It promises to become one of the most widely used on our wards.

May 17, 1972

Edward Eager, Ph.D.
Chief Psychologist
Midtown State Hospital
Midtown, Illinois

Dear Dr. Eager:

I just heard about your appointment to Midtown as chief psychologist. Congratulations!

We will all miss George. He was a real friend to us all. Nevertheless, I am sure that we will all lend our support to you as you take over the reins.

As you probably know I have been attending the psychoanalytic meetings and planned to take two weeks' vacation following this. However, I've decided to cut the time short and report for work next Wednesday, May 23.

I am looking forward to meeting you then.

Sincerely yours,

William Wister

M E M O R A N D U M

May 21, 1972

CONFIDENTIAL

TO: E. Eager, Ph.D.

FROM: E. Endall, M.D.

SUBJECT: M. Melton, Ph.D.

A situation has arisen relative to Dr. Melton, who has been seeing Thomas Small on Ward 18 in psychotherapy for the past year. Last Thursday Mr. Small has an acute anxiety attack, refused medication from the ward physician, but asked—even begged—to see Dr. Melton. When the nurse called Dr. Melton at 9:30 p.m., he refused to come in to talk with the patient, saying that it was after hours and he was not officially in a professional category which compensated him—in time off or shorter working hours or paid overtime—for emergency night duty.

After the nurse told me what had happened (and especially that Mr. Small was in a severely agitated state all night long until Dr. Melton saw him at 8 the following morning), I admit I was burning mad. I was so mad, I didn't think of calling you in on the matter.

In my talk with Dr. Melton, however, he said that the blame for this situation resides not with him but with the hospital administration because it refuses to recognize or admit that such a relationship can develop between a psychologist and his "client" and to make time repayment provisions as it does with physicians and dentists for night or emergency duty performed. His arrogance and logic were disgusting, for he kept raising issues of professional "responsibility," "recognition," "peer status," "hampering authoritative pronouncements," and so on. He said that in the past he frequently came in evenings to see patients, but no allowances were made in his basic work to compensate for this time. He had a most irritating legalistic series of examples and indications in the case of other psychologists of how the hospital rigidly adhered to the regulations concerning the basic work week and working hours. In other words, he placed the burden of what I consider his basic breach of professional ethics and his downright inhumanity right back on the hospital.

I am afraid that I invited him, if he was unhappy with the working conditions, to resign. He has otherwise had an exemplary record, and I know he is a competent psychologist. I might have acted too hastily.

MEMORANDUM

May 18, 1972

TO: Dr. Eager

FROM: Dr. Levine

SUBJECT: Drug Research Project

I have been working up an extensive proposal for a research project designed to measure the effectiveness of the new drug Xenofil. Due to the generous support offered by the Xeno Drug Company, this promises to be a really fruitful project, not only in terms of the evaluation of the drug, but also because of the possible implications some of the basic assumptions—especially the principle of conditionability as a function metabolic accumulation—will have for psychology in general.

Since the company representative will be here Friday, I want to get your go-ahead before you leave. Unless I finalize the arrangement with him on Friday, we will loose our chance to get the grant.

MEMORANDUM

May 21, 1972

CONFIDENTIAL

TO: Dr. Eager

FROM: Michael Master

I wanted to see you this afternoon, but I had to leave to get to my Rorschach class. While it may not be any of my business, I feel that I should speak my piece about something.

I think Bill Wister is being victimized by some nasty rumors originated by a very neurotic attendant on the female admission ward. Many people have had trouble with this person, but since Bill has commenced an extensive therapy program on the ward, he has come in for the worst of it. Several of us have speculated that this female attendant is homosexual and that she resents professionals coming in and working with some of her favorite patients.

I've heard that Dr. Holloway got in on this affair. This is unfortunate because he has it in for people in the clinical services. Since you're new here, I should warn you that Dr. Holloway is the real power around here and you should avoid crossing him.

Nevertheless if Bill goes, there's going to be a lot of unhappy psychologists around here.

M E M O R A N D U M

Monday 3:00 p.m.

TO: Ed

FROM: Tim

RE: Training Meeting

I'm sorry I didn't get to see you before you left for your ABEPP's. Anyway, good luck with them! I've got to leave now for the meeting at the university.

Since I won't see you until next Monday and our hospital training meeting is scheduled for that day, I wanted to alert you to a situation that may arise. John has hinted that he'd like to be included in the meeting. I have no strong objection to his going, but you should make the decision. John is an excellent trainer and highly competent technically, but he has some strong ideas that I just can't buy about certain aspects of the program. I'm afraid that he might louse things up for our psychology training program unless you hold the reins on him in a meeting such as this.

Incidentally, thanks for permitting me to take the couple of days leave Wednesday and Thursday. I can't wait to get back on the golf course—it's been a long winter.

See you next Monday.

MEMORANDUM

May 21, 1962

TO: Dr. Edward Eager, Psychology

FROM: Dr. Holloway

SUBJECT: Mr. Wister

It has come to my attention that Dr. Grater told Mr. Wister to go on leave while he looked into some problems that Mr. Wister was creating. While I have no firsthand information pertaining to the situation, I have talked with those who do. Mr. Wister has made it difficult for all psychologists by his actions.

I will support dismissal proceedings if you decide on this. In any case, I strongly advise he should not be permitted to come back to work until you have investigated the situation.

There are many loyal and conscientious employees in our institution, and we have little room for a professional employee who doesn't act like one.

MEMORANDUM

May 18, 1972

TO: Edward Eager, Ph.D.

FROM: Mortimer Melton, Ph.D.

SUBJECT: Resignation

This is to notify you that I am submitting my resignation to the personnel office, to be effective May 30, 1972. By this date I will have discharged all remaining leave time. My last day on the job will be May 24.

12 Winding Lane
Midtown, Illinois 60619
May 17, 1972

Chief Psychologist
Midtown State Hospital
Midtown, Illinois

Dear Sir:

I am a graduating senior at Midtown High and am writing to seek your advice on a college. I intend to major in psychology, and I thought you could tell me which is the best school.

Also, how long does it take to become a psychologist?

Is a medical doctor higher or lower?

Isn't it possible to help people without studying psychology?

I hope you can write me soon, as I will need to mail my applications for college in next week. I will have to write to a large number of universities because my grades haven't been very good.

I think I could do well in psychology though!

Thank you.

Yours truly,

Henry Happen

MEMORANDUM

May 18, 1962

TO: Edward Eager, Ph.D.

FROM: Dr. Mellow

I trust that by now you are feeling quite at home with us here in the hospital. I regret that my busy schedule has not permitted us time to sit down together and talk at length, beyond our first brief meeting. We must do this very soon.

Prior to your coming, I met with Dr. Levine who told me of his proposed drug project with Xenofil. This sounds very promising, and I want you to know that the project has my approval. We need more of these well-designed evaluation projects if we are to maintain our forward looking treatment program.

You should, of course, get the go-ahead from Dr. Lucid on this research since you will require the participation of some of his people.

MEMORANDUM

May 21, 1972

TO: Dr. Edward Eager, Psychology Department

FROM: Hannah Hook, Social Service Department

I am sorry that our meeting had to be so brief last week, but I can understand how busy these first few days have been for you.

Due to the physical proximity of our departments, I feel very close to psychology and have been an interested observer of the growth of the Psychology Department.

I feel that I should bring to your attention certain practices that I have noticed during the period after Dr. Grater left and before you arrived. While I am really not concerned with the time schedule which psychologists observe, certain obvious infractions have caused some dissention in my department. Due to the pressure brought upon me by my own people, I feel that I must discuss this matter with Dr. Mellow in my conference with him this week. However, in all fairness, I feel that we ought to have a chance to discuss the matter first. Would you call me on this?

Allow me again to express my warmest welcome to you in your new position. I look forward to a rewarding collaboration.

MEMORANDUM

May 21, 1972

TO: Dr. Eager, Psychology

FROM: Dr. Lucid

SUBJECT: Training Committee Meeting

The meeting of the training committee originally scheduled for next Monday has been moved up to Wednesday, May 23. I want to emphasize that the attendance of you and Dr. Trainor is vital. Dr. Mellow has asked us to develop a master training plan by which we might better utilize our total training resources in the hospital, and he needs our recommendations prior to his discussion with the Commissioner concerning the necessary program modifications. As we have discussed, a number of advantages will also accrue to the psychology training program in particular.

MEMORANDUM

May 21, 1972

TO: Dr. Eager

FROM: Miss Kaper

SUBJECT: Training Committee Meeting

Dr. Lucid's secretary called me late this afternoon and dictated the following message over the phone from Dr. Lucid:

"The meeting of the training committee originally scheduled for the 28th has been moved up to Wednesday, May 23. I want to emphasize that the attendance of you and Dr. Trainor is most important. Dr. Mellow has asked us to develop a master training and development plan by which we might better utilize our total training resources in the hospital, and he needs our recommendations prior to his discussion with the Commissioner concerning the necessary program modifications.

"The new team approach in handling our patients also makes it imperative that everyone in the hospital be trained to understand their exact role. As we have discussed, a number of advantages will also accrue to the psychology training program in particular."

P.S.   I knew that you were going to be out of town for the rest of the week and told Dr. Lucid's secretary that you wouldn't be able to make the Wednesday meeting. She was unable to recheck with Dr. Lucid since he had gone golfing with Dr. Trainor.

MEMORANDUM

May 18, 1972

TO: Dr. Eager, Psychology Department

FROM: Dr. Salter, Ward 12A

SUBJECT: Assignment of Psychologist to Female Admission Wards

Your predecessor, Dr. Grater, somehow precipitated some difficulty with Mr. Wister who is the psychologist assigned to my female admission wards. According to what I hear, Mr. Wister was mistreated, and I want you to know that I am anxious to have him back. In fact, I am unwilling to have any substitute.

Mr. Wister is a highly skilled therapist who is especially effective with females. We work well together and I would like to have him back as soon as possible.

MEMORANDUM

May 18, 1972

TO: Dr. Eager

FROM: Lucifer Latter

SUBJECT: Work Schedule Arrangement

This is to let you know that I would like to leave at 2:00 p.m. each Wednesday to get to class at NWU. With this current course, I will complete all course work for my doctorate. I was fortunate to get a departmental stipend for it.

I had obtained Dr. Grater's approval for this arrangement, and he stated that he had cleared it with the administration.

Your approval will be appreciated.

M E M O R A N D U M

May 17, 1972

TO: ALL DEPARTMENT HEADS

FROM: Dr. Holloway

SUBJECT: Working Day Schedules

Once again I find that I must remind all department heads of Section 12D of the Time and Attendance Rules which specifies the working day. Deviations from this are allowed only in very unusual circumstances, and in no case are any special arrangements to be made without my specific approval.

XENO PHARMACEUTICALS CORPORATION

DETROIT, MICHIGAN

May 17, 1972

R. Gerhardt Schmidt, M.D., Ph.D.
President

AIR MAIL

Edward Eager, Ph.D.
Chief Psychiatrist
Midtown State Hospital
Midtown, Illinois

Dear Doctor Eager:

I am so pleased to be able to contact you and to wish the best of everything on your promotion. You are no doubt aware by now that a breakthrough of gargantuan dimensions in chemotherapy has taken place at Midtown State Hospital. Dr. Levine, whose energies and intensive imagination have been so productive, especially deserves the gratitude of the mentally disturbed and, of course, their families. Your predecessor, Dr. Grater, should also share in the credits, but, unfortunately, he has left Midtown Hospital. We at XENO, naturally, look to you, as Dr. Levine's superior, to partake in a share of the fruits of our collective struggles to prove Xenofil's value.

You may be aware that Xenofil is about to be cleared for widespread experimental use by both FDA and NIMH. We are currently completing our final plans for a nationwide news and ethical educational campaign describing the positive values of Xenofil in mental health rehabilitation. And, as I've indicated, we would want you to enjoy a significant role in these plans.

At 8:00 p.m. on June 4, I am asking you, your wife, Dr. Mellow (whom I am also writing and who has been most generous with his time) and Dr. Levine to join a few of us at the XENO family for a small, intimate party. We shall be getting together at the Philador Manor for a little celebration. Dr. Herman Horne, our senior vice president in charge of research, will be at Midtown Hospital on the 25th—and he'll fill you in on the details.

In closing, my very best wishes to you on your new assignment. I know that in the future we shall be able to expand on our present cooperative efforts.

Cordially yours,

MEMORANDUM

May 21, 1972

TO: Dr. Eager

FROM: Dr. Lucid

SUBJECT: Xenofil Project

In response to your memo concerning the feasibility of Dr. Levine's proposed research, I must be rather discouraging. Recent results with this drug have shown it to be of modest value and with moderately harmful side effects. I would say that the project ought not to be done at this particular point in time.

Monday, 4:00 p.m.

Dr. Eager

Dr. Smith called in relation to attached referral [Figure 10.7]. He wanted to remind you that this was urgent. Patient, Rollo Roster, Ward 6-G, is a court com-

MIDTOWN STATE HOSPITAL

Requested by **S. Smith MD**   Date **5/21/62**

Location	Patient's Name	Age	Sex
Ward 6-G	**Roster, Rollo**	**26**	**M**

Referred for EVALUATION of (check)*

☒ Prognosis
☒ Change after treatment
☐ Vocational fitness
☐ Educational fitness
☐ Other:

☐ Intellectual functioning
☐ Personality dynamics
☐ Organic impairment
☐ Differential diagnosis

Referred for COUNSELING and PSYCHOTHERAPY (check)*

☐ Vocational, educational counseling
☐ Psychotherapy, individual
☐ Psychotherapy, group
☐ Other:

Other Pertinent Data

Exhibitionism

*Elaborate here:

Patient has shown remarkably positive response to treatment using Xenojil. He has shown no real evidence of former exhibitionistic behavior.

Figure 10.7. Request for psychological services.

mitment and will be presented at staff tomorrow for consideration of release.

Dr. Smith asks that the patient be examined the first thing in the morning if at all possible.

Kay

MEMORANDUM

May 18, 1972

TO: Dr. Eager

FROM: Dr. Lucid

SUBJECT: Referrals from Dr. S. Smith

I have asked Dr. Simon Smith (senior psychiatrist on geriatric ward) to channel all of his psychology referrals through me so that I might screen out those that are less important. Dr. Grater spoke to me about this, and I well recognize that you people have lots to do without doing relatively unnecessary work.

Therefore, no referrals are to be accepted from Dr. Smith without my specific authorization, indicated by my countersigning the referral form.

Appendix

Instructional efforts should be planned to ensure the attainment of instructional objectives. As they plan for instruction, trainers are concerned with:

1. Bridging the time gap between separate training sessions and also between these sessions and the work environment
2. Presenting the instructional materials in a logical, orderly fashion
3. Arranging the time available to attain maximum attention and concentration on the most important subject elements
4. Building suitable trainee participation
5. Structuring the total effort with the proper mixture of methodologies

Perhaps the most desirable and practical approach for helping the trainer achieve the items noted above is the development and use of a lesson plan. While we undoubtedly know experienced trainers with talented verbal facilities, this quality does *not* automatically provide for a sound instructional outcome. When working with case studies particularly, trainers may fail to achieve what it was that they considered attainable.

The inherent nature of case studies and the requirement for considerable trainee participation may well cause the trainer to overlook the necessity for sticking to a planned approach. Lesson planning, though seemingly a tedious process, mandates that the trainer lay out *what* it is he wants to do and *how* he intends to accomplish it.

The material which follows illustrates how to build a lesson plan based on a case study. The reader will recognize, as he studies the lesson plan, that the case study selected was chosen as a practical follow-up to a *previous* training session dealing with the JIT method.

Lesson Plan	
Course Title: Objectives:	Basic Supervisory Practices At the conclusion of this session, trainees will understand: (a) the importance of applying a systematized method when instructing a new worker and (b) the potential consequences to the organization of failure by supervisor to accept his instructional responsibilities.* *If this is to be handled as a case situation in problem analysis and decision-making, see Major Topic 7.* Naturally, the objectives would be revised to reflect this emphasis.
Session Title: Materials:	Job Instruction Responsibilities (continued). Case study entitled, "The Involuntary Dropout" (See below.)

The Involuntary Dropout

Joanne has been crying. Her eyes are red and she'd walk off the job now, if it wasn't for the fact that she desperately needs her pay check. As soon as the checks are distributed, around 2:00 p.m., she's picking up and leaving. And good riddance too—especially to that bitchy boss, Bertha.

Today Joanne was due to complete her probationary term as a file clerk. She then would have become permanent. Instead, she was called in soon after reporting to work and told by Bertha that her work was unsatisfactory; that she had not learned what she should have learned during her probationary period. Therefore, she was being "dropped." She broke down crying and could get no real answers from Bertha as to why . . . .

The only thing that Bertha told Joanne was that she wasn't quick enough in picking up the organization's filing system; that she was too slow in doing her work, especially in retrieving materials from the files for some of the executives.

On Joanne's first day on the job, three months back, Bertha had taken her through the file room and shown her how the files were organized and where new, incoming materials were obtained for filing. Bertha also explained how the retrieval system worked. She had also demonstrated the use of the microfilm reader. However, Joanne had trouble using the reader and often called on one of the other three girls to help her. Because of the rush of work, this often was impractical. When Joanne asked Bertha for help, she was told "Take your time and

---

*The reader will recognize, as he goes through this material, that the case study has been selected as a practical follow-up to a previous session on the JIT method.

reread the instructions on the machine." Although Joanne finally learned to handle the reader, she preferred to let someone else do this work—unless she couldn't avoid the assignment. Joanne realized that she was slow—but she always got the file asked for. She never had been reprimanded for poor work. Her attendance was better than Bertha's.

Joanne is 22 years old; Bertha (who has been in the organization for 15 years) is 40.

Instructions

1. Construct a list of three broad questions (and responses) which should be asked after this case has been read carefully. Questions should be stated as broadly as possible. For example: "What principles of supervision are involved in this case?"
2. Each group is then to develop responses to its own questions.

Major Topic 1: *Summary of Previous Session*

Subject Matter	Techniques
Remind group that previous session covered four-step method of job instruction training (JIT). Preparation Presentation Application Follow-up	Ask group to summarize four-step method. Write on flip chart or board.

Major Topic 2: *Supervisor and His Training Responsibilities (Overview)*

Subject Matter	Techniques

Why is four-step method important?
    Saves time. Training ensures that material is covered adequately. Provides a systematic method for ensuring that *knowledge* and *skills* are covered. More responsive *attitude* by trainees (subordinates).
Where does foreman, supervisor or manager "fit" in the training process?
    Major supervisory responsibility is development of subordinates.
	Ask group to respond.
	
	Ask group for views.
	
	Discuss.

Major Topic 3: *Case Study—Introduction*

Subject Matter	Techniques
Consider what happened in real life when training and development of subordinate—such as a new employee—is not carried through effectively. Explain to class that one way of studying this situation is to analyze a case. (They have had experience with this method during a previous session.)	Distribute case of "The Involuntary Dropout." Read case to trainees while they follow along on their individual copies. Divide total group into subgroups of four or five. Each group may designate a leader-recorder (they have one minute to do this).

Major topic 4: *Case Study—Group Activity*

Subject Matter	Techniques
The case: "The Involuntary Dropout" (see p. 249).	Small group activities continue. *Each group should be developing questions, per instruction at end of case.* Circulate among groups during discussion—listen in (do not participate).

Major Topic 5: *Case Study—Group Responses to Negative Attitudes*

Subject Matter	Techniques
This case concerns a new employee, Joanne, who is hired, put to work and then released, just before achieving "tenure." The reason given by the supervisor (Bertha) for making this employee an "involuntary dropout" is that the employee had not learned her job properly. Explore the essentially negative attitude exhibited by Bertha toward having to instruct. Consider the ways that some supervisors react when having to teach:	Allow small groups to remain seated together as groups and not to reassemble into a whole. Group may or may not use spokesman. Permit "minority views" during discussion.

1. Learned the job the hard way; "no one taught me!"
2. Teaching is not his bag. Supervisor's job is to get the work out.
3. Teaching time cuts into production time.
4. Does not want to give the impression that he's playing favorites.
5. Did not spend much time instructing other employees (who may have been experienced when they moved into jobs).
6. Feels foolish trying to act as an instructor.
7. It takes too long to prepare to teach.
8. Does not like to tell people that they're slow in catching on.
9. Too busy with other things to devote time to instructing.

Ask groups to comment on each of these attitudes and to provide a *positive* rebuttal to each; i.e., if groups were asked to "sell" training as a supervisory function, how would they do this?

> ## Major Topic 6: *Case Study—Group Questions Relating to Principles*

Subject Matter

Now, let us look at questions which each group has developed. Some typical questions and responses for discussion follow.

1. How are training and communications related?
   (A trainer is an effective communicator. He is perceptive and alert as to how subordinates are progressing. He keeps learners informed so they know where they stand. He does not keep them in the dark or at arm's length. He maintains effective rapport by being both a good listener and a clear, concise communicator.)
2. What is apt to happen when someone like Bertha runs the show?
   (If he or she cannot handle the teaching responsibility, the supervisor may develop low trust levels within the work unit because he failed to assign this to another subordinate. There is a lack of teamwork leading to reduced productivity and efficiency. Also, morale is apt to be affected.)
3. What kind of feedback is needed for new employees?
   (Employees have to be told how well they are doing. They need to have an opportunity to ask questions, to receive responses, to make mistakes and to learn from such mistakes and to progress to higher levels of responsibility. They need positive reinforcement

Techniques

Request group leader-recorders to read a single question. Go around room until all *different* questions are exhausted. Proceed this way:

Examination of questions and discussion.

Trainees remain with their small groups.

when they are doing well. Praise and recognition are critical during the learning process.)

4. How often do new employees need to receive such feedback?

(Information on progress on the job may have to be provided on a daily basis, particularly in the early period of employment. Recognition and facilitating acceptance into work unit is a prime supervisory responsibility. Employees cannot be thrown in, on a sink-or-swim basis, within a new unit and told, in a cursory fashion, what needs to be done.)

5. If an employee is doing unsatisfactory work after having been provided with adequate training, how should this be handled?

(The supervisor is not the only individual who can handle the instruction. Often another employee may be more effective in getting the training message across to new employees. Unsatisfactory performance has to be examined on a step-by-step basis. It may be that there is some key aspect of the work which the employee has not mastered and needs additional practice on. Refer back to JIT principles relating to critical aspects of a job. In other words, Joanne may be hung up on one item which is acting as a kind of block toward advancement.)

6. To what extent may a supervisor delegate his instructional responsibilities?

(The supervisor may designate a key subordinate, who has an excellent understanding of the job, as the individual charged with duty for job training within the unit. Individual must acquiesce in this assignment and, of course, be properly instructed on how to train. In other words he should be trained in JIT principles. Note that in this type of situation the supervisor is still responsible for the required training, even though it is done by someone else.)

7. What is loss to organization when employee is kept on payroll for lengthy period and then dropped as unsatisfactory?

(Average employee recruitment and placement is an expensive matter. Paper work on payroll and tax deductions, as example, are costly. Employee requires reasonable period to become productive in organization. For a time most new employees are a loss. Excessive turnover is, therefore, wasteful. Also, it may give organization a reputation as undesirable place to work—turning off above average candidates for employment.)

At this point, a summarization would be called for, pulling together all major principles covered. See Major Topic 12 as an example of summary. (*Major Topics 7-11*). *12 summarizes only those materials dealing with problem analysis and decision-making.*

Major Topic 7: *Problem Analysis—Facts and Inferences (General Concepts)*

Subject Matter	Techniques
Discussion: Why look at facts and inferences during problem analysis? *Fact:* What we *know* or what we accept as truth or as real. *Inference:* What we *deduce,* using logic and reason, from given data. An inference may be *rebutted* with other information. Inferences are based on *probabilities.*	*Ask groups:* 1. Definitions of facts 2. Definitions of inferences List responses on board or flip chart.
Refer, for additional reading, to "Language Habits in Human Affairs," by Irving J. Lee (New York: Harper & Brothers Publishers, 1941).	Get agreement.
Need for separation of facts from inferences. We accept Inferences on basis of *reasonable* risk (i.e. are these likely to be accurate and do they fit in with total picture?).	*Ask groups:* What is essential difference between a *fact* and an *inference*?
	Ask: Why must we recognize the distinction when becoming involved in problem analysis and decision-making? Discuss.

Major Topic 8: *Problem Analysis—Facts In Case of Involuntary Dropout*

Subject Matter	Techniques
Joanne told by Bertha her work was unsatisfactory on final day of probationary period. Bertha had provided Joanne with some instruction during first day on the job. Joanne had trouble with microfilm reader. Joanne never reprimanded for poor work. Joanne's attendance record satisfactory. Joanne had asked other girls for help with microfilm reader.	Ask each group to cite *facts.* Obtain agreement that each meets criteria. Refer back to case as necessary.

Major Topic 9: *Problem Analysis—Inferences in Case of Involuntary Dropout*

Subject Matter

1. Bertha provided little job instruction to Joanne.
2. Bertha gave Joanne little, if any, feedback on her work performance.
3. Bertha is not interested in subordinates as people (i.e., insensitive).
4. Bertha believes each subordinate is responsible for his own progress.
5. Bertha is a poor communicator.
6. Bertha is not accountable to her manager on the progress of subordinates.
7. Bertha's work group is understaffed.
8. Bertha is an unpleasant person.
9. Sloppy evaluation or appraisal methods of new employees by Bertha.
10. Bertha had received complaints about Joanne's work which she had not acted on.

Rank inferences as to probabilities.

Techniques

Each group cites *inferences*. Obtain agreement that each meets criteria. Use case as required.

Free group discussion.

Use vote, if needed, to gain ranking.

Major Topic 10: *Defining the Problem*

Subject Matter

Combine inferences with facts. Remind participants that degrees of correctness in problem definition (and resulting decisions) will vary. (There may be more than a single problem.)
Possible problem definitions:

1. Members of Bertha's work group not exposed to organized training on the job.
2. Supervision of Bertha, by her manager, is unconcerned with employee training and development.
3. No apparent system of keeping employees informed as to their development or where they stand.
4. Bertha's work group is understaffed.
5. Poor distribution of work within the work group.

Techniques

Small group discussions. Each small group to work up several problem definitions *and* decisions.

Call on groups to report on

Problem definitions.

List and discuss each. Gain consensus.

Major Topic 11: *Decision-Making*

Subject Matter

Decisions are *alternative* courses of resolving problems.

Each decision must have a *reasoned* basis. *Consequences* of each decision must be considered.

Possible decisions:

1. Have conference with Bertha to get more data. More facts are needed.
2. Introduce MBO and train Bertha in her training responsibilities, after a mutually agreed upon listing of objectives.
3. Refer matter to personnel office (if there is one).
4. Move Bertha to another unit.
5. Fire Bertha.

Techniques

Ask groups to report on decisions.

Discuss and evaluate.

Major Topic 12: *Summarization*

Subject Matter

Recap principles involved in problem analysis and decision-making:

1. Study situation.
2. Separate facts and inferences.
3. Inferences which may be combined with facts.
4. List probable problems.
5. Define problem(s).
6. List alternative decisions.
7. Select decision and implement.
8. Evaluate outcome or decision.

Techniques

Lecture-discussion.

Use board or flip chart.

Annotated Bibliography

The following listing is intended to alert the user of this publication to selected books which (a) discuss theory or principles of case study and roleplay utilization, (b) assist in the writing of learning exercises and (c) may be sources of cases, roleplays, complex exercises, or in-baskets.

Additional sources of exercises may be found by reviewing professional publications, such as *Management Review,* the *Training and Development Journal* and by consulting the catalogs available through such firms as Didactic Systems, Inc. (Westbury, New York 11590) and Development Dimensions, Inc. (Pittsburgh, Pennsylvania 15243).

Athos, Anthony G., and Coffey, Robert E. *Behavior in Organizations: A Multidimensional View.* Englewood Cliffs, New Jersey: Prentice-Hall, Inc., 1968.

As the authors note, this book contains textual materials (covering principles or concepts), readings and cases. The 30 cases, all in the private sector, will be particularly helpful to trainers or educators concerned with organizational behavior. Many of the cases are typical of those used in the Harvard Business School, where indeed they originated.

Barnlund, Dean C., and Haiman, Franklyn S. *The Dynamics of Discussion.* Boston: Houghton Mifflin Company, 1960.

The management of formal group communications in a discussion setting is the concern of this volume. It was added to this bibliography because it contains some 40 pages of "exercises in discussion," covering cases and roleplays in discussion-leadership development.

Beal, George M.; Bohlen, Joe M.; and Raudabaugh, J. Neal. *Leadership and Dynamic Group Action.* Ames, Iowa: The Iowa State University Press, 1962.

For training trainers and discussion group leaders, this utilitarian volume is a must. It is particularly valuable in its explanation of commonly used instructional methods; the authors cite the "shoulds," the "should nots" and "cautions" for each. The cartoons accompanying the text brighten and clarify the language. Available in both hardcover and paperback.

Byers, Kenneth T., ed. *Employee Training and Development in the Public Service.* Chicago, Illinois: Public Personnel Association, 1970.

A compendium of current developments, including theory, methods and techniques, encompassing all phases of employee and managerial training. Directed, of course, to the public sector environment. However, the valuable explanations, in uncomplicated language, make this helpful for trainers in the private sector as well. Several chapters provide good working definitions of various participative methodologies.

Coghill, Mary Ann. *Games and Simulations in Industrial and Labor Relations Training* (Key Issues Series #7). Ithaca, New York: New York State School of Industrial and Labor Relations, Cornell University, 1971.

A useful source of recent simulation materials for training managers and supervisors in collective bargaining, grievance handling and related subjects. Contains a helpful listing of references and catalogs of business games.

Corsini, Raymond J.; Shaw, Malcolm E.; and Blake, Robert R. *Roleplaying in Business and Industry.* New York: The Free Press of Glencoe, Inc., 1961.

One of the few books directed especially to the subject of roleplaying and written in clear, nontechnical language. Where technical terms are used, these are explained lucidly so that a nonspecialist may understand what is meant. This book contains helpful examples of the roleplay in action in various settings.

Farmer, Richard N.; Richman, Barry M.; and Ryan, William G. *Incidents in Applying Management Theory.* Belmont, California: Wadsworth Publishing Company, Inc., 1966.

A collection of 99 short "incidents" (in reality, most are traditional case studies), with two or three questions at the end of each. These materials are arranged by broad subject classifications. Most situations are those in the private sector, although a few public and nonprofit cases are to be found in this paperback publication.

Fordyce, Jack K., and Weil, Raymond. *Managing with People.* Reading, Massachusetts: Addison-Wesley Publishing Company, 1971.

The subtitle of this paperback recites its purpose: "A Manager's Handbook of Organization Development Methods." This is a useful book for the experienced trainer. Whether the manager who has been inquisitive about OD can get his answers here, well—that's a bit dubious. Four descriptions of OD applications in different settings may offer supportive data for trainers attempting to sell this approach to management.

Gordon, Thomas. *Group-Centered Leadership*. Boston: Houghton Mifflin Company, 1955.

An excellent book, covering the interrelationships between the leader and the group. Included are two lengthy "case study" recitations, one covering a religious-based workshop and the other, an industrial setting. The cases refer to group-leader interactions in these two different environments.

Graham, Robert G., and Gray, Clifford F. *Business Games Handbook*. New York: American Management Association, Inc., 1969.

Essentially a catalog of slightly over 200 business games and simulation exercises, this publication provides authoritative summarizations covering descriptions of the exercises, their training purposes, actions to be taken by participants, methods of administration and sources. The authors have also included a valuable discussion on the uses of business games.

Greenberg, Ira A. *Psychodrama and Audience Attitude Change*. Beverly Hills, California: Behavioral Studies Press, Thyrsus Publishing Company, 1968.

While this social psychological study is generally intended for the professional practicing psychologist, the author's explanations of roleplaying (and its attendant vocabulary), as used for therapeutic purposes, make it a desirable addition to this bibliography. J.L. Moreno's introduction to the book also helps commend it.

Guth, Hans P. *Words and Ideas*. 3rd ed. Belmont, California: Wadsworth Publishing Company, Inc., 1969 (1972 printing).

Writers all depend on a dictionary, a thesaurus and a book such as *Words and Ideas*. While this publication is used primarily as a text in a college English course, its contents (such items as style, grammar, handling facts and opinions, etc.) make a worthwhile addition to a trainer's library.

Haiman, Franklyn S. *Group Leadership and Democratic Action*. Cambridge, Massachusetts: Houghton Mifflin Company, The Riverside Press, 1951.

A useful publication about various approaches to leadership and the leader's impact on group dynamics. Some desirable items included for trainers are the "Barnlund-Haiman Leader Rating Scale," as well as case studies about leader effectiveness. Most of the examples provided relate to nonprofit organizations.

Hicks, Herbert G. *The Management of Organizations.* New York: McGraw-Hill Book Company, Inc., 1967.

A sound basic text embracing an introduction to organization theory, elements of human behavior in organizations and managerial functions and concepts. Some useful case materials are included at the end of each chapter.

Ivens, Michael, and Broadway, Frank, eds. *Case Studies in Human Relations, Productivity and Organization.* London: Business Publications Limited, 1966.

Written primarily for the United Kingdom management education market, this book is directed toward work situations and cultures which are somewhat different than those found in America. Nevertheless, despite these dissimilarities—mostly of a minor nature—we strongly recommend its inclusion in a trainer's reference library. Many excellent, well-thought-out cases and roleplays are included. Available in the United States through Cahners Books, 221 Columbus Avenue, Boston, Massachusetts 02116.

Ivens, Michael, and Broadway, Frank, eds. *Case Studies in Marketing, Finance and Control.* London: Business Publications Limited, 1967.

See comments under *Case Studies in Human Relations, Productivity and Organization.*

Jaffee, Cabot L. *Problems in Supervision, An In-Basket Training Exercise.* Reading, Massachusetts: Addison-Wesley Publishing Company, Inc., 1968.

Two complete in-basket exercises have been devised by the author to be applied in courses in supervision and management training or in related areas. Each exercise is provided with follow-up questions for the trainees plus a prepared multiple-choice quiz which the instructor may choose to give to the trainees. Some 25 individual problem items have been included in each in-basket. Both relate to the same fictional company.

Jahoda, Marie, and Warren, Neil, eds. *Attitudes.* Baltimore, Maryland: Penguin Books, Inc., 1966.

An inexpensive paperback containing pertinent writings by such acknowledged authorities as Allport, Bettelheim, Janowitz and Gordon. Trainers display genuine skill and proficiency when their personal knowledge of the research in such subject areas as attitudes is more than skin-deep. This book contains an informative article on how roleplaying affects the opinions of roleplayers.

Kepner, Charles H., and Tregoe, Benjamin B. *The Rational Manager.* New York: McGraw-Hill Book Company, Inc., 1965.

Case studies often entail problem-solving objectives. This book—recommended reading for those who teach problem solving and decision making—details fundamental concepts and procedures in clear, intelligible prose.

Kirkschbaum, Leo. *Clear Writing*. Cleveland: The World Publishing Company, 1950.

This is included as example of an inexpensive paperback ready reference for the writer of case and roleplay materials. Originally published in 1950, this book has gone through several reprintings.

Lee, Irving J. *Language Habits in Human Affairs*. New York: Harper & Brothers Publishers, 1941.

This is *not* specifically a case book; rather, it provides the reader with an introduction to general semantics. But, Lee's presentation format gathers together, as examples, many treasured literary sketches and yarns—all having usefulness in the area of communications. The inventive trainer using learning exercises will be able to capitalize on these without difficulty.

Lopez, Felix M., Jr. *Evaluating Executive Decision Making—The In-Basket Technique*. New York: American Management Association, Inc. (AMA Research Study 75), 1966.

Felix Lopez is one of the unquestioned experts in the use of the in-basket, both for testing and training uses. Drawn together is much practical and theoretical information relating to the in-basket. (The English sometimes refer to this method as the "in-tray.") Trainers seeking to learn where and how this method has been applied will find it all here.

Luft, Joseph. *Of Human Interaction*. Palo Alto, California: National Press Books, 1969.

The definitive discussion of the Johari Window by one of its inventors. Trainers should be acquainted with this "model of interpersonal behavior" and its implications for self-awareness learning.

Maier, Noram R.F., Solem, Allen R., and Maier, Ayesha A. *Supervisory and Executive Development—A Manual for Role Playing*. New York: John Wiley & Sons, Inc. (Science Editions), 1964.

Where would some trainers be without their "The New Truck Dilemma" or "The Truck Seating Order?" Here we have the classic—if we can use that term—approach to group roleplay materials. There are twenty cases. Included with each are instructions for observers, advice for trainers and valuable comments on the intrinsic content of the case. All cases relate to private sector problems.

McLarney, William J. *Management Training—Cases and Principles*. 4th ed. Homewood, Illinois: Richard D. Irwin, Inc., 1965.

A standard text intended for college-level courses in supervision or basic management. Loaded with short, conveniently constructed cases, each with a few questions for the instructor's benefit. A teacher's guide, in the form of a "conference leader's manual," is available with this edition.

Pfeiffer, J. William, and Jones, John E. *A Handbook of Structured Experiences for Human Relations Training*. 3 vols. Iowa City: University Associates Press, 1969.

Although the "structured experiences" in these three spiral-bound volumes are copyrighted by the publisher, we note in the preface that the reader is free to copy or reproduce any and all materials therein. A total of 74 learning exercises, of varying levels of utility, are included. Many relate directly to OD and laboratory (sensitivity-type) training. Others cover the more traditional "human relations" areas, as well as race relations. One well-known exercise included is the "NASA Exercise." One caution about these three volumes: this material is *not* for novices in the training business. The exercises are stated in very sparse language and may readily be misused by an inexperienced instructor.

Pigors, Paul, and Pigors, Faith. *Case Method in Human Relations: The Incident Process*. New York: McGraw-Hill Book Company, Inc., 1961.

A definitive interpretation of the incident process as it relates to the case method. The cases, discussions and schematic diagrams are particularly valuable to the trainer and educator seriously intent on broadening their knowledge and skills in the use of these methods.

Shostrom, Everett L. *Man, the Manipulator*. Nashville, Tennessee: Abingdon Press, 1967.

An enjoyable book, directed at the broad audience of sophisticated readers. It possesses some of the same thrust as Berne's *Games People Play*. Educators and/or trainers who will be applying methods which are intended to influence human behavior will find many riches herein.

This, Leslie E. *The Small Meeting Planner*. Houston, Texas: Gulf Publishing Company, 1972.

According to Les This, both "science and art" are involved in the outcome of successful meetings and small group sessions. Here is a very basic book for those who plan meetings, seminars, workshops, conferences and training activities for 100 or less participants. It will also be a valuable reference for individuals responsible for the individual sessions of a large assemblage. Charts and diagrams covering topics such as seating arrangements and the use of audio-visual equipment are especially well done.

Towle, Joseph W.; Schoen, Sterling H.; and, Hilgert, Raymond L. *Problems and Policies in Personnel Management, A Casebook*. (2nd Edition) Boston: Houghton Mifflin Co., 1972.

Over 50 different cases relating to various types of personnel management functions are contained in this useful paperback. Also available is an instructor's manual. For the most part, this publication is designed for a college level course in personnel administration. For the trainer, however, it contains much of value; excellent suggestions on topics, case format and case construction, plus background information on how to use the individual cases.

Wegner, Robert E.C., and Sayles, Leonard. *Cases in Organizational and Administrative Behavior.* Englewood Cliffs, New Jersey: Prentice-Hall, Inc., 1972.

Designed as an adjunct to "texts in organization and administrative behavior," the contents of this paperback may be easily adapted for use in a variety of in-service training settings. The 32 cases have been cataloged for 22 different topical areas. Each case has been identified as to its "major" and "subsidiary" issues.

Willings, David R. *How to Use the Case Study in Training for Decision Making.* London: Business Publications Limited, 1968.

This book details the advantages of using case studies as a method in decision-making training. It also delineates practical cautions: where the case method may be inapplicable; selection of cases and how to apply. While this book has Great Britain as its principal intended market, its witty style (for a technical publication) recommends it to a broad readership. Six cases, several of which fit the description of complex learning exercises, are included. One of these cases represents an unusual combination of the in-basket and roleplay exercise. Available in the United States through Cahners Books, 221 Columbus Avenue, Boston, Massachusetts 02116.

Zoll, Allen A., III. *Dynamic Management Education.* 2nd ed. Reading, Massachusetts: Addison-Wesley Publishing Company, Inc., 1969.

A comprehensive compilation of the methodologies available to trainers: case studies, roleplaying, in-baskets, the "action maze" (a feedback learning technique developed by Zoll) and several business games. Each section contains examples and a commentary on how to apply the stated methods. Most examples relate to the private sector.

Index of Learning Exercises

This handbook contains 50 different learning exercises: cases, roleplays, complex exercises and in-baskets. Most of this material was developed and included in order to illustrate principles of creating learning exercises and how best to use these. The reader is encouraged to apply this material in whatever setting he considers suitable. But, the cautions about "canned" material are as appropriate for exercises in this book as they are for someone else's.

Abbreviations:

CS	Case Study
RP	Roleplay
CE	Complex Exercise
I	Incident
IB	In-Basket

Subject Index

Author's Index